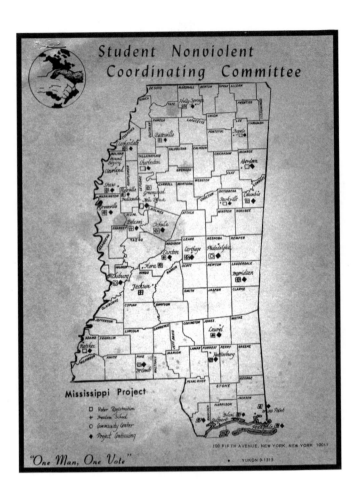

Student Nonviolent Coordinating Committee

Mississippi Project

- ☐ Voter Registration
- ✦ Freedom School
- ○ Community Center
- ◆ Project Continuing

"One Man, One Vote"

100 FIFTH AVENUE, NEW YORK, NEW YORK 10011

YUKON 9-1313

Letters from Mississippi

Edited and with a preface by
ELIZABETH MARTÍNEZ

Introduction by
JULIAN BOND

ZEPHYR PRESS
BROOKLINE, MA

Publication was assisted by a grant from
the Massachusetts Cultural Council

massculturalcouncil.org

An earlier version of Julian Bond's essay appeared in *Monthly Review*

Front cover photo by Herbert Randall from *Faces of Freedom Summer*

Cover and book design by *typeslowly*

Printed in Michigan by Cushing-Malloy

Photo credits: pp. 14, 39, 230 courtesy of Mark Levy; pp. 102 and 121
courtesy of Donna Garde; pp. 36, 100, 112 courtesy of Kathie Sarachild;
pp. 71, 78, 196, 224 courtesy of Tom Pugh; p. 133 courtesy of Chude
Pamela Allen (photo taken by Michael McClure); pp. 134, 172, 189, 223,
235, 237 courtesy of John Maurer.

Library of Congress Cataloging-in-Publication Data:
Martinez, Elizabeth Sutherland, 1925-
    Letters from Mississippi / edited and Introduced by Elizabeth Sutherland
Martinez ; preface by Julian Bond. -- 1st pbk. ed.
        p. cm.
    Includes bibliographical references and index.
    ISBN 978-0-939010-92-9 (pbk : alk. paper)
    1. African Americans--Civil rights--History--20th century--Sources. 2. United
States--Race relations--Sources. 3. Civil rights workers--Mississippi--
Correspondence. 4. Mississippi--Race relations--Sources. 5. African Americans-
-Civil rights--Mississippi--History--20th century--Sources. 6. Civil rights
movements--Mississippi--History--Sources. 7. Student Nonviolent Coordinating
Committee (U.S.) I. Title.
    E185.61.M363 2007
    323.1196'0730762--dc22

                                        2007003752

FIRST PAPERBACK PRINTING IN 2007

ZEPHYR PRESS

50 KENWOOD STREET / BROOKLINE, MA 02446
WWW.ZEPHYRPRESS.ORG

Table of Contents

DEDICATED TO FANNIE LOU HAMER

Introduction

Julian Bond was Communications Director of the Student Nonviolent Coordinating Committee (SNCC) from 1960 until 1965, when he was elected to the Georgia House of Representatives. Today, he is Distinguished Professor in Residence in the School of Government at American University in Washington, D.C., and a Professor in History at the University of Virginia. In February 2000, he was elected to a third term as Chair of the National Association for the Advancement of Colored People (NAACP).

This introduction is adapted from an article that appeared in *Monthly Review.*

What We Did

Of all the work done by the Student Nonviolent Coordinating Committee (SNCC) in the southern freedom movement of the 1960s, one effort is probably better known today than any other: the Mississippi Summer Project of 1964, the subject of this book. It is often called Freedom Summer, but that was not its name at the time.

Indeed that summer was about freedom and people dying in its name, but so much more. *Letters from Mississippi* reveals some of this deeper story in unforgettably immediate, personal terms. We can all celebrate that it is back in print. We can also be glad that its editor is someone who worked in Mississippi herself that summer and remained on SNCC's northern staff.

One comment about Freedom Summer that we hear today was true both then and now. It was a time when nobody stopped to wonder, "What is the meaning of my life?" For people in and around SNCC, the answer seemed obvious; it lay in what we tried to do and what we did. Ella Baker, whose vision served to found SNCC, used to say "Strong people don't need strong leaders." We were strong people, we did strong things.

This is a good place to talk about what SNCC did.

* * *

It began for me as it did for many others in early 1960. On February 4, I was sitting in a café near my college campus in Atlanta, Georgia. It was our hangout, a place where students went between — or instead of — classes. A student named Lonnie King approached me with a copy of that day's *Atlanta Daily World*, the local black daily newspaper. The headline read: GREENSBORO STUDENTS SIT-IN FOR THIRD DAY!

In exact detail, the story told how black college students from North Carolina A&T University in Greensboro had, for the third consecutive day, entered a Woolworth's Five and Ten Cents Store and asked for service at the whites-only lunch counter. It described their demeanor, their dress, and their determination to return the following day — and for as many days as it took to gain the service they were denied.

"Have you seen this?" Lonnie demanded.

"Yes, I have," I replied.

"What do you think about it?" he inquired.

"I think it's great."

"Don't you think it ought to happen here?" he asked.

"Oh, I'm sure it will happen here," I responded. "Surely someone here will do it."

Then it came to me, as it did to so many others in those early days of 1960 — a query, an invitation, and a command: "Why don't we make it happen here?"

The two of us and a friend, Joe Pierce, canvassed the cafe, talked to students, invited them to discuss the Greensboro events and to duplicate them in Atlanta. The Atlanta student movement had begun.

We recruited schoolmates and with them formed an organization, reconnoitered downtown lunch counters, and within a few weeks, seventy-seven of us had been arrested.

Years later, former President Jimmy Carter told former SNCC worker and author Mary King, "If you wanted to scare white people in southwest Georgia, Martin Luther King and the Southern Christian Leadership Conference wouldn't do it. You only had to say one word — SNCC."

SNCC was founded in April 1960 by southern student protesters engaged in those sit-in demonstrations against lunch-counter segregation. Within a year, it evolved from a coordinating agency to a hands-on organization, helping local leadership in rural and small-town communities across the South to participate in a variety of protests, as well as in political and economic organizing campaigns. SNCC's members, its youth, and its organizational independence enabled SNCC to remain close to grassroots currents that rapidly escalated the southern movement from sit-ins to freedom rides, and then from voter drives to political organizing.

Ironically, one consequence of segregation was the development of institutions in close-knit communities, churches, schools and organizations that nurtured and encouraged the fight against white supremacy. The young people who began the 1960 student sit-in movement lived and learned among such institutions.

The student movement's goals were described to the Democratic Convention Platform Committee in 1960 by SNCC's first Chair, Marion Barry, as "seeking a community in which man can realize the full meaning of self, which demands open relationships with others." Barry declared that southern students wanted an end to racial discrimination in housing, education, employment, and voting.

SNCC's goals were set out in similar terms by Executive Secretary James Forman in 1961 as "working full-time against the whole value system of this country" and "by working toward revolution." Later he would describe its program as one of developing, building and strengthening indigenous leadership." SNCC's third chair, John Lewis, would say at the 1963 March on Washington that SNCC was building "a serious social revolution" against "American politics dominated by politicians who build their careers on immoral compromises and ally themselves with open forms of political, economic and social exploitation."

For much of its early history, SNCC battled against the fear that had kept rural southern blacks from wholeheartedly organizing and acting on their own behalf. It strengthened or built aggressive, locally led movements in the communities where it worked. While organizing grassroots voter-registration drives, SNCC workers offered themselves as a protective barrier between private and state-sponsored terror and the local communities where the SNCC staffers lived and worked.

The rural South that SNCC encountered in 1961 had a long history of civil-rights activism; in many instances, however, SNCC staffers were the first paid civil-rights workers to base themselves in isolated rural communities, daring to "take the message of freedom into areas where the bigger civil rights organizations fear to tread." SNCC workers were more numerous and less transient than those from other civil-rights organizations, and their method of operation was different as well.

SNCC pioneered first-time electoral races by blacks in the deep South in the 1960s while adding foreign-policy demands to the black political agenda, thus broadening the acceptable limits of political discourse. SNCC was in the vanguard in demonstrating that independent black politics could be successful. Its early attempts to use black candidates to raise issues in races where victory was unlikely expanded the political horizon. SNCC's development of independent political parties mirrored the philosophy that political form must follow function and that nonhierarchical organizations were necessary to counter the growth of cults of personality and self-reinforcing leadership.

By the spring of 1963, SNCC had eleven staff members in southwest Georgia, as well as twenty staff members — and six offices — in

Mississippi. By August, SNCC had projects and permanent staff in a dozen Mississippi communities; in Selma, Alabama; in Danville, Virginia; and in Pine Bluff, Arkansas. There were twelve workers in the Atlanta headquarters, sixty field secretaries and 121 fulltime volunteers.

Typically, SNCC began campaigns by exploring the economic and political history of a target community. Field workers were supplied by SNCC's own research office with detailed information on a community's economic and financial power structure that traced corporate relationships from local bankers and business leadership in a local White Citizens Council to the largest U.S. banks and corporations. Other research, like the report on "The Economic Status of Blacks in Alabama," provided invaluable intelligence on the conditions of the state's black population.

SNCC organizers spent their first weeks in a new community meeting local leadership, formulating with them an action plan for more aggressive registration efforts, and recruiting new activists through informal conversation, painstaking house-to-house canvassing, and regular mass meetings. Registering rural southern blacks, a SNCC worker wrote, "would greatly liberate American politics as a whole. At the very least, these new voters would defeat the powerful, hidebound Southern Democrats who were holding the reins of Congress and the Senate on the basis of being elected year after year from districts where Black citizens were denied the franchise. The Southern Democratic legislators weren't just holding up civil rights legislation, they were a serious impediment to any kind of meaningful social or economic changes."

SNCC and other organizations fought white terror and helped create a willingness to risk danger in order to register to vote. By one estimate, reported in Pat Watters' and Reese Cleghorn's *Climbing Jacob's Ladder: The Arrival of The Negro in Southern Politics*, a majority of the unregistered had at least been confronted with registration's challenge by 1965.

By that time, SNCC fielded the largest staff of any civil-rights organization in the South. It had organized nonviolent direct action against segregated facilities, as well as voter-registration projects in

Alabama, Arkansas, Maryland, Missouri, Louisiana, Virginia, Kentucky, Tennessee, Illinois, North and South Carolina, Georgia, and Mississippi; built two independent political parties; organized labor unions and agricultural cooperatives; and given the movement for women's liberation new energy.

It also inspired and trained the activists who began the "New Left." It helped expand the limits of political debate within black America, and broadened the focus of the civil-rights movement. Unlike mainstream civil-rights groups, which merely sought integration of blacks into the existing order, SNCC sought structural changes in American society itself.

And How We Did It

SNCC's broader definition of the civil-rights movement's purposes was obvious from the beginning. At its founding conference in April 1960, SNCC Executive Committee member Charles Jones declared, "this movement will affect other areas beyond [lunch-counter] services, such as politics and economics." A report from the conference concluded with a warning about America's false preoccupations at the time. "Civil defense and economic power alone will not ensure the continuation of Democracy," it said.

Democracy itself demands the great intangible strength of the people able to unite in a common endeavor because they are granted human dignity. This challenge cannot be met unless and until all Americans enjoy the full promise of our democratic heritage — first-class citizenship.

Another recommendation noted SNCC's emphasis on winning political power:

Students have a natural claim to leadership in this project. They have pioneered in nonviolent direct action. Now we can show we understand the political implications of our movement — that it goes far beyond lunch counters. We are convinced of the necessity of all local areas joining in the campaign to secure the right to vote. No right is more basic to the American citizen, none more basic to a democracy.

Within four months of these declarations, SNCC volunteer worker Robert Moses was planning a student-staffed voter-registration project in all-black Mound Bayou in the Mississippi Delta for the summer of 1961. The state of Mississippi became a laboratory for SNCC's unique methods of organizing. SNCC's work began in southwestern Mississippi in 1961, but when its workers were driven from the area by violence, state repression, and federal indifference, the organization regrouped in Jackson and in the state's Delta counties in early 1962.

Earlier in 1961, SNCC's Nashville affiliate had continued the Freedom Rides, a direct-action campaign launched by the Congress on Racial Equality (CORE) to integrate interstate bus lines, when Alabama violence threatened to bring them to a halt. After being released from Parchman Penitentiary, many jailed Freedom Riders joined the civil-rights movement in McComb, Mississippi. Several became part of the organizing cadre for the Mississippi movement that followed.

Unencumbered by allegiances to the national Democratic Party, which frequently constrained other, older organizations, SNCC encouraged two black candidates to run for Congress from Mississippi. Moses served as unofficial campaign manager. They ran, wrote James Forman, "to shake loose the fear" among blacks and, through their progressive platforms, gave their intended constituencies an expanded notion of the meaning politics might have in their lives. They talked about issues that no white Mississippi politicians had ever dreamed of mentioning — ideas that resonate even today. In his book, *Jackson, Mississippi*, John R. Salter described these as legislation to improve the school system, a broader plan of medical coverage, and special training facilities to develop industrial skills among the great mass of Mississippians who completely lacked them.

To demonstrate that disenfranchised Mississippi blacks did want to vote, SNCC mounted a "Freedom Vote" campaign in November 1963. Over 80,000 blacks cast votes in a mock election for Governor and Lieutenant Governor. One hundred white northern students worked in this campaign, attracting attention from the Department of Justice and the national media as black registration workers had never done.

That experience with white volunteers paved the way for the

Mississippi Summer Project of 1964, the subject of this book. "Freedom Summer," as it came to be called, brought one thousand mostly white volunteers to Mississippi for the summer of 1964. They helped build the new political party SNCC had organized, the Mississippi Freedom Democratic Party (MFDP); registered voters; and staffed twenty-eight Freedom Schools intended by their designer, Charles Cobb, "to provide an education which will make it possible for them to challenge the myths of our society, to perceive more clearly its realities, and to find alternatives, and ultimately new directions for action."

At the end of the summer, SNCC workers and many of the volunteers went on to the Democratic Party's convention in Atlantic City. There they worked to support the challenge mounted by the Mississippi Freedom Democratic Party, demanding it be seated, instead of the regular, lily-white delegation from Mississippi. That challenge ended in failure when pressure from President Lyndon Johnson erased promised support from party liberals. An offer was made of two convention seats-at large, to which Fannie Lou Hamer replied "We didn't come for no two seats when all of us is tired."

SNCC also organized the founding in 1966 in Alabama of the Lowndes County Freedom Organization in response to the racism of local and state Democratic parties. Like the MFDP, this new, independent party was open to whites but no whites in Lowndes County participated in a black-dominated political effort. The party raised the political consciousness of some Lowndes County black people to such a degree that it played a significant role in Alabama politics for years.

Each challenge served as an object lesson for strengthening black political independence (and for defining the concept of Black Power popularized by Chairman Stokely Carmichael/Kwame Ture). The organizing and lobbying efforts for each laid the groundwork for congressional passage of the Voting Rights Act in 1965. MFDP's legal efforts against white resistance to political equality proved important to black political efforts across the South. An MFDP-directed lawsuit resulted in the Supreme Court's 1969 landmark decision in *Allen v. State Board of Elections,* 393 U.S.544 (1969). Frank Parker, in *Black Votes Count,* wrote that this victory was "critical to continuing black progress throughout the South. For the first time," he asserted, [although in the context of interpreting the Voting Rights Act rather than applying constitutional principles] "the Supreme Court recognized and applied the principle of minority vote dilution — that the black vote can be affected as much by dilution as by an absolute prohibition on casting a ballot."

SNCC's electoral work continued all over the South. During the next several years, SNCC-backed candidates for Congress ran in Albany, Georgia; Selma, Alabama; Danville, Virginia; and Enfield, North Carolina. SNCC helped candidates for Agricultural Stabilization and Conservation Service Boards in Alabama, Arkansas, Georgia, North Carolina and Mississippi. It also aided school board candidates in Arkansas in 1965. On the economic front, it organized the Mississippi Freedom Labor Union and Poor People's Corporation and mounted economic boycotts against discriminatory merchants.

The Mid-Sixties: A Turning Point

The mid-sixties were a turning point in the southern struggle for human rights. Federal legislation passed in 1964 and 1965 accomplished the immediate goals of many in the civil-rights movement to outlaw public segregation and win the vote for Blacks in the South. SNCC had long believed its work ought to be expanded in larger cities of the South and outside the South. Executive Committee minutes from December 1963 record James Forman asserting that "SNCC is going to have to go into the poor sections of large cities to work."

We knew that victories at lunch counters and ballot boxes meant little to blacks locked in northern ghettoes. They demanded results, concrete results, as the urban riots in the North would later make very clear.

At a retreat in May 1966, Ivanhoe Donaldson argued in favor of SNCC's replicating its successful southern political organizing efforts in the North, and the staff agreed. Donaldson and Robert Moses suggested that techniques learned in southern campaigns could be employed to ease SNCC's passage into northern cities. Organizing for political power and community control could mobilize northern urban dwellers, they contended. Michael Thelwell proposed that the organization move "to the ghetto and organize those communities to control themselves. The organization must be attempted in northern and southern areas as well as in the rural Black Belt of the South."

My campaign for the Georgia House of Representatives in 1965 was an attempt to take the techniques SNCC had learned in the rural South into an urban setting. In keeping with SNCC's style, a platform was developed in consultation with the voters. The campaign supported a $2 minimum wage, repeal of the so-called "right-to-work law," and abolition of the death penalty.

After I was elected, the state legislature refused to seat me on the grounds of my support for SNCC's position against the Vietnam War. The two resulting campaigns gave SNCC a chance to successfully test its critique of U.S. imperialism at the ballot box. As in the MFDP campaign, SNCC was enabled to provide a political voice for the politically powerless black poor. In 1966, the McComb branch of the MFDP had become the first black political organization to express opposition to the war. State MFDP officials not only refused to repudiate the McComb anti-war statement; they reprinted it in the state MFDP newsletter, giving it wider circulation and laying the groundwork for future black opposition to the war.

As the focus of the southern movement had changed, so would the goals and programs of our northern organizers. In Columbus, Ohio, a community foundation was organized. In Harlem, SNCC worker William Hall helped a Harlem group striving for community control of Intermediate School 201 in 1966. His efforts laid the groundwork for later successful protests demanding community control of public schools throughout the city. In Los Angeles, SNCC helped monitor local police and joined an effort to create a "Freedom City" in black neighborhoods. Cliff Vaughs of SNCC described that work as "a manifestation of self-help, self-determination, power for poor people." In Chicago, SNCC workers began to build an independent political party and demonstrated against segregated schools. In all of these cities, the southern experience of SNCC organizers informed their work.

The best-known urban effort is probably the Washington, D.C. movement to provide self-government to the vote-less residents of our nation's capital. As SNCC Chair, Marion Barry had written members of Congress in 1960 urging immediate action to that end. In February 1966, Barry, then Director of SNCC's Washington office, announced the formation of the "Free D.C. Movement" (FDCM). He wrote, "The premise … is that we want to organize Black people for Black power." Barry and the FDCM conducted a successful boycott of Washington merchants who did not support home rule.

Just as its concern for social change had never been limited to the southern states alone, SNCC's concern for human rights had long extended beyond the borders of the United States. From its first public statements, SNCC had linked the fight of American blacks with the struggle for African independence. At its founding conference, SNCC announced its identification with the African liberation struggle. "We identify ourselves with the African struggle as a concern for all mankind," they said. At SNCC's Fall 1960 conference in Atlanta, a featured speaker was Alphonse Okuku, an Antioch College student and brother of Kenyan labor leader Tom Mboya. The mass meeting program, said Okuku, "brings to our attention the great significance of the African struggle and its relationship to our fight." SNCC Chairman John Lewis told the 1963 March on Washington, "One man, one vote is the African cry. It must be ours!"

In December 1963, SNCC workers in Atlanta conferred with Kenyan leader Odinga Odinga and, in September 1964, an eleven-member SNCC delegation went to Guinea as guests of that country's President Sekou Toure. Two members of the group toured Africa for a month following that visit. In October 1965, two SNCC staffers attended the annual meeting of the Organization of African Unity in Ghana as representatives of SNCC.

SNCC's January 1966 anti-war statement charged the United States with being "deceptive in claiming concern for the freedom of colored people in such other countries as the Dominican Republic, the Congo, South Africa and the United States itself." Singer Harry Belafonte organized a supportive reception at the United Nations with fifteen African diplomats and myself in early 1966. On March 22, 1966, seven SNCC workers — John Lewis, James Bond, James Forman, Cleveland Sellers, Willie Ricks, Judy Richardson and William Hall

— were arrested at the South African Consulate in New York, preceding by twenty years the "Free South Africa Movement" that later saw hundreds arrested at the South African embassy in Washington.

At a June 1967 staff meeting, SNCC declared itself a human-rights organization, dedicated to the "liberation not only of Black people in the United States but of all oppressed people, especially those in Africa, Asia and Latin America." At that meeting, Forman became director of SNCC's International Affairs Commission; in this capacity he visited Tanzania and Zambia. In mid-1967, SNCC Chair Stokely Carmichael went to Algeria, Syria, Egypt, Guinea and Tanzania; he also visited Cuba with other SNCC staffers Julius Lester, George Ware and Elizabeth Sutherland Martínez. In November 1967 Forman testified for SNCC before the United Nations' Fourth Committee against U.S. investments in South Africa.

There are many reasons for the demise of SNCC despite its clear historical importance. The current of nationalism, ever-present in black America, widened at the end of the 1960s to become a rushing torrent that swept away the hopeful notion of "black and white together" that the decade's beginning had promised. SNCC's white staff members were asked to devote their energies to organizing in white communities; some agreed but most believed this action repudiated the movement's hopeful call to "Americans all, side by equal side." For many on the staff, both white and black, nearly a decade's worth of hard work at irregular, subsistence-level pay, in an atmosphere of constant tension, interrupted by jailings, beatings and official and private terror, proved too much to bear.

Nonetheless, when measured by the legislative accomplishments of the 1964 Civil Rights and 1965 Voting Rights Acts, SNCC's efforts were successful. But the MFDP's failure to gain recognition at Atlantic City presaged the coming collapse of support from liberals. The murders in 1963 of four schoolgirls in Birmingham and of Medgar Evers in Jackson, of civil-rights workers and others in Mississippi in 1964, and Martin Luther King, Jr., in 1968 demonstrated that non-violence was no antidote in a violent society. The outbreak of urban violence at the decade's end further reflected a sense of frustration and alienation among African Americans in general as well as many

SNCC veterans.

Throughout its brief but momentous history, SNCC insisted on group-centered leadership and community-based politics. It made clear the connection between economic power and racial oppression. It refused to define racism as a solely southern phenomenon, to describe racial inequality as caused by irrational prejudice alone, or to limit its struggle solely to guaranteeing legal equality. It challenged U.S. imperialism while mainstream civil-rights organizations were silent or curried favor with President Lyndon Johnson, condemning SNCC's linkage of domestic with international poverty and racism with overseas adventurism.

SNCC refused to apply political tests to its membership or supporters, opposing the redbaiting that other organizations and leaders endorsed or condoned. It created an atmosphere of expectation and anticipation among the people with whom it worked, trusting them to make decisions about their own lives. Thus SNCC widened the definition of politics beyond campaigns and elections; for SNCC, politics encompassed not only electoral races but also organizing political parties, labor unions, produce cooperatives, and alternative schools.

SNCC initially sought to transform southern politics by organizing and enfranchising blacks. One proof of its success was the increase in black elected officials in the southern states from seventy-two in 1965 to 388 in 1968. But SNCC also sought to amplify the ends of political participation by enlarging the issues of political debate to include the economic and foreign-policy concerns of American blacks. SNCC's articulation and advocacy of Black Power redefined the relationship between black Americans and white power. No longer would political equity be considered a privilege; it had become a right.

A final SNCC legacy is the destruction of the psychological shackles that had kept black southerners in physical and mental peonage. SNCC helped break those chains forever. It demonstrated that ordinary women and men, young and old, could perform extraordinary tasks.

They did then and can do so again. This book is about the inspiring example they set for dozens of young people, mostly northerners of relative privilege, who had the great fortune to briefly share their lives during a long, unforgettable summer. Some of those young people went on to work for social justice at home or wherever they might be, as long as they could. May the letters they wrote that summer bring the same inspiring message to the youth of today.

A note on sources and suggestions for further reading:

This essay has made extensive use of the papers of SNCC, interviews with Ivanhoe Donaldson and William Hall, and letters from and between SNCC staffers.

Important books utilized and recommended for further reading are the following:

Braden, Anne, *The Wall Between*. Maryville, TN: University of Tennessee Press, 1999.

Branch, Taylor, *America in the King Years*, vols. 1 & 2. New York: Simon & Schuster, 1988.

Carson, Clayborne, *In Struggle: SNCC and the Black Awakening of the 1960s*. Cambridge: Harvard University Press, 1981.

Forman, James, *The Making of Black Revolutionaries*. Seattle: Univ. of Washington Press, 1997, 3rd edition.

Forman, James, *High Tide of Black Resistance*. Seattle: Open Hand Publishing, 1994.

Grant, Joanne, *Ella Baker: Freedom Bound*. New York: John Wiley and Sons, 1998.

King, Mary, *Freedom Song, A Personal Story of the 1960s Civil Rights Movement*. New York: Morrow, 1987.

Marable, Manning, *Race, Reform, and Rebellion: The Second Reconstruction in Black America, 1945-90*. Jackson: University of Mississippi Press, 1984.

Sellers, Cleveland and Terrell, Robert, *The River of No Return*. New York: William Morrow and Co., 1973.

Sullivan, Patricia, *Days of Hope: Race and Democracy in the New Deal Era*. Chapel Hill: University of North Carolina Press, 1996.

Zinn, Howard, *SNCC: The New Abolitionists*. Boston: Beacon Press, 1968.

Preface

Who could have imagined that youth today would want to know about a bunch of mostly white northerners who went to Mississippi almost 40 years ago to help Black folks against that state's rock-hard racism? But it seems they do, and so this new edition of the 1964 volunteers' letters home.

It was largely the energetic commitment of young people, who formed the majority of those 1,000 volunteers, which made the 1964 Mississippi Summer Project possible. In the Black civil rights movement, as in the Chicano, Asian/Pacific American, Puerto Rican, and Native American movements of those years, youth led the way in fighting oppression. Before that, the Black struggle in this century had usually centered on professionals or community leaders and middle-class or working class adults, often profoundly brave, persistent and self-sacrificing people. Young activists were everywhere but not the base of rebellion and not the recognized leadership. All that changed in the 1960s.

During those years a vision of justice, and commitment to that vision, defined reality for many people of all colors. With it came the sense of empowerment that flows from being part of a massive movement of righteous humanity. It enabled idealistic youth to ground themselves in communities and work with communities, often across generational lines, as happened in Mississippi 1964. Today, when optimism comes hard, knowledge of such possibility is treasured. Stories that affirm living for yourself by way of living for something bigger than yourself — as in this volume — speak eloquently to youth who demand a new society now more than ever.

The Student Nonviolent Coordinating Committee (SNCC), which initiated the Mississippi Summer Project, had all the hallmarks of youth. Its young black field secretaries and other staff set a tone and style of work that celebrated boldness, energy, untraditional creativity, informality, democratic procedure, and sometimes breathtaking courage. Another reason for today's youthful interest in that era probably rises from the idea of "black and white together, we shall overcome." No matter how complicated or flawed, that goal resonated powerfully through the southern freedom struggle. As an ideal, black/white unity inspired thousands of people from north to south who dreamed of equal rights and opportunity won by joint struggle.

The Mississippi Summer Project thereby continued a historic tradition of white anti-racist activism that stands as an alternative to the tradition of white racist activism. Such an alternative does exist and whites can choose to join an honorable tradition or a hateful one. Such a choice demands to be made yesterday, today, and at all times every day.

Amongst whites representing the anti-racist tradition, John Brown remains the best known martyr. But there are more to be researched, documented, and taught about. Today who even knows the name of William Moore, the ex-Marine postal worker from Baltimore who had grown up in Mississippi and thought its people were basically good? In April 1963, he walked down Deep South highways, wearing a sandwich-board bearing anti-racist slogans, with the goal of hand-delivering a letter, a civil rights plea, to the governor of Mississippi. After 70 miles he was shot dead at close range on U.S. Highway 11 in Alabama. People blamed the victim: "He should have known better. Must have been crazy." We need to honor such "craziness."

Rev. Jonathan Daniels, a young northern minister who had been working with the black community, was shot dead in Lowndes County, Alabama, in 1965. That same year, Viola Liuzzo, a civil rights volunteer from Detroit who had come to join the Selma-Montgomery march, was shot dead by Klansmen while driving a local black youth home after the event. We hear a little more about two white Summer Project volunteers, Mickey Schwerner and Andrew Goodman, murdered together with Black activist James Chaney at Philadelphia, Mississippi.

An important reminder of that monstrous act comes from Sally Belfrage, who wrote a beautiful book about her volunteer experience, *Freedom Summer* (1965). "Because two of the boys were white, there was a world reaction ..." she recalled, "but for James, no picture, no name." Again and again the media reduced Chaney to "a Mississippi Negro youth."

After the mid-1960s, the alternative tradition faded along with "black and white together." As racist whites nationwide resisted yielding anything more than the vote — and not always that — many activists of color became focused on their own history, culture and liberation work with a nationalist analysis indifferent to white support. During those later years, SNCC advised its white members "Go organize in your own communities against racism," and a few did. They and other anti-racist white activists continue that alternative tradition today in various forms, with activist/educator Anne Braden of Kentucky a tireless example. This book raises their banner and asks: What, then, will you do?

For readers of *Letters* who might wonder what became of the volunteers, Professor Doug McAdam says in his 1988 study, also called *Freedom Summer*, that by then half were uninvolved in social justice work. Former volunteers now pessimistic about the prospects for social justice outnumbered the optimists two to one. But we should remember that those were the Reagan years, when the rightwing backlash against gains of the '60s roared ahead leaving despair or cynicism in its wake.

Also, numbers do not tell the whole story. The influence of former Summer Project volunteers spread throughout progressive activism in the late 1960s and 70s. Awareness grew of the linkage between southern racism and U.S. imperialism around the world. Among the best known examples of the volunteers' influence is Mario Savio, who returned from Mississippi to fire the Free Speech Movement based in Berkeley, California, and made history. From lessons learned during the summer of 1964 — some of them painful — women like Kathie Amatniek (who coined the slogan "sisterhood is powerful") and Pam Parker (Chude) Allen went on to create and define the women's movement, again making history. Heather Tobis Booth started the Midwest Academy in 1973, an organizer-training center that became widely known for helping to build influential national organizations.

An even fuller picture now emerges from other volunteers whose letters appear here and who were located through months of effort by Zephyr Press staff. Many of them are still doing work that reflects the same hunger for social justice that sent them to Mississippi. Some worked in the anti-Vietnam war movement or against U.S. intervention in Central America, or traveled to Cuba with the Venceremos Brigade. Other former volunteers now, for example, head a national abortion-rights project, fight against the death penalty and for prison reform, do union organizing, or work to provide legal services to the poor.

Quite a few have achieved recognition in academia, the medical or legal world, as authors of books in their fields, and even on a major national newspaper. More than one have worked specifically against racism on a campus, in the field of voting rights, at a major foundation or within government. Even where the volunteers have blended back into the dominant society, as some of them vowed never to do, they brought an altered consciousness. That consciousness is much needed today in the United States. More than ever, we can say.

This book was compiled from letters submitted by volunteers and their families to the Parents Committee, which turned them over to me as editor. The letters included here represent only a fraction of all the volunteers who went to Mississippi, yet they are of an amazing richness, often beautiful, and fearless in talking about the many contradictions of the Summer Project. An important and greatly regretted omission from the book is more letters representing the Black volunteers in the Summer Project; only a very small number appear here. Too often their role in the 1964 project is forgotten and must be reaffirmed.

The book does tell readers about black Mississippians like Fannie Lou Hamer, and the word goes out loud and clear: they must not be seen just as victims! They were and are protagonists, fighting for their daily lives, fighting to determine their own future.

For them as for so many others, the anti-racist struggle in Mississippi has its steps forward together with its steps back — like any other struggle. So much has changed and yet remains unchanged. As of 1998, Mississippi had 10 black sheriffs (more than any other state) but chose in 2001 to retain the Confederate symbol of flags and bars in its flag.

Racism lives, and not only in Mississippi. From the criminal injustice system to attacks on affirmative action, from environmental racism to intensifying poverty and the prison system, today's struggles often seem not so different from four decades ago. Denial of Black voting rights, a crucial southern issue in 1964, turned out to be very crucial nationwide in 2000, when it may well have decided the presidency, as Florida's voting records confirm. The role of racism in U.S. foreign policy and its domestic consequences became unmistakable with the government's response to the tragedy of September 11, 2001. Many people see more clearly today than before that ending racism is central and essential to any transformation of the human condition. The only fatal mistake in this long, hard struggle is cynicism.

* * *

The secret of continuity became clear to me that summer in Mississippi, where my SNCC assignment was to visit every project headquarters and encourage volunteers to continue working. Late one moonless night, I was driving through the Delta, notorious for white supremacist violence. Alone in a rented car, on an empty road with many miles yet to go, I wondered why I did not feel more afraid.

Then the answer surfaced: I was not really alone. The spirit of resistance of black Mississippi enfolded me, the spirit of that summer was strong enough to hold off evil. And so the night quietly passed.

Today the sense of connection, of collectivity, is more needed than ever. It is the opposite of the self-centered, competitive, alienating value system that dominates the national ideology. This book goes back to press in an era that celebrates the United States as the world's only super-power, with a passion for domination and no sense of humanity's absolute interdependence. Within that world view youth are often seen apprehensively rather than as our most consistently idealistic social force, on the move again today.

Let this new edition of *Letters from Mississippi* remind us all that another value system, another world view, another passion, does exist.

A last gift of the letters should be mentioned. They show how vital is the need, especially though not only, for young whites to take the initiative in changing their consciousness about racism. To seek out a different perspective from the one they have always known. To listen to what Black, Latino, and other oppressed peoples say in one way or another. For a new consciousness does not come automatically but with persistent effort.

Now read these letters and be inspired, and learn, and dream. What more could one ask of a book?

— *Elizabeth Martínez*

Acknowledgments

Acknowledging the people who helped bring about this new edition begins with those who insisted the book should be back in print after almost forty years. Thanks should go first, then, to Mike Thelwell, a former SNCC staffer now writing and teaching at the University of Massachusetts, who called one day and urged a new edition. When I approached Anthony Arnove at South End Press about doing it, he was ready to go—another supportive voice.

Still later we collectively decided an even better publisher would be Zephyr Press, whose co-director is himself a former 1964 Mississippi Summer Project volunteer. Jim Kates became much more than the publisher; he almost single-handedly tracked down over sixty of the original letter-writers to find out what had become of them, no small feat after almost four decades, and also added endnotes explaining many references in the letters to help young readers today.

Of other former volunteers who helped on this new edition, special thanks go to Chude Pam Allen, who also has letters in the book. Journalist Joanne Grant also helped to fill out unwritten histories; she covered the civil rights movement at the time and later wrote *Ella Baker: Freedom Bound,* the biography of the guiding spirit of the Student Nonviolent Coordinating Committee (SNCC). Finally, the San Francisco Bay Area Veterans of the Civil Rights Movement assisted in tracking down elusive information.

Proper credit can also be given at last to the woman who made this book happen in the first place. Jean Kates headed the Mississippi Project Parents Committee, which collected most of the letters that summer and arranged for the book's publication. Once started, I received wonderful suppport from Betty Garman and others in SNCC. A special word, finally, for my daughter Tessa, a child at the time, who endured many lonely hours while this book took shape. Like the others, she understood that history was in the making that summer, and the historians included the letter-writers. Let us all remember: history makes us and we the people make history.

— *Elizabeth Martínez*

A Special Note to Readers

Reading this book in the 21st century, you may be surprised to see the term Negro used. In both the letters and the narrative. It may well sound dated and it is certainly not the word that I, and probably the volunteers,would use today. But at the time of writing, 1964, it was generally considered respectful — and still is. Especially in the South. As Willie (now Wazir) Peacock, a former SNCC Field Secretary from Mississippi said with a laugh recently, remembering the ugly, racist terms that once abounded, "You were doing GREAT if somebody called you a Negro!"

* * *

The publishers would also like to thank those who helped in securing the rights and compiling the end notes and the biographical notes for *Letters from Mississippi* — not only all the contributing volunteers and former staff workers with SNCC/COFO, but also Alana Clear, Michael Collins in the office of Congressman John Lewis, George Gensler of McGraw-Hill, Chris Graeser, John Howell, Laura Love at the University of Mississippi, Peter Kates, Steve Lary, Margie Raine, Norma S. Riser and the volunteers of the Batesville Public Library, Bobs Tusa and Toby Graham of the University of Southern Mississippi, Gerald Walton, Chrissy Wilson, and staffs at the Hattiesburg, Mississippi, and Brookline, Massachusetts, Public Libraries. Thanks also to *The Nation* for printing our call to hear from former volunteers. In addition, publication would not have been possible without generous financial support from anonymous donors, David and Linda Blair, Esther Kates, Jean Kates, Jane Pincus, and The Massachusetts Cultural Council.

Letters from
Mississippi

And that freedom train's a-comin', comin', comin'
And that freedom train's a-comin', comin', comin'
And that freedom train's a-comin', comin', comin'
Get on board.

It'll be bringing nothing but freedom, freedom, freedom
It'll be bringing nothing but freedom, freedom, freedom
It'll be bringing nothing but freedom, freedom, freedom
Get on board.

They'll be coming by the thousand, thousand, thousand
They'll be coming by the thousand, thousand, thousand
They'll be coming by the thousand, thousand, thousand
Get on board.

The Road to Mississippi

They were called "the volunteers": 650 young people, mostly northern-ers and mostly white and mostly students. They were the largest single group of the many people who went to Mississippi in the summer of 1964. They were the nonprofessionals. The kids. And they wrote the letters that make up this book.

Most of them knew why they wanted to go to Mississippi before they left home or school to join the project. Some found out at the orientation sessions held in Ohio, Tennessee and other nearby states. Some learned the best reasons in Mississippi itself. And perhaps a few understood only when they had left.

All of them realized that the eyes of the nation were fixed upon their undertaking: from almost every side came the voices of skep-ticism as well as admiration. Hostility was not limited to white Mississippians like Mayor Allen Thompson of Jackson, who stood ready to greet the "invaders" with his specially built tank and riot squads. A Louis Harris public opinion poll taken in June among Americans across the nation indicated that 65% opposed the Mississippi Summer Project.

The doubts and criticisms ranged wide:

Why Mississippi when there is so much racial injustice in their own backyards?

Let Mississippi do its own house cleaning.

Let the government do the job.

They'll just stir up a lot of resentment among the whites and make matters worse.

They are being used to foster violence and thus force federal intervention.

They're just doing it for publicity.

They're wild-eyed radicals, they're naïve idealists, they're beatniks, they're misfits.

But some voices said: They are the cream of our youth. The hope of this nation.

The first contingent of volunteers — about 250 strong — poured in from all parts of the country for orientation at Western College for Women in Oxford, Ohio, during the weekend of June 13-14. A second orientation period began the following week when the first group left. The lush, 200-acre Oxford campus included an oddly symbolic bird sanctuary; the dormitory rooms were attractive and the modernistic dining hall of glass and wood served unusually good food. In these surroundings the volunteers spent a week learning how to avoid being beaten or killed.

A hundred facts of Mississippi life were thrown at them one day, real tear gas another. They learned how the racist Citizens Councils operate, what sort of work they might be doing, how to talk to a group of threatening whites, how not to dress. But their first real discovery had little to do with all this.

Dear Mom and Jo,   Oxford, Ohio, June 14

The reception at Western College was not warm. I was surprised at how unfriendly and unextending people were. Small groups formed or had been formed and people seemed concerned with "fitting in." I went to bed. Later that day (to-day) I went to register. I still felt uncomfortable but attempted to shake a few hands. (It wasn't too bad.) Some people were friendly and helpful. Tremendous enthusiasm was generated when we all began singing after dinner. It was the spiritual revival type of singing and you know how I love that. We all must have sung for about 2 hours, and the previous in-grouping of Negroes and reservedness of whites seemed to disappear — but not really … Maybe we'll be able to at the end of the summer, but right now we don't know what it is to be a Negro and even if we did, the Negroes here would not accept us. It's the old case of having to prove ourselves. In their eyes we're rich middle or upper-class whites who've taken off a summer to help the Negro.

Intellectually, I think many of us whites can understand the Negroes' resentment but emotionally we want to be "accepted" at face value. We want this acceptance because this is part of our reason for going down south, i.e., the basic worth of the individual. I've always thought that my relations with Negroes have been fairly honest. I've gone to a predominately Negro high school and participated in athletics with them. I've gotten to know Negroes in college.… I haven't gone out of my way to meet them but those I have met I have gotten along well with, if not intimately. What I mean to say is that I never detected a "difference," or an inability to communicate with one another.… But what I am finding here is a different situation and perhaps a more honest one …

Love,
Lew

June 15

... Us white kids here are in a position we've never been in before. The direction of the whole program is under Negro leadership — almost entirely. And a large part of that leadership is young people from the South — Negroes who've had experience just because they're Negroes and because they've been active in the movement. And here "we" are, for the most part never experiencing any injustice other than, "No, I won't let you see your exam paper ..."

Dear Peggy:

... All whites who read Baldwin ask, "Is he right? Do they really hate us?" I have never before talked to a Negro about his feelings toward whites. A wonderful Negro man from Detroit named Joe Harrison told me here at Oxford, "I always feel much more comfortable with Negroes than with whites. But I can become good friends with white people."

And one SNCC [Student Nonviolent Coordinating Committee] worker — Frank Smith — said, "I grew up hating all white folks. It wasn't till a couple of years ago that I learned that there could be good whites — and even now I sometimes wonder."

So, there is this great reluctance and distrust, born of generations of oppression and slavery.... It seems that if more whites understood this — especially white liberals — race relations might be a lot less strained.

I have also discovered a lot about my own feelings about race. I grew up in an upper middle-class Westchester home, where my parents were good liberals, but I never knew any Negroes except the woman who cooked and cleaned for us. I loved her very much and she, me.... We all called her "Sarah" while she called me "Ellen" and my parents "Mr. and Mrs."

Consequently, although my parents told me that Negroes were just as good as whites — I must have seen them in the role of servants. Once, my mother tells me, when I was little, we were driving along a road near our house and passed a Negro woman waiting for a bus. "There's somebody's maid," I said.

To arrive in Ohio, where there were 60 or 70 Negro kids my age — all close friends and rather cliquish at first — was a frightening experience. It was not that I looked down on them at all — quite the contrary: I was awed by them. For the first few days, I mostly hung around with the kids from Harvard. I sat with them at meals or in meetings, walking by the groups of Negro kids who also sat together at the table or under a tree on the grass.... But as the week wore on, things began to change.

Ellen

The turning point came with the showing of a film on June 16.

Dearest,

For the first two days there was a noticeable tension between the volunteers and the staff.... Then, Tuesday night we saw a movie made by CBS Reports ["Mississippi and the Fifteenth Amendment"] describing how the Negro was discriminated against in Mississippi with regard to voting. Some of the film was absolutely ridiculous and ludicrous — a big, fat, really fat and ugly white county registrar prevents Negroes from voting; the stupid, really completely irrational and dishonest views of some white Southerners and so on. Six of the staff members got up and walked out of the movie because it was so real to them while we laughed because it was so completely foreign to us — if anyone had said what they did in the movie, we in the North would lock them up or dismiss them completely, but this is the way many white Southerners think.

After the movie one of the staff told us why they had walked out and it shook some of us up. We were afraid the whole movement was going to fall apart ...

Love,
Wally

Dear Folks,   June 16

... We had the whole thing out in the living room, with everybody sitting on the floor or standing along the walls. The kids brought out their gripes: the staff was distant, they didn't let us know what was going on or who would be assigned where, or how we would be assigned, and they looked down on us for not having been through what they had. They shouldn't walk out like that, saying in effect you white people are too stupid to understand how serious all of this is.

Other people argued that we should take into account all of the hardships they were going through, and the fact that they had a lot on their minds. Others again demanded that the staff respect us more: we were after all products of our environments, and did not understand Mississippi, and had not been beaten. Could we do something really concrete down there, or are we just pawns? If so, why should we go down there indeed? Did the staff trust us, could we learn?

Staff members began drifting in from a meeting and entered the discussion. "We did not walk because of you, necessarily. We have seen too much of that stuff in the flesh. We know that bastard and don't have to see him on the screen." One guy said "if you get mad at us walking out, just wait until they break your head in, and see if you don't have something to get mad about. Ask Jimmy Travis over there what he thinks about the project. What does he think about Mississippi? He has six slugs in him, man, and the last one went right through the back of his neck when he was driving a car outside Greenwood. Ask Jesse here — he has been beaten so that we couldn't recognize him time and time and time and time again. If you don't get scared, pack up and get the hell out of here because we don't need any favors of people who don't know what they are doing here in the first place."

"We cried over you in the staff meeting because we love you and are afraid for you. We are grown men and women who have been beaten and shot at, and we cried for you. Somebody walked out of a movie, but you won't see anybody walk out on your picket line. When you get beaten up, I am going to be right behind you. The song we sang yesterday was dedicated to a couple of people now in jail, and they know we are singing and thinking about them. As long as there is one person alive wearing a SNCC pin they know. And you had better know it too, or else get out. I was a good soldier in Korea. I can stick a bayonet in your back in the right spot so that you don't make a sound. I know how to use piano wire around your neck and then let you fall to the ground soft. And all the time I was in Korea I was sick to the guts because I was being taught to kill so good. Don't tell me that you are coming down to help me because you are saving yourselves. We are proud of you, and love you. Don't worry when we don't have time to shake hands, because that's not the SNCC greeting anyway. We hug and kiss you because we love you."

Here is what I said: people have been talking about Americans, and how there is more than just the black man's problem. Somebody said that we sounded like a sick bunch of people with all of our complaints. Well, we are all sick, black and white, because we are Americans, and that fat bastard on the screen has poisoned all of us. The whole god damn country has gone to hell, and we are the only ones who can save it. Isn't it sick when we have to see an in-group sitting together at lunch and feel that they are suspicious of us because we are white? That is why we are going down, not to help the Negro, but to get rid of those guys for all of us. It is natural that these things should come out, because that bastard put it into all of us. That is why the training is a week long and not just two days ...

Then some of the staff people came in singing, and we all sang together, and the first time really together. The crisis is past, I think.

Love,
Bill

With the tension between Negro staff and white volunteers broken,
if not resolved, the volunteers began to see Mississippi through the
eyes of those who knew it all too well. Their understanding of what
lay ahead grew stronger — as did their fear.

Dear People at home in the Safe, Safe North,   June 17

Mississippi is going to be hell this summer. Monday, Jim Forman, executive secretary of SNCC, stood up during one of the general sessions and calmly told the staff (who already knew) and the volunteers that they could all expect to be arrested, jailed, and beaten this summer, and, in many cases, shot at. There is a quiet Negro fellow on the staff who has an ugly scar on his neck and another on his shoulder where he stopped .45 slugs.... Another fellow told this morning how his father and later his brother had been shot to death.... I'd venture to say that every member of the Mississippi staff has been beaten up at least once and he who has not been shot at is rare. It is impossible for you to imagine what we are going in to, as it is for me now, but I'm beginning to see ...

Please talk up Mississippi up North, pass around the materials I am sending, and begin petitioning the Federal government for intervention ...

                              Love,
                              Xtoph

Dear God, also dear me, and anyone else interested,   June 19

I want to write everything down now, while I have time and can and before I leave Oxford....

My feelings are many and mixed and are not always the same.... When I began this letter I was feeling quite calm and relaxed, then the butterflies started in the pit of my stomach, they subsided somewhat and then continued to my hands.

Whenever I am scared or terribly excited about something, I have always gotten this feeling in my stomach and then often in my hands. But this afternoon I felt it so that I ached — my whole stomach, my chest, my arm, hands, legs and even down to my feet. That is pretty near all of me....

A Negro girl said to me in the john a few minutes ago that she wondered if I had a match. I said No. And she said, "You don't smoke yet?" I replied, "no." "You will before the end of the summer," she said.

She went on to tell me, "I do because I'm nervous. No, I'm going to quit saying I'm nervous. I'm scared. Sometimes I smoke two packs a day."

She also said she had been told that many of the girls, especially in a certain other dorm, cried all by themselves at night, that they really didn't want to go. "If I didn't really want to go I wouldn't go," she said. And I said, "Sometimes there isn't a really don't and a really do." She continued, "And sometimes you've told the people back home you were going to help and what will they think if you come home now." I said, "Well, that would present a problem too."

Perhaps I should have said "that does present a problem too." I actually have thought about the feelings or thoughts of others should I back out. So this is one of the pressures. But only one, and who can say how large or small ...

With much love, a very (calm right now) me,
Virginia

Monday night,

June 15

I turned down a chance to work in the southwest part of the state, the most dangerous area. I talked to a staff member covering that area for about fifteen minutes and he told me about the five Negroes who have been taken into the woods and shot in the last three months.... I told him that I couldn't go in there because I was just too scared. I felt so bad I was about ready to forget about going to Mississippi at all. But I still wanted to go; I just didn't feel like giving up my life. After thinking about this seeming contradiction, I decided that I have not discovered just how dedicated I am to the civil rights cause and that that is the purpose of the trip....

Amidst the apprehension, the volunteers went on listening and learning. The days were packed from morning to night, the week from beginning to end, with new knowledge and new songs and especially new people.

Dear family and friends,   June 18

Sunday evening, the first program was a solemn memorial service for Medgar Evers conducted by Ed King, a native Mississippian who is Methodist chaplain and dean at Tougaloo — the Negro college outside of Jackson. Monday morning King led off the first session with a run-down of some of the factors which contribute to making Miss. a police state. King is a soft-spoken man with large scars from an auto accident disfiguring one side of his face. He ran for Lieutenant Governor in the Freedom Election run last year by SNCC. He told about the techniques the White Citizens Council, which receives state funds, has used to keep control of the state. No politician can afford to be a moderate. Three were voted out recently for voting against an extreme piece of anti-Negro legislation. In the past six years over 60 Methodist ministers have been forced out of the Southern half of the state alone. Merchants who meet the terms of the civil rights groups are economically coerced to change or leave. All widely read newspapers simply deny the white guilt for violence and usually ignore incidents entirely. National news on TV is interrupted by local commercials or by saying, "The following is an example of biased untrue Yankee reporting." King says that he sees how there can be some truth to the contention that many Germans didn't know about the treatment of the Jews under Hitler.

Next Bob Moses talked to us in his quiet, reasoned manner about the project and the situation in various parts of the state. Bob warned us that we are all victims of the plague of prejudice but must not make the mistake that the authorities in Camus' *Plague* made by resisting the recognition of the disease because recognition would have made action necessary.... He then sketched some of the goals of the summer. He said that the mere fact of our spending the summer in Negro homes would be a very important victory. It is also hoped that we, through our connections back home will give the project more protection, and bring the Justice Dept. into Mississippi in a bigger way.

In the next session the body was broken down into small groups in which project directors from the local projects described in some detail the conditions in their counties. I happened to be assigned to a group where Charles McLaurin was talking about Sunflower and Bolivar counties. He is a dynamic, clear speaker whose determination, good humor and calmness are massively impressive. These SNCC staff people must really stand out against the background of a lazy dead-end society. It becomes almost understandable how they can persuade people to risk house, job and life to go down and attempt to register.

That evening we went back into the same groups and discussed race relations. This was a painful rather intimate discussion.... One boy from West Virginia confessed that he is quite embarrassed when confronted by a group of Negroes and asked how he should act. A little blond Smith girl said she knew what he meant although she didn't have the problem herself, in fact she didn't know whether it was environment or heredity but she found Southern Negroes quite attractive. The discussion was very valuable in posing the problem of how does one adapt without selling out his own identity ...

Tuesday we had more regional briefings. Then there was an informal general session to discuss various problems. The most interesting discussion was how we should confront the white kids in Mississippi who want to talk to us and persuade us to go back home. Should we insist that a Negro come along. If their minds are closed what is the use of talking to them.... On the other hand it is so important, I feel, to get into the white community and let somebody know what we are like. I imagine the rumors about the invasion of Communists are getting pretty wild.

Bob Moses

Tuesday evening was a talk by Charles Morgan, the courageous Birmingham attorney who stood up at the time of the bombings and made a strong public statement in favor of sanity. He has since been forced out of Birmingham by economic coercion and published a book, *A Time to Speak*. He warned us gravely about the dangers of Mississippi. Said he thought that atrocities don't soften but harden the local people.... He said one thing that might help was that Mississippi is very concerned about its image. He laid the slow movement of the civil rights movement in the South not to the strength of Southern opposition but to the weakness of the North on the issue.... He ended by solemnly stating that he admired our courage. From a guy like that who has seen a lot of fire, this was really frightening. We have all lived under the increasing weight of fear and the struggle to come to terms with the possibility of death consumes much of our emotional energy ...

Just the security precautions are scary: beware of cars without tags — they are always danger; never go out alone; never go out after dark; never be the last one out of a mass meeting; watch for cops without their badge; listen for an accelerating car outside; if you wake up at night thinking there is danger, wake everybody up. There seems to be a very good type instinct for preservation. Some of the Negro field secretaries I was talking to informally told how they played like real Uncle Toms to the cops when in danger....

Wednesday, Rev. James Lawson presented and skillfully defended Christian revolutionary nonviolence as a way of life. Most of the staff and volunteers were agnostic nonviolent technicians. The discussion was hot but very real. It became clear that not all nonviolent techniques could be practiced by certain personality types. Only perhaps 10% can talk successfully with someone who is going to beat you. For the rest, withdrawal seems the best reaction....

Thursday we got some practical legal counsel from one of three Negro lawyers in Mississippi who takes civil rights cases. He is a wily old fox with a wonderful sense of humor and a great gift for diplomacy (no, not Uncle Tomming). Also heard from head of legal defense fund and others. There will be 150 lawyers in the state this summer! Friday morning we heard John Doar, Burke Marshall's assistant in the Justice Department, talk about what they will be doing there. He said they would keep very close watch on us and try to watch for trouble brewing. However, he said unless there is a Federal court order to bring

Federal troops into an area, responsibility for maintaining law and order is left up to the local law enforcement agencies. The kids' questions and statements were quite burning. There is a law which gives the FBI power to arrest and protect people from intimidation of their right to vote....

Love,
Mike

P. S. A word about the group. A surprising number of young married couples. One school teacher who left wife and kids at home. Maybe a majority of Young Democrat types with a good representation of people from the left. It is hard to tell how we will turn out till we have seen action.

Dear Folks,

A great deal of tension and a great deal of camaraderie here at Oxford. Workshops and role-playing are constant. We staged one situation, a screaming mob lining the steps to the courthouse while a small band of registrants tried to get through. The inevitable happened — what will actually happen in Mississippi happened. The chanting mob (instructed to be as brutal as possible, and to pull no punches) turned into a clawing, pounding mob, and we volunteer registrants were down in our crouched-up ball. Casualties?

A couple of scratches, a sprained ankle, and one cameraman who got swept up was a little bit shaken. It seems like brutal play, and it is. We've got to be ready for anything, and we must prepare for it ourselves. Once we get south we are nonviolent; we must get whatever there is in our systems out now, and we must also learn to take the worst. Some of the staff members walk around carrying sections of hose. This strangely terrifying training in brutality may well save lives. (I must confess, I have not been able to take part in even the screaming of a mob scene, much less the pummeling. Wherever possible, I am among the victims.)

We have registration workshops, too. And lecturers came from all over the country to speak to us. And we sing. What "We Shall Overcome" is to the national movement, "We'll Never Turn Back" is to the Mississippi workers. It is a slow song, measured out in grief and determination. The final verse goes,

> We have hung our head and cried,
> Cried for those like Lee who died
> Died for you and died for me,
> Died for the cause of equality,
> But we will never turn back
> Until we've all been free
> And we have equality, and we have equality.

Love,
Jim

Dear Mom and Dad,

A lot of the meetings have been run by a Negro Mennonite minister from Georgia, a member of the National Council of Churches. (The NCC is paying for this orientation, and has some excellent staff people here.) His name is Vincent Harding, plump, bespectacled, a brilliant moderator in discussions because he reacts so honestly and humorously to every question. Yesterday he gave a long talk about people using each other and where to watch out for this within the movement itself (Negro man accuses white girl of being a racist if she won't go to bed with him, or vice versa; or white girl looking for "my summer Negro;" or Negroes in the community using volunteers as the only available victims of their suppressed hostility to whites in general, etc., etc.) These are examples of the kind of honesty that characterizes the whole training session. His main point was that people within the movement must not use each other because it is that very exploitation of someone else, which turns him from a human being into an object, that the movement is fighting against.

Love, Susan

Dear John and Cleo,

... I feel such a need for you and really crave to somehow have you experiencing what is important to me. So look, please, at the enclosed material.

In *The Student Voice*, look especially at Mrs. Hamer's face.... She was a timekeeper on a cotton plantation. When she registered to vote she was fired from a job she had held for 18 years and made to leave the plantation. Soon her husband, who had been there about 30 years was also fired. In the course of her work for civil rights which followed, she was jailed. Her jailers brought in black prisoners to beat her. One of the black men's hips had been so thrown out of joint that it was jutting out several inches. He and his fellows had been given corn liquor. He was told that if they didn't beat her his other hip would be thrown out ... To watch her limp around here, encouraging the prayer sessions in which we remember Sen. Eastland and Gov. Johnson and all the brutal people they sanction, is almost too much to take. But it's also a never-failing source of courage and determination....

Does America really know about these people and these places and about incidents of terror that occur every day? I didn't really. And I still don't sometimes. And I expect that even you really don't. As Robert Moses told us: When you're not in Mississippi, it's not real and when you're there the rest of the world isn't real ...

Love,
Jo

The people here, most particularly the top-level directors of the entire project, are impressive. They are wise, caring, courageous, honest, and full of love. All those adjectives in a list don't mean much. The point is, I trust them and believe in them not only more than I expected to, but more than I trust any other group organizers I can think of. The director of the Summer

Project, as you probably know, is Bob Moses. He is about thirty, married to a Negro girl, comes, I think, from New York, but has been a SNCC staff worker in Miss. for some time. He is a careful thinker, expresses himself with great economy and honesty, and with every word one is amazed at the amount of caring in the man. He is more or less the Jesus of the whole project, not because he asks to be, but because of everyone's reaction to him. (I forgot to say, he's a Negro.) He has a very intelligent face, wears glasses, blue denim overalls....

June 18

... he was not in the least dynamic, but he forced you by what he said and by his manner of saying it, to want to partake of him, to come to him. He was not in any way outgoing, yet when he spoke you felt close to him.

Dear Lynne,

The organization here is a real student movement. And it looks like it will be around a long time. I would not be surprised if it really does, with time, influence the course of American history through the leaders it produces and develops — for that is one of its main objectives....The savvy of the organization is a marvel. It is shrewd, calculating, and geared for years of struggle. Its members ... have the strange ability to discuss, plan, scheme, openly and honestly disagree, and then come to a definite decision which all follow....

Now these people are only students. They are taking on a state and perhaps a nation which they think has ignored the heritage of the United States and has violated the fundamental rights of man. They have acted when few others would. They are speaking about a festering sore in this nation. The people who are bugged by this are responding. The sore is not just segregation but the general de-humanization of American life ...

Right now the church and Christians are politically impotent. Unless they do something soon, they will become more and more so, until they are snuffed out. That is why to peel off the layers of do-nothing spiritualists, apathetic worshipers, navel-gazers, and to institute people who will make a sacrifice, a radical … witness for comfort and "happiness" is imperative for the church …

                              Love,
                              Dave

Dear Mom and Dad,

… I had no idea that so many young people of the age and education of the people here had any serious commitment to religion in this country. It is disturbing, and reassuring. Disturbing, because I'm afraid the faith of some of these nice little girls may run into difficulties if things start happening. Reassuring, because if it survives or already has survived such things, it will be a mighty stay for those of us whose commitment is mostly intellectual.…

                              Love,
                              Gene

… These people — the Mississippians and the SNCC staff members — are the ones who are really free. More free, certainly, than the Southern white imprisoned in his hatred for the Negro. Maybe you have to see the people's faces, hear them talk and sing and struggle, to understand the Movement. You should — you must — understand this Movement, for it is the most important thing involving people in America today …

Dear folks,

June 21

… One sees a freedom here that is so much more than just the ironical fact that the enslaved people are, at least relatively, the liberated ones. Some "white" people sit at their feet wondering at this sorrow freed and made beautiful, sensing dimly in themselves a similar pain but knowing, dimly, that they have bound and frustrated it by their fear of it.… I think what is at the root of what I experienced today with these black people was a sense of tragedy. And I mustn't forget how joy and deep humor are involved in that sense, how they are all one and how that is why it is the key. If we realize that safety is a myth, aren't we in a sense "saved" by that knowledge and acceptance of death?

… I begin to realize that it is a war that I will enter and that the enemy is even lunatic, even driven into frenzy by his fear. But I also learn that the enemy is very much myself and all of America and, perhaps, of humanity.… I cannot agree with that "sympathetic" American who from his "safe" and carefully maintained distance says that we must slow up, that we must not push. I suspect this attitude, as I suspect that part of it which I see in myself, because it says that something abnormal and therefore ominous, a naked reality, is drawing too close and threatening the sacred status quo. I think that there is too much piety and wise head-shaking about "Mississippi".… Has everybody in the U. S. asked himself — asked himself! — am I prejudiced? asked himself persistently until he arrives at that prejudice that is inevitably there by the nature of our society?

Love,
Bret

While the volunteers searched their minds and hearts, the outside world watched. The volunteers were half glad that national attention had been focused on the project, half angry at the kind of attention …

Dear people,

All around the campus swarm reporters and photographers. Claude Sitton is here from *The New York Times*; Karl Fleming from *Newsweek*; Homer Bigart from CBS; Dick Cunningham from the *Minneapolis Tribune*; Nick von Hoffman from the *Chicago Daily News*. They are not here to watch the SNCC staff; as Bob Moses said in a speech the first morning, the press is interested in the students, not the staff, and not the people of Mississippi.... *Look Magazine* is searching for the ideal naive northern middle-class white girl. For the national press, that's the big story. And when one of us gets killed, the story will be even bigger.

But the big story out of Mississippi this summer ought not to be about my participation in the movement, or even my death. The big story ought to be Life in Mississippi. If that life is ugly, then its creators must be villains, and those who endure must be beautiful.... The purpose of this summer's program is to spotlight oppressed Mississippi; if northern college students dominate the spotlight, the project will, in large measure, have failed.

Geoff

Not only wrong emphasis troubled the volunteers, but also the attacks and inaccuracies. They answered the many naysayers with logic or anger or the truth of their own observations.

... Not one of us northern volunteers would deny the existence of oppressive systems in the North — especially in the city slums.... But it is stronger and more oppressive in Mississippi. Another thing — Mississippi is just a start — this whole country needs changing so that everyone can live a life in which he is able to realize his full capacities as a human being. Perhaps the reason we are going to Mississippi rather than New York or Philadelphia or even Seattle or Minneapolis is that here is an organized program through which we can use our skills and our lives to bring some measure of justice, maybe even love, to this state and the rest of the country.

One other question — from my point of view the most important and at the same time, the most disturbing — is why not leave the whole problem to the Federal Government?...The federal government is not doing the work that needs to be done to change Mississippi. This very question, though, is a reflection of the whole country's attitude of let someone else do it....

Dear Al,

June 29

As you expressed in your letter, you and your law partners believe the effect of outsiders coming into Mississippi will be negative and a great amount of resentment will build up (only to be released by violence — my parenthesis). I cannot deny the fact that some resentment has developed in the white community — but our purpose is to work and develop the Negro community....

As far as changing the white folks, I've already expressed my doubts about what can be accomplished. These folks have deeply entrenched values about a certain way of life. But you and I both know the effect which enforced law has upon changing people.... The major fault so far is that the laws have not been enforced, especially in the south, and more subtly in the north....

Best,
Lew

Dear Mr. M.:

A letter from you to Miss Sharon Anderson was read over the loudspeaker in our dining room at the Mississippi project orientation sessions at the Western College for Women. Some found it amusing. Some found it disgusting. I did not find it amusing ...

You say among other things that this Mississippi project should be left to experts. What experts? Experts like you? Experts have done nothing for three hundred years. Many Negro people in Mississippi are no better off than they were in the days of slavery. Furthermore, did Jesus Christ say, "Let the experts preach the gospel?" No! He commanded everyone who loves Him to "take up thy cross and follow me." Christ said to love one's neighbor. And do you remember that a lawyer tried to trick Christ by asking, "Who is my neighbor?" And what did Jesus answer? He told the story of the Good Samaritan. Many people are our neighbors. But especially, our neighbor is a person of a different race.

You are quite right that there is plenty to do in the field of race relations right in our own back yard. That's one of the favorite excuses of those who don't want anything done. I have done a great deal in my own back yard, which is New York City. I have helped Negroes to get a decent apartment which was denied them merely because they were Negroes. I have helped get five-day trash collection on some streets in the Negro ghetto area of Brooklyn. I have helped break down the hiring discrimination practiced in New York City. There is still much to be done. But that in no way alleviates anything that must be done in Mississippi....

Suppose you had lived at the time of the French Revolution. Which side would you have been on? Or suppose you had lived at the time of the American Revolution? Which side would you have been on? Of course we can easily say nowadays which side we would have been on because those battles have been fought and won so that it's now perfectly safe to take sides. But there is a battle to be won now today.... Has it ever occurred to you that George Washington was a criminal at the time that he fought the Revolution? Of course he was.... His army was a bunch of rabble-rousers. Isn't that always the way? Yesterday's fools are tomorrow's heroes — that is, if they win. Well, we intend to win. And while we're winning, you'll sit on your comfortable hind parts and tell me that we're doing it all wrong....

What are you afraid of? Are you afraid that your position in society is so precarious that if anyone rocks the boat, you'll fall in and drown? What a pity! If I live to be 76 years old, I hope that I will have become more intelligent than I am now, not less. You may call me a naive, white college student.... It might be that some of us are naive. But you ought to praise God that they can do what they're doing in spite of their naivete. Did you ever do any such thing when you were their age? Maybe that's why you resent their doing this great thing....

But, Mr. M., it's not too late even at 76.... Your body might be too old to run with a teenager but the wisdom of a person of your years should enable you to have ideas that can run ahead of all these eager youth. Please, Mr. M., don't sit beside the road of life and moan and groan because the younger generation is passing you by. Get up and run!

Sincerely,
Than R.P.

And then the volunteers had their own families to contend with. The grandmother of one student had written to the boy's father: "I do not understand what he is trying to do in Mississippi. I hope he finds something pleasant and what he wants. Mississippi never sounded interesting to me."

Some parents were sympathetic. But many were uncomprehending, others were simply afraid for their children. Thus a number of volunteers had gone to Oxford secretly. Or against the wishes of their families. They tried to explain.

Dear Dad,   June 24

By now you know that what I told you about my plans for the summer was in part a deliberate lie. I'm sorry about this. I thought it was a necessary evil at the time but now I wish I had faced you and told you what I was up to.

The trip through the south was genuine ... We saw almost every battle-field in the south, in addition to New Orleans, a few Georgia beaches and a grand old plantation outside Natchez, Miss.

Now the trip is over. I am at the orientation session for the "Mississippi Summer Project" with the Student Nonviolent Coordinating Committee (we are called "Snick" for SNCC, kind of a rotten name).

... I am sure that you are convinced that I have fallen in with agitators and a dangerous brand of screwballs. Well for some time I feared the same thing myself. I have found the fact to be otherwise ... And there will be no mass demonstrations, there will be no picketing and no sit-ins. We are not even dreaming of total integration this summer and in this decade ...

I am, of course, living hand to mouth now. I expect that you are so disgusted with this whole business that you will try to starve me out. You may succeed. I receive no pay from SNCC. If in fact, I have completely misjudged your reaction I would be only too happy — ever grateful indeed — for support.

I will write you once a week. I am sorry if this frightens or saddens you.

Bill

Dear Mom and Dad,   June 27

This letter is hard to write because I would like so much to communicate how I feel and I don't know if I can. It is very hard to answer to your attitude that if I loved you I wouldn't do this — hard, because the thought is cruel. I can only hope you have the sensitivity to understand that I can both love you very much and desire to go to Mississippi. I have no way of demonstrating my love. It is simply a fact and that is all I can say....

I hope you will accept my decision even if you do not agree with me. There comes a time when you have to do things which your parents do not agree with.... Convictions are worthless in themselves. In fact, if they don't become actions, they are worse than worthless — they become a force of evil in themselves.

You can't run away from a broadened awareness ... If you try, it follows you in your conscience, or you become a self-deceiving person who has numbed some of his humanness. I think you have to live to the fullest extent to which you have gained an awareness or you are less than the human being you are capable of being ... This doesn't apply just to civil rights or social consciousness but to all the experiences of life ...

Love,
Bonnie

Dear Folks,

Concerning the "practicality" of such a venture: nothing could be more "lucrative," "profitable," than teaching in Mississippi this summer.... I want to fulfill myself, not to prove myself. I do not want to spend my life in the pursuit and enjoyment of comfort and security; I want to pursue my spiritual growth. It is all ultimately selfish: I "save" myself by committing myself to the concerns of other men.... I want to teach in Negro schools after graduation. The freedom schools could be the most practical kind of preparation for such a career — and of more value than the life I lead at Stanford among the rather insipid and spoilt, egocentric products of the middle class.

You should know that it would be a lot nicer in Hawaii than in Mississippi this summer. I am afraid of the situation down there, and the beaches and the safety are very alluring. But I am perhaps more afraid of the kind of life I would fall into in Hawaii. I sense somehow that I am at a crucial moment in my life and that to return home where everything is secure and made for me would be to choose a kind of death. I fear the kind of lethargy that I fell into in Munich ... I feel the urgent need, somehow, to enter life, to be born into it....

Love,
Bret

The time to leave for Mississippi came near. Some of the volunteers tried to catch hold of the week's meaning.

The past week has been, without doubt, the most amazing of my entire life. Now that I've felt what it is to be involved and committed, it seems hard to believe that I could be content with any other kind of life. I've thought about death a lot and what death means about life, and I know that right now I don't want to live any way but the way I am ...

... I wish I could see you for just a few hours to tell you what has happened here this week, and what might happen this summer — both inside and outside of me and this environment. It's an intense and frightening but deeply human and both ugly and beautiful world. I think I've never felt so strangely exhausted and exhilarated, scared to death and aching to get down there....

Dear Mom and Dad,

If the rest of the summer is a failure, this week alone will have been enough. Of course there's been a terrific amount of tension and anxiety, but of a constructive kind, by and large, the kind that enables you to understand yourself and what you're doing. Bob Moses said that when no one had dropped out by Wednesday, he was very worried, it didn't seem real. Since then a few have left, but not too many ...

It's time to go. I know you'll worry, and we will worry with you. In many ways it's harder to be in NY waiting for news than in Miss. doing things ...

                                Joe and Nancy

June 19

The time for departure is about 24 hours away. The atmosphere here is very tense and yet amazingly calm considering what may lie ahead … I find out that I function almost normally (despite what I am prepared to face) except for brief intervals when the situation, with its full implications, suddenly focuses before my eyes.

I hope the Mississippi Summer Project creates a national crisis of a positive nature. This is probably impossible. The press wants blood and that is what you will hear about.…

The first bus and carloads of volunteers left for Mississippi on Saturday, June 20, looking like a strange mixture of kids going to camp and soldiers off to war. Others departed the next day. At the same time there were new arrivals and a new week of orientation began.

That Sunday, a volunteer already arrived in Meridian, Miss., sat down to write a letter.

Dear Stark …   June 21

Hi. As you said, no picture postcards to be had, or at least not anywhere I've been, so this'll have to do.

They said that Meridian was an easy town. Comparatively speaking, of course, meaning that the police aren't altogether that terrible, and they try to hold down the vigilante types. Right now, tho, we're all sitting here in the office being quietly nervous as hell. This morning Mickey, who's the project director, and Chaney, a local staff member and Andy, who's a volunteer, all went out to one of the rougher rural counties to see about a church that was burned down a few days ago. They said they'd be back by four, and now it's coming on to ten. We've been calling the Jackson office all day, and have checked all the jails around, and they're not in any of them. No word from them of any kind. We've had people out looking for them and they haven't found anything. We've been in touch with the FBI and DJ [Department of Justice] but I don't quite know if they're doing much of anything. Philadelphia, Miss., that's where they went to see about the church. The city of brotherly love. Everywhere you go here, there's hate. Just now when some of us went down the street for coffee, they were followed by a carload of white hoods. Now that we're back inside, there are two carloads of hoods and one carload, no two, of police, following each other around in low circles outside. Sometimes when the hoods pass they yell something. "White nigger lover" seems to be a favorite. I wish I knew more what the intentions of the police are. In this town, they probably are trying to keep the hoods from shooting us or something, but it's hard to tell. It's funny, you know, to come from a place where the police are expected to protect you into one where either you're not sure or else you know very well they're against you.

Still no word from the missing people. It must be 11 by now. No one has really said anything about the kinds of things that we're all thinking could have happened to them. The people who've been out looking just came back. Now we talk about the Klan. The FBI is trying to find some grounds to get into the case full strength. Wish they'd hurry up about it.

Hot here, down to 95 now in the office, which is an improvement. Everyone now is very quiet, just sitting, and watching out of the darkened windows a little bit, watching the cars that circle. There's a couple of people standing around on the corner. One of them is a little kid who gets the license number of the circling cars. Besides that, there's nothing out there, just a kind of brightly lit street, with the electric wires crisscrossing in front of the window, and the darkness behind you when you sit in the window. Nothing to do but play ping pong or read and wait for the phone to ring. I've been reading *All Quiet on the Western Front*. Somehow it's appropriate, or maybe not. We'll see …

Love,
Edna

At Oxford, on Monday morning, Mrs. Rita Schwerner announced to
the new group of volunteers that her husband Michael was missing
in Philadelphia together with James Chaney and Andrew Good-
man, a New Yorker who had just arrived after attending the first
orientation session.

   The volunteers rushed to wire or call their congressmen and
demand federal protection for civil rights workers in Mississippi.
There was little else to do about the disappearance except wait for
news. And think, or write …

Dear Mom and Dad,

   I cannot begin to tell you how it feels to be here.… know-
ing about them. You feel like it couldn't be real. No — uh-huh.
They were in Oxford only a few days before — they couldn't
already be in such danger. But then all of a sudden — the dis-
belief is countered by a vivid picture of reality — that it could
be you. And then there's this weird feeling of guilt because it
wasn't you — and here you are on a beautiful campus trying
so hard to understand just what danger is anyway. Everyone
suspects the worse to have happened to the men but no one
says anything …

   A lot of kids are trying to be real casual and cool and funny
about everything so they don't worry their folks. This seems
silly to me — especially with you — because you're in this with
us in the sense that unlike a lot of parents — you realize the
significance of this summer as much as I do.…

                                             Love,
                                             Barbara

Dear Dad,   June 24

   The mood up here [in Oxford, Ohio] is, of course, very
strained with those three guys who disappeared Sunday, dead,
most likely. Saturday night, I ate dinner with the wife of one

of them. She was telling me about all the great things she and her husband were working on. She looks younger than me. What does she do now? Give up the movement? What a terrible rotten life this is! I feel that the only meaningful type of work is the Movement but I don't want myself or anyone I've met to have to die. I'm so shook up that death just doesn't seem so awful anymore, though. I'm no different from anyone else and if they're risking their lives, then so must I. But I just can't comprehend why people must die to achieve something so basic and simple as Freedom ...

Love,
Sylvie

... Most of the regular SNCC workers didn't show much emotion in the open. To us it was something new, something unbelievable, that we were putting our lives on the line, that some of our team-mates had been killed; but to them it was not new.... I got the impression that their feelings did not differ much from those of a soldier who sees death around him....

... You probably heard about our three workers who are presently missing in Mississippi. At first this, too, was unreal ... but today the tension broke through.... We had a white lawyer from Birmingham [Charles Morgan] speaking on the white Southerner. In the question period ...

... a SNCC worker by the name of Jimmy Travis, who has been in the movement for years and has been shot up with a machine-gun, suddenly opened up and started to give one of the most moving statements I have ever heard ...

... "It's hell in Mississippi," he repeated again and again. "We've got to change the system, to change the system!" he cried repeatedly. He talked for about a half hour, saying the same things over again, but each time it struck each of the listeners or at least me like a poison dart filling each of us with the realization of what we were getting into and the dedication needed to do it …

… After his words, everyone broke out in applause and Travis left the room in disgust. Then another SNCC worker stood up and said that no one should have clapped — that Jimmy was not giving a speech. But people in the audience wanted to somehow express that they felt for and with him — and so when someone started clapping everyone joined in even though they knew that they shouldn't …

… He said what I knew all along, but it has made this place seem like a funeral parlor. People just walk around and sing, or are silent. It would be better for everyone if we just got busy and started learning techniques and policies. So far we have discussed "Why I want to go to Mississippi" for 2½ days. Damn it! I don't want to go; I just want to know the best way to do it …

What had happened in Philadelphia gave new significance to the concept of nonviolence, which was much discussed at Oxford. For some it had philosophical value; for other only a practical one.

Dear Mommy and Daddy and Toni: June 27

… We've been told over and over again of brutality and beating and murder. Hank says none of us really believe it inside. We probably each feel we have a lucky charm which will give us a halo of sanctity. I think we do. Part of it is the nonviolent philosophy, especially the part I now understand, which I didn't before. That is the part that teaches you to love your "enemy," how to feel true compassion for the cop who is using a cattle-prod on you, how to understand him as a human being caught in a predicament not of his own making. I think, although I'm not explaining it to you, that I now know how. When I came I thought that M. L. King and his "love your enemy" was a lot of Christian mysticism. Now I can see it as a force and support, helping those who understand it. It makes me think that maybe I can take what is coming this summer …

Love,
Judy

Dear Folks:

Yesterday was non-violence day here. In the morning we heard Jim Lawson of Nashville, who gave us the word on non-violence as a way of life. Lawson speaks of a moral confrontation with one's enemies, catching the other guy's eye, speaking to him with love, if possible, and so on … "Violence always brings more harm to the people who use it; economic and political forces have no place in the Movement … etc." These are the things that Lawson came up with … I feel very strongly that he does NOT represent the Movement.

Stokely Carmichael of SNCC rebutted him in the afternoon session: Nonviolence used to work because (1) it was new; (2) the newspapers gave it top coverage week after week, and most important (3) the demands were minor and the resistance to change was not hard-core. Now the North is tired of demonstrations, a very vigorous backlash has emerged, and the papers will only report major violence. Now we are responsible for what we do, and have to explain the stall-in instead of having it welcomed on the front pages of the press. Again most important, the movement has grown up, and is now aiming at the places where the white society really feels threatened — at jobs and at voting.

There comes a point when you get tired of being beaten and going back the next day for your beating for 5 days in a row. You get tired of being asked whether you are a Negro or a nigger, and ending up on the floor of the police station screaming at the top of your lungs that yes, you are a nigger, boss. You get tired of seeing young women smashed in the face right in front of your eyes. Stokely does not advocate violence. No SNCC workers are armed, nor are there guns in any SNCC office. What he is saying is that love and moral confrontations have no place in front of a brute who beats you till you cry nigger.

My feelings, and I think these are common, is that non-violence is a perverted way of life, but a necessary tactic and technique. It is harmful to the human person to feel that he must love a man who has a foot in his face. The only reason that I will not hit back is because then I will be in the hospital two weeks instead of one, and will be useless to the movement during that extra week when I can only read Gandhi's latest book on how to win friends and influence people ...

Bill

Bayard Rustin [told how when he was] ... in prison as a conscientious objector during the second World War, he was constantly harassed by a prison-mate, a thief, who kept throwing stones at him. One day, he went up to this man, and said, "Look friend, I'm tired of this, and so must you be. If you'd like to kill me, take this stone and bash my head in with it. Otherwise, let's stop ..." He [added] that he hadn't been courageous, because he chose a moment when there were many people around. The man was very confused. He stood there glaring for a long, long minute, and then walked away, never to throw stones again. Now the point of this ... the efficacy of non-violence ... was minor to me in comparison with the impact of what he said as an indication of the kind of person I felt him to be. That is, when he said it, I actually believed the story ...

The last night of orientation for the second group of Oxford arrived. The first bus stood waiting to leave; the volunteers traveled at night so as to arrive in Mississippi during the daytime. There was little doubt in anyone's mind that the missing three were dead.

Jim Forman of SNCC spoke, and then Bob Moses.

1st Oxford orientation session (Pam Jones singing at far left, Annelle Ponder in foreground, Julian Bond at far right, and Karen Kunstler standing between Annelle and Julian)

June 27

... Before the first bus pulled out last night Bob Moses, his head hanging, his voice barely audible, tried to tell us what he feels about being responsible for the creation of situations in which people get killed. His only rationales (and obviously they don't satisfy him) are that he asks no one to risk what he himself will not risk and that people were getting killed before Civil Rights workers became active. Looking at us sitting in the same room where the 3 missing men had been last week, Moses almost seemed to be wanting all of us to go home.

... He talked of the problem of good and evil ... of a book which is one of my greatest favorites, a rather unknown book by the Englishman, J. R. R. Tolkien, *The Lord of the Rings* ... the hero gains a means of ultimate power which he does not want. Yet this power becomes a necessity to him until in the end he is unable to yield it voluntarily, and in a very great sense, he must sacrifice that which is best in himself ... For those of us who knew the book, it was a great and beautiful moment and it gave us an understanding which we might otherwise never have had ...

... He talked about how, when you spend all your times fighting evil, you become preoccupied with it and terribly weary. There may be more people killed this summer, but that won't in any way deter us from what we are trying to do. Negroes who have challenged authorities in Mississippi have always been harassed or killed and we're trying to change that, not succumb to it. We're going to do the job we have to do.

... Then Bob talked directly to the freedom school teachers. He begged them to be patient with their students. There's a difference between being slow and being stupid, he said. The people you will be working with aren't stupid. But they're slow, so slow.

He finished, stood for a moment, then walked out the door. Inside the auditorium there was total silence. Finally, from far in the back, a single girl's voice started to sing: "They say that freedom is a constant sorrow ..."

... Slowly the voices in the room joined in. We stood with our arms around each other and we sang for each other. I stood between a boy I knew from Morehouse and a girl I knew from Carleton. And I felt the boy reach across behind me and hold the girl as well as me. I felt his love go through me, whom he knew and loved, to a girl he did not know well but whom he loved also. On the other side of this girl stood a woman who had taught at Spelman whom I knew and loved and who gave her love to this girl she did not know ...

The group sang in one voice, each individual singing not for himself but for the group ... As I sang and I felt the love of the group I realized that I loved all equally and that the difference was that I knew some better than others. And I knew better than ever before why I was going to Mississippi and what I am fighting for. It is for freedom — the freedom to love. It is something that none can have until everybody has it. Freedom to love all people equally and unselfishly, freedom to be a man with integrity so that there is no need to try to take others' integrity from them …

… As we sang, we all must have thought of our three who already died this summer in Mississippi. Everyone cried; either inside or out. We sang more, all kinds of songs, but the mood remained sad — sad because we have to do what we have to do, but not pity …

June 26

… Must write — thoughts are going crazy. Bob Moses just told us now is the time to back out. Should I? I don't know — I am scared shitless. I don't want to go to Mississippi. Why? Is it because I am scared or because the program isn't for me? No, program is good — people are dedicated — means of project conform with the end says Mario. Civil Rights Bill won't help — people are being killed — got to help. Pray. Forman says much of the tension will leave when we reach Mississippi. Father Keating says stick it out, give the project a chance. Perhaps I should only write down optimistic things to reduce dissonance but I must be honest. Little Negro kid said I would be killed in Mississippi and not to go if they weren't paying me. He's too glib. Nevertheless, he really shook me up. Damon isn't going. Wish I knew why. I have no one to turn to but me — and God. Perhaps He will give me a sign — Iwo Jima — cat who raised the flag is still living. But I ask for too many signs. Tomorrow I am leaving.

Volunteers in Oxford, Ohio, including Massachusetts Congressman Barney Frank (*second from right in back row*)

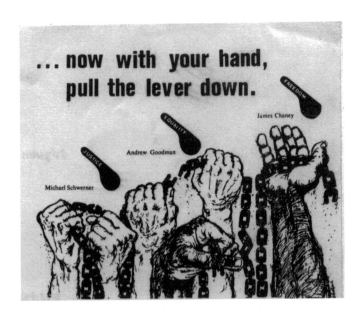

Before you all came, Mississippi was white man's land.
Now it will become human land.

Freedom School pupil
Greenwood, Mississippi

At Home in a Black World

Now it is one o'clock and our bus is traveling down a Tennessee road, far into the country. I have always thought that between the hours of one and three a.m. America comes closest to realizing her promise. There is a unity among all her travelers ...We all inhabit the same night in the same land. But somehow that is not enough.

The entry of the volunteers into Mississippi — mostly by bus and singing together on the way — was very different from the first lonely trip made there by Bob Moses four years earlier. Civil rights workers hadn't even tried to enter the state until 1952; the first "agitator" was shot and killed, the second was shot and run out of the state. Moses' foray turned out to be the seed of the Mississippi Summer Project. Between August 1961 and the fall of 1963, voter registra-

tion workers — mainly from the Student Nonviolent Coordinating Committee — spread into several parts of the state. That November, a Freedom Vote took place in which 80,000 disenfranchised Negroes cast their ballots for their own candidates in a mock state election which demonstrated that they would vote if they could. Students from Yale and Stanford came down to work on the Freedom Vote, thus extending civil rights work into seven more counties and establishing a successful precedent for the 1964 volunteers.

The needs of the Mississippi Negro clearly called for a campaign which could be waged only with the help of a lot of outsiders and a lot of outside money. After a long winter and spring of analysis, debate, recruitment, confusion and scrambling for funds, the Summer Project of 1964 finally began. Over 1,000 people entered the state of Mississippi. There was, first, the core group of 650 volunteers from 37 states (with a sprinkling from England, New Zealand and Australia) who are represented in this book. Then came the hundreds of ministers, doctors, nurses, lawyers and performing artists, to lend their abilities for two weeks or longer. Of the entire band, a very large majority were white people from outside the South, not so much because they were chosen that way as because more whites than Negroes applied and were financially able to come. (Every volunteer was supposed to bring $150 for his or her stay in Mississippi plus guaranteed bail money.)

The mechanics of the project's administration bewildered more than a few observers. Nominally, it was run by COFO — the Council of Federated Organizations — a Mississippi-based union of local groups, SNCC, CORE, King's Southern Christian Leadership Conference, and the Mississippi State Conference of NAACP branches (not the national NAACP). COFO had administered the Freedom Vote of 1963.

In actuality, SNCC and CORE did almost the entire job. Mississippi's five congressional districts were divided between those two organizations, with SNCC staffing and financing the work in four of them. Of the 100 staff members on the Summer Project, 76 were from SNCC. Robert Moses of SNCC was the director of the project and Program Director for COFO; Dave Dennis from

CORE held the post of Assistant Program Director; Dr. Aaron Henry, state President of the NAACP and a long-time resident, served as President of COFO. Headquarters for the project was a hectic office in the Negro neighborhood of Jackson, with almost as many telephones as people and 1017 Lynch Street for its address. Up in the town of Greenwood, about a two-hour drive away, SNCC established its national headquarters for the summer. Nobody was quite ready for action when the first wave of volunteers hit.

Dear friends,   Ruleville, Miss.

Last Saturday four of us took the long ride from Oxford to Memphis in a small Corvette which was rigged with a mike so that a CBS sound car behind us could record our profound thoughts as we went into battle.... We were all too tired to be the least bit profound. I felt quite relaxed during most of the 14 hour drive. Mississippi seemed very remote! At midnite we pulled up to a Howard Johnson's Motel just a few miles from the border. The CBS crew went through great contortions in arranging rooms for us all which could be written off on their expense account. An old man who was in the office asked us what CBS was doing. We told him. He asked why we wanted to stir up trouble. Why didn't we take care of Harlem. People in Mississippi could take care of their own problems. We were too tired to answer, but the feeling that we were in enemy territory swept in on me.

Sunday morning after the dead sleep of exhaustion I awoke with fear gripping my gut. I had a hard time forcing down breakfast. At 10 a.m. we left for the most direct route to Ruleville. When we got to the state line the camera car told us to stop at the side of the road while they went to set up a shot at the big sign that welcomes motorists to the Magnolia State. Waiting there as cars streamed past with all their occupants craning their necks to look at us, we got quite spooked. We finally got the go-ahead but then had to go back past the sign for a second run. All this time we noticed a big yellow car pass back and forth. We were quite angry at the newsmen's lack of planning and precautions.

After the first ten miles across the sun-bathed delta, the acute tension started to give way to a loose-limbed anxiety. Instead of being braced for what might come, I was ready to give with it. But the fear still clutched at the back of my neck as a car full of white men approached.... At one point the photographer was shooting us from the back of his car ahead when a car full of white rowdies passed us on the left and observed the whole thing. Well, we made it to Ruleville and Mrs. Fannie Lou Hamer's house where some of the volunteers plus a whole lot of press and some local people were gathered. Oh, were they a welcome sight!

Love,
Mike

Moss Point, June 30

I arrived by bus with the two other girls in Moss Point yesterday afternoon. After we waited a few minutes and nobody met us, we made a call to a number we'd been given and were told a ride was coming. We were then approached by a big heavy double-chinned drawling Southern stereotype, who turned out to be the chief deputy sheriff, one "Caesar" Byrd. He claimed he was looking for "a bunch of runaway girls from the North" and had us hand over our identification. After some prolonged verbal fencing which went something like this ... "What part of town you staying in?" "With some friends." etc., it became clear that he knew damn well who we were and we knew that he knew when he finally gave up the circumlocution with, "You come straight down from Oxford?"

I must confess I was scared silly at first, and was already fumbling in my pocket to make sure I had a dime for my one call from jail, but actually it's just as well it happened — he'd find out about us anyway ...

Shortly after this little interview, a car picked us up, and a fat laughing Negro woman drove us to our destination. Sheriff Byrd followed us in his car most of the way. The police drove past the COFO office six times in half an hour tonight, and this afternoon a car full of whites stopped and took down all the license numbers of cars in front of the office. But we got theirs, too, even-stephen....

Canton, July 3

Sunday saw the arrival of about 25 Freedom School teachers in Canton. They came in on the train about noon and we had six or seven cars there to meet them.... A couple of car-loads of cops pulled up suddenly and stood around while we unloaded all the suitcases and equipment and put them in the cars.... The county Sheriff and the chief of police asked us to go down to the police station to register. We decided we would cooperate so that our lack of cooperation couldn't be held against us in case of trouble. [*This was not COFO policy, which generally advised against agreeing to register.*] We were all registered, giving our names, home addresses, local addresses, intentions, ages, and various other identifying details. We also had our pictures taken with a little blackboard with our name written on it hanging around our necks. Then we were issued cards which signified that we had been duly registered with the Canton police department.

As a part of the show at the police station we were asked to listen to a tape which had been prepared by the attorneys of the city of Canton.... We were told that the girls might be raped by the very Negroes whom we have come to help and that the men might be stabbed or worse by the same people. The tape [*said*] that our presence here is very much resented by the white citizens and that they would be extremely happy if we were to change our minds and go home. We were told that we are uninvited guests in the county — which remark was challenged by one of the workers who reminded the chief of police that we had been invited by the Negro citizens of the county, if not by the whites. This would seem to constitute a rather good invitation as the county is 72% Negro....

But usually the whites just stared — sullen or curious or hateful — and the volunteers found their fear receding.

Ruleville, July 5

...We were really expecting much worse. Most of us would not have been too surprised if everybody had been arrested as we crossed the Miss. border and/or beaten. The disappearance of the three boys, tragic as it is, is mild compared to what we expected.

Their new homes were with Negro families or on Negro college campuses, but always in a Negro community. Some of the families had their own farms, some had no security at all.

Dear Anne,   Itta Bena, June 28

It's a hot lazy Sunday afternoon. I want to try to give you a description of Itta Bena and the place where we're staying.

The Negro neighborhood is literally "on the other side of the railroad tracks." To get over to the white and downtown area you have to either walk past several warehouses, small factories, etc., or cross the railroad tracks. The Negro neighborhood hasn't got a single paved street in it. It's all dirt and gravel roads. The houses vary from really beat-up shacks to fairly good looking cottages. The beat-up places predominate. There are lots of smelly outhouses and many of the houses have no inside water.

During the day it seems as if there is nothing but small children, hordes of them, and old people sitting on porches. There are quite a few churches. These have the most uncomfortable benches imaginable. I really can't do a good job of describing it; but then I don't have to — you've seen places like this town in movies and magazines a hundred times. But to see the place in the real is so different from seeing pictures of it. It's really there — you feel the heat, breathe the dust, smell the outhouses, hear the kids and the chickens.

John and I are staying with a 67-year-old woman named Rosa Lee Williams. She owns her place, so she doesn't have to worry about being thrown out.

Her house is on East Freedom Street. The street runs along the RR tracks. Across the street is a row of corn and then the RR tracks and a cotton field beyond. The house has a living room, with a double bed that John and I sleep in, a bedroom where Mrs. Williams sleeps and where we eat, then a small kitchen. The only running water in the place is in the toilet. No sinks are hooked up, so we wash out of buckets etc., but at least we have a flush toilet. Those outhouses are too much!

Mrs. Williams gets $4.00 a week from each of us for room. Originally she said she wasn't going to cook for us, but she's always doing it anyhow, so we're giving her another $4.00 a week. She said she didn't want the extra money, but she's on a pension and welfare, so she probably needs the money. She's really gotten crazy about us. She calls us "Lil' Bro'" and "Big Bro'" (Bro' is brother). She had a broken leg which wasn't set quite right, so she sort of limps. She also has an improperly set collarbone; it was broken when she was fighting with someone over a shotgun. She's still mad at the Deputy Sheriff for not giving her back the shotgun.

There's an old preacher, Mr. Bevel, two doors down. Another preacher in Itta Bena decided that it would be better for John and me to move in with him because he has a phone. When we mentioned it to Mrs. Williams, she was furious with Bevel for trying to take us away and we had to stop talking about it for fear she'd start a fight with him.

She's really a fiery and fast moving old woman. The first night we were here, Willie, John and I moved the bed into the living room. She was in the bedroom about 3 seconds before us and had the bed half apart before we were in the room. While we were setting it up in the living room she was running around mopping under where we were putting the bed. Before we went to sleep she brought in a can and put it under the bed. She said it was for "spittin" (she chews tobacco).

She keeps as clean a house as is possible with all the dust from the road blowing in. She's meticulous about flies and mosquitoes and usually sprays the place at night.

She's sort of a lonely old woman and I guess she enjoys having people around the house. She said that the last of her children died after the influenza epidemic of 1918. Her husband was a preacher and she's a retired midwife.

John and I both started having diarrhea last night. Must be due to new bugs in the water, food, etc. It should be over in a few days.

I love you,
Roy

Greetings Ed, from the Delta —   Tchula, July 6

My views on ruralfucking America are well known. Yet here I am living on a farm for the first time in my life — and enjoying it ... The Negroes here are independent farmers and live in small wooden houses with no running water and no sanitation facilities but they generally have a TV set, a freezer, a truck and a tractor — luxury that few sharecroppers or casual workers in Mississippi can hope to attain.

In the two bedroom house in which I live we have 5 small girls, a baby, 3 teenage girls, the mother and the father, one 11-year old boy and a grandmother, plus the two of us volunteers. The five children sleep in pinwheel fashion in one bed. Cephas (the other volunteer — a Negro) and I share a room all to ourselves. The house is kept immaculately by the three girls. Many

Northern women could take lessons from them. The food is unbelievable, the proverbial farmhand's meal with biscuits, eggs, rice, cornbread, sausage for breakfast and so much dinner that no three people could eat it ...

Best,
Mike

... Shaw is a small town (1,500) sharply divided into Negro and white sections ... I stay with five other girls in a house of ten people, two dogs, a cat and an assortment of several thousand bugs. An ants' nest in my bed the first night, a bees' nest in the kitchen, a wasps' nest in the bedroom ... Two of the girls left within a week ...

Hattiesburg, July 4

I am spoiled here in a solid, middle-class type home, and feel guilty about not sharing the more primitive living conditions of many other volunteers. Living with so many people — there are 16 here — has been surprisingly easy, but I got some insight into what it would be like without plumbing the other day. I had the misfortune of waking up with an urgent need to urinate. Of course there is only one bathroom, and the man of the house was in the tub. I paced the floor as long as I could and finally ran for Mrs. —. She got the pot, and I took it into the bedroom. Now my room-mate was still asleep, and she is a terror in the morning. You can't imagine how terrified I was of her wrath and my humiliation as I squatted above the ringing tin!...

Love,
Susan

Mileston, June 30

Man, like I don't even believe what I just did. You really had to be here to appreciate it. I took a bath. But no ordinary bath 'cause there's no running water. No, we take this bucket out in the back yard and fill it with water warmed over a fire. It's pitch black so we shine Mr. Clark's truck lights on the bucket. Then I strip down naked and stand in the bucket wash. That is the way you take a bath around here.

But the most significant new experience for the white volunteers was their reception by the Negro community.

Dear people,   Batesville

Batesville welcomed us triumphantly — at least Black Batesville did. Children and adults waved from their porches and shouted hello as we walked along the labyrinth of dirt paths and small wooden houses that characterize the Negro section of any Southern town. In a few days scores of children knew us and called to us by name. We had been warned to expect fear and hostility, but we were immediately invited to live and eat in Negro homes and to speak in Negro churches. For many local citizens our coming was a religious event; I found it difficult to be cynical. Sometimes when we pass by, the children cheer....

Geoff

Gulfport

... Fifty times a day people come up to us and thank us and tell us what we're doing is so fine, so good. The kids, playing with boards in the dust, have the greatest smiles. When we're out going from door to door to get people to register, we see a kid get up and run inside. "There they is" we hear. We are "they" and everyone knows who "they" is.

Greenville

It's amazing how you can grow to almost love a place so quickly. The Negro community has been so receptive and welcoming. The other night, a woman who has 17 children invited 20 of us over for dinner. It was a good dinner, too.

Canton, July 10

We are constantly on display when we're at the house; neighbors file in and out to have a look at us. The older ladies like to feel our skin; the kids are fascinated by our hair; everybody makes an appraisal of some sort — either we're "skinny" or "pretty" or "clean" or "young." When we go walking with [*the two*] widows [*we're staying with*] one of them invariably greets each passerby with "have you seen my girls yet?"

Meridian

There are the old men and women in old clothing whom you know have little money and none to spare, who stop you as you are leaving the church after addressing the congregation and press a dollar into your hand and say, "I've waited 80 years for you to come and I just have to give you this little bit to let you all know how much we appreciate your coming. I prays for your safety every night, son. God bless you all." And then they move down the stone steps and disappear along the red clay road lined with tall green trees and houses tumbling down.

Gulfport

Time and again when we go into a restaurant or bar, we start to pay, only to be told that the bill has been taken care of. People bring over a dozen eggs or cake and invite us to dinner.

The hospitality seems like that of the old frontier, with its house raisings and quilting bees.

Hattiesburg

Sometimes I think that all the decency the Mississippi human contains is encased in black walls. They're slow and talkative, but they'd shake hands with a mule if it came up to speak to them; if they had one cigarette left, they'd offer to halve it with you before they'd smoke it in front of your face. All this from people to whom $20 is a fortune …

And a medical student assigned to Meridian wrote:

I gave "medical" advice earlier this week to a father, whose son had an abscess on his chest. I told them to take the kids to a doctor. The father thanked me and kissed my hand. I was embarrassed and didn't know what to do, so I kissed his hand.

Sometimes, during the first days of the project, the local men showed their concern by standing guard unasked — at offices and homes where the volunteers were staying. Once in a while the offers of protection created awkward situations....

Gulfport, July 25

We had a problem with a man, and some of his friends, who took it upon himself to protect us from the white men who visited us yesterday. He came over at night with his friends and brought along a machine gun and ammunition. And told us not to worry. But he finally got ticked off at us, because we got ticked off at him. That machine gun made us edgy....

But as the volunteers lived longer in Mississippi, the guns seemed more understandable. They learned on the spot — from the things that befell their own hosts and hostesses.

Dear John and Cleo,   Canton, July 10

Our hostesses are brave women. And their fear is not at all mixed with resentment of us, but that makes it none the easier for them. The other morning a local newscaster said that someone was reported to have offered someone else $400 to bomb all the houses where volunteers are staying. I'm not convinced that that particular story has any basis, but it touched off the terror that must lie latent always in our sisters' hearts. I overheard one of them on the telephone: "My guhls probly think I'm out of mah head; I been singin' all mornin, every song I knows — I just has to." And she had been, moaning "Lord have musee" in between the songs. I talked with her a little bit. She told me she knows people have suffered and died too long and that we must take risks now so it won't go on forever. But that doesn't make the risk any less painful to bear. She sleeps with a hatchet under her bed. She told me she used to have a gun under her pillow until one night when she almost accidentally shot a neighbor boy....

Jo

The Negroes here have been pretty courageous, taking us into their homes and churches. Many of the homes we are staying in were shot up when the people went down to register during the past two years. One family got scared and asked two of us to leave after a car parked all night in front of their home a couple of nights ago — imagine having somebody sit in front of your home all night. Another person was fired from his job yesterday because two of us were staying with him.

Ruleville, July

... we have been given a wonderfully warm welcome wherever we have gone. In Ruleville the mayor had spent a week warning the Negroes that we were coming to kill them. (The mayor was told by one of the Negro ministers, "You're so low you're going to need a step ladder to climb into Hell.") Yet we were given the best of everything, and housing was found for all forty of us. Two people have already lost their jobs for housing us, and yet in each case half a dozen families begged us to stay with them after we had had to leave....

More and more, the volunteers found that the people they had come to help were helping them; those whom they had come to teach grammar and history were giving them lessons in life and love.

Dear Mom and Dad,   Gulfport, July 4

... You both know how critical I always have been of other people — always expecting a high level of performance and rather arrogant when the level is not reached. Thus I was a little worried, coming down here, where — because of a completely different cultural environment —people couldn't possibly meet those standards, or even aim toward them. That is, I was worried that I would tend to be extremely critical of the people around me, even though intellectually I knew how ridiculous it was.

But this has not occurred.... When I talk to someone while I am canvassing, I am able to accept them completely as they are.... If Mrs. X can read, fine; if not, I can enjoy talking to her about her life and experiences. Perhaps I've been finding that people everywhere have more in common than I once thought: humanity is so much more basic than education or intellectual achievement.

Related to this — I have met some of the most amazing, great people. Out of nowhere, seemingly, come little old women with so much warmth and wisdom that I almost cry. There's little Mrs. Rachel Fairley, who is about 65 and wonderful and crisp and brisk, yet full of God and sympathy. She's always praying for me — and for the three lost near Philadelphia....

Yesterday, around 7 p.m. I marched up on the steps of a

dark little falling apart house. Mrs. Brotherns — the lady of the house, I later learned — invited me in. (I keep being invited in for "some barbecue or a cold drink or a rest on the front porch.") Her husband was a beautiful man of about 59, great masses of graying hair. He was crippled with arthritis and thus could not write and could not read either.

It began to rain. We sat in a small dark room, lighted only by a brief flame in the fireplace where Mrs. Brotherns was cooking dinner. Their three adopted children sat on the floor and read from schoolbooks or counted bottletops, while the two old people looked on with love. The whole scene was from another century — especially because the little boy had a self-made bow and arrow, bent from a stick and tied with some cord. He proudly shot an arrow into the bushes across the street as I watched....

Love,
Ellen

Meridian, August 11

This is a very front porch community. People seem to know all the details of their neighbors' lives but there is very little judgment. This is not a puritanical society. Pity is somehow blended with complete acceptance of sensuality, sexuality, except if it's interracial — a white girl talking to a Negro boy is terrifying to them and with reason ... By sensuality I guess I mean what Baldwin meant — a way of being present in everything they do.

Tchula, August 30

There is some strong ambivalence which goes with this work. I sometimes fear that I am only helping to integrate some beautiful people into modern white society with all of its depersonalization (I suppose that has something to do with its industrial nature). It isn't 19th century pastoral romanticism which I feel, but a genuine respect and admiration for a culture which, for all the trouble, still isn't as commercialized and de-personalized as is our Northern mass culture. It is somewhat annoying to see a grubby little Negro cafe with a four foot by six foot tall full color picture of a young handsome Negro in a white dinner jacket next to his beautiful young Negro wife in a $200 cocktail dress in the backyard of their $40,000 brick home standing in front of a massive barbecue with prime ribs of beef and tender young duckling in beautiful glistening cop-perware serving Pabst Blue Ribbon Beer. A typical American Negro couple on a typical Sunday afternoon. Let's all escape and be like the white man ...

Dear Mom,   Holmes County, July 8

I have become so close to the family I am staying with — eleven people — that Mrs. H. finally paid me a great com-pliment. She was introducing me to one of her Negro women friends and said, "This is Nancy, my adopted daughter!" I baby-sat for her one night and in general we have become very close friends. She is a beautiful mother. My favorite picture of her is sitting peacefully in a summer chair with her 2-year-old baby girl in her lap; the baby, sucking her bottle, with one hand inside her mother's dress resting on her bosom. It is such a human sight; such love oozes from this house I can't begin to explain. All evening I have little children crawling over me and big boys, 16, my buddies, combing my hair, confiding in me, appreciating me, because I will open my heart and mind to them and listen and care for them and show my concern. I may be sex- and love-starved, as some like to picture me, but at least I have faced the problem and have found my own inner peace by being with people who have not forgotten how to love.

Really, to tell you the honest truth, I am just a little bit tired of hearing how you and others, and for a long time even myself, think, worry, discuss, write and talk about all the deep down psychological reasons for your personal problems. When I see these simple people living lives of relative inner peace, love, honor, courage and humor, I lose patience with people who sit and ponder their belly buttons....

Love,
Nancy

The happiness of the white volunteers sometimes suggested a feeling of assuaged guilt: "these people who should reject me for what my race has done to them are not full of hatred but warm acceptance." It was a surprise, and a relief...

Hattiesburg, July 8

I am not yet sure that I know why Southern Negroes seem to be less suspicious of our intentions than would Harlem Negroes for instance, but I definitely believe it is there.

Vicksburg

One day when I was canvassing I met Mr. Brown. I told him my name is Ann. He said yes, Miss Ann, pleased to meet you. He is a young Negro teacher in the all-Negro Temple High School and of course he had had no contact with white people before, except as Mr., Mrs., "Massa," — well, I said please call me Ann — and Ran, there was nothing so beautiful as the rest of the conversation. At every opportunity he had, he said Ann — he didn't just say Ann — he rolled the name around his tongue, savored the taste and sang it, listening to the echo in the back of his mind. He played with the word as a child would play with a new and fascinating toy, as a person would delight in the ecstasy of a new-found love. And that conversation has left a mark on me. I hear the name — a loved word — the start of something so big, so beautiful, so new....

Ran, this is something really big — yes, a revolution — a New Way of Living and Being. It's so different from the North where there is the intense, bitter hatred which makes working in Harlem or Roxbury or Philadelphia so heartbreaking because there is this invisible wall. Here there is Fear (I am referring now to the Negroes altho the whites are included) and when you reach that fear and stop it — as you can with some of the college and high school-age kids — there is a clear path — and this is where that great Change will come.... There is hope here that does not exist in the North ...

One of the several reasons for this hope seemed to be religion. Nothing made a deeper impression on the volunteers than the black Mississippian's sense of God.

Hi again,   Flora, July 13

... Jim and I have moved in with a little man who looks like Mr. Magoo and who bakes wonderful bread. He must be 75 years old, but he's tough, still working, and willing to undergo danger. He spends nearly all his spare time in reading the Bible, and like many of the people here, he takes its teachings to heart. The faith of these people here is amazing and not a dead form, like in most Northern churches. The services are lively, and it seems like the people follow the theory of Love Thy Enemy better than any people I've come in contact with. They have every reason to hate the white man, but I think they really don't....

                             Doug

                         Holly Springs, July 6

... Sunday I went to a real whoop and holler church, with people shouting, screaming and stomping. The sermon began as a talk and ended as a song. The preacher jumped up and down and had tears running down his face. He finally was overcome by the sheer power of his words and started to sing "This Little Light of Mine" in the middle of a sentence. We joined him, and people came up to grab his hands. I was one of them. This was the only House of God I had ever run into in my life. Amen! It was real, powerful and glorious.

Vicksburg

I went to Church today, the third time since I've been here … It's just like the scene in *Go Tell It on the Mountain* — but it's real — there's a direct tie between every person in that church and God, and every person with me and I with them.

Tonight was different from the first time … I left the church, wondering the eternal question of God, which we so easily answer with terms of science and evolution and theories of the Beginning … I cannot say God, I cannot think God, yet I cannot so easily dismiss the thought of some higher order of things — and after so long I cannot accept it and I want to run to some Wise One and plead "Tell me, tell me — what is the answer?" And there is no Wise One to answer me — and now I shall never know and I am afraid to read again what I am writing to you now with such speed because I know two weeks later, I will say to you — well, I was very tired when I wrote this to you and I will forget how I felt and I will sink back into that middle class existence you and I and our clan live in. No — I do not mean that exactly, for we do think and really wonder and worry and hope and weep and feel — but it's sort of a rut. For we think more or less in the context in which we were brought up — Aye, liberal and thought-provoking though it is, it is still enslaving us.…

Moss Point, July 8

... On Sunday I heard a very fine preacher in a little ram-shackle church down the road. A congregation of about twelve adults and a few children, scattered around to look like more, in flowered hats, little girls in bright pink dresses, sat listening and mostly fanning themselves with stiff cardboard fans which said "Friendly Funeral Home" on the back. This one gesture I would pick to show a big piece of Mississippi life; this slow fanning in the heat, the head cocked sideways, eyes half-closed, lazy, feeling the wind on wet skin....

The preacher was a visiting bishop, a great orator, almost a black nationalist, shouting out about Africa ... no Uncle Tom he, and Pharoah he said was "not a man, but the symbol of a government, a system, like Uncle Sam, the man with the long beard, always there even if the President gets shot." He spoke like this, loudly and earnestly, to the little fanning congregation, which answered now and then with a quiet "oyeslord" and "ain't it the truth" to the rhythm of their fanning.

Ruleville

At the service this morning, in the interminable prayer of thanksgiving, I was ready to gag. These people — who for sincerity and simplicity of belief are unrivaled by ten times as many Central Churches — have no reward for their faith. I wanted to tell them, but of course I won't, because it's all they have, and I admire them for it ...

Dear Mom,   Hattiesburg, 3:30 a.m.

... I really can't understand role of God and 'His will be done.' I think we should stop mouthing that cliche and start looking at vast sickness and decay in organized religion. Outside of the National Council of Churches which breathes a little fresh air (some of the ministers are really sharp)* and men like Mallette, Clemens, and Sheehan, religion bugs me so … Been reading that 'liberal' encyclical. Not very impressed. Also, big news from Jackson: Bishop of Mississippi declares all first grades [in parochial schools] should be opened on non-racial basis. Too bad most schools just happen to have their quotas filled up already. Bless our monsignor. He thinks with such foresight. Yea, social justice!

Love,
Dick

It was difficult to talk about Negro faith without coming back to the facts of Negro life. The first gift of black Mississippi to the white volunteers had been a sense of human beauty; the second was an education in some aspects of America which most of them had never confronted before.

Ruleville

There are people here without food and clothing. Kids that eat a bit of bread for breakfast, chicken necks for dinner. Kids that don't have clothes to go to school in. Old old people, and young people chop [*hoe*] cotton from sun up till sun down for $3 a day. They come home exhausted, it's not enough to feed their family on. It's gone before they earn it.… Some people down here get welfare. It amounts to about $45 a month. Pay the average $15 rent and you have a family "living" on $30 for four weeks.…

In Sunflower County alone there are 4,270 Negro families and 720 white families living in poverty. At the same time there are just over 100 families who own and control most of the county. Negro people are being kicked out of jobs, off sharecropping etc. to remove them from Mississippi. Mechanization of

---

*The NCC sent ministers for consultation by the volunteers when needed.

farms (plantations), usage of agricultural sprays, etc. provide the excuse and the agency to force the Negro to leave Mississippi. By no means is this the only means used, though.... Mississippi might be described as a state where people are harassed and intimidated — once because they were black and the means of production; now because they are black and a challenge to the status quo.

The other day a shipment of food and clothing arrived for the Negroes. Man, you don't know the "trouble" that something like this makes. The needs down here have to be measured by the truck loads or train loads. The shipment does not bring enough to go around....

Tchula, July 16

One lady I talked to last Saturday makes $2.50 a day working 7 days a week from 7 a.m. to 10 p.m. as cook and maid in a white home. She is old and alone and afraid to do anything for fear she will lose her only income and with it the tiny wooden house she saved for through many years of chopping and picking cotton. She never drinks a coke but fixes instead a penny Kool-aid on a hot day, to save the 9 cents she needs for her house and bills.

Dear Mom, Dad and Shari,   Mileston, July 23

We've been learning a little about conditions on some local plantations.

One plantation worker secretly left the plantation to come and ask us for help. He gets up at 3:30 a.m. and works on a tractor until dusk — for $5 a day, six days a week. His wife picks cotton for $2.50 a day. Two years ago he borrowed $250 from his plantation owner; since then, his "owner" has taken $10 a week out of his pay and hasn't stopped. A year and a half ago, when the debt had been paid, he asked the "owner" how much he still owed, he was told $100, and got the same answer ten weeks later (with the $10 a week still being deducted). He asked once too often, because the next week, after his boss discovered that he attended citizenship classes, the boss came to him with a note saying he owed $650. His boss and a local deputy sheriff are co-owners of the plantation ...

Love,
Joel

Dear Mom and Dad, Shaw, July 4

One day has passed in Shaw and the other America is opening itself before my naive, middle-class eyes. The cockroaches draw patterns across the floor and table and make a live patchwork on the bed. Sweat covers my skin and cakes brown in my joints — wrist, elbow, knee, neck. Mosquito bites, red specks on white background.

The four-year-old grandson is standing by my side. I wonder how our presence now will affect him when he is a man?

I saw other children today who bore the marks of the Negro in rural Mississippi. One had a protruding navel the size of the stone he held in his hand. Several had distended stomachs.

Is America really the land that greets its visitor with "Send me your tired, your poor, your helpless masses to breathe free ..."?

There is no Golden Door in Shaw.

Every statistic stood now for things the volunteers had seen with their own eyes, for people they lived with, people who fed them and protected them.

Hattiesburg, July 4

Every time I talk to people, I hear about things which bring tears to my eyes. I have begun, finally, to feel deep inside me this horrible double existence Negroes have to lead in both North and South ... the strategies they must learn to survive without either going crazy or being physically maimed — or destroyed. Mr. Reese describes how a Negro must learn to walk through a crowd: weaving, slightly hunched — shuffling helps — in order to be as humbly inconspicuous as possible....Then I hear from men who served in Korea or elsewhere, that they alone had no flag to fight for ... I talked with a fellow whose closest buddy [*in the Army*] had been a white man from Mississippi; when they were homeward bound on the train and they crossed the Mason-Dixon line, the white man left his seat beside the Negro to change seats with another Negro.

I could go on and on about all the people I've met ... Baby, it takes coming down here to grasp all this, no matter how many books we've read.

Ruleville, July

Most of us ... are from schools and families where sensitivity to pain is a very important virtue. I have made here the discovery that sensitivity is one of those virtues that depends upon the certainty of food and roof.... Here, one who is sensitive to pain will soon be reduced to a mass of wounds and hurts....

Dear Stark,   Meridian, June 30

... About the three missing men: there have been so many things like this that have never made any difference because no one has heard of them. Like the Negro [Herbert Lee] who was shot on the front lawn of the Liberty courthouse three years ago by a member of the state legislature. A Negro witness [Louis Allen] testified that it was self-defense, because of course he was scared. Then in January for some reason the sheriff or someone beat him up and broke his jaw. So he called up the FBI and told them he'd lied before, but the FBI wouldn't protect him and

he was killed within 24 hours. Maybe you've heard this, most people haven't. But of course he was a Mississippi Negro....
Love,
Edna

There are almost no sidewalks in the Negro neighborhoods. The red clay dirt is hard and the sun won't quit ... The poverty and sorrow of the neighborhoods doesn't leave you. I've been to hundreds of houses I could kick down with my feet and a small hammer. And I've seen the hands of these people, swollen and bruised, hard and calloused from years of work at practically no pay and whatever the pay was, it was always half what a white man would get for the same job. And I realized very suddenly and forcefully that these are my people and their sorrow is mine also. And since we are of this country our grief is collective whether the rest of the country admits it or not ...

What had happened, in a very short time, was that the Negro's world had become the volunteer's world, while the white world — in most cases, their own — had become an alien, frightening and ugly place.

Greenwood, July 11

I really cannot describe how sick I think this state is. I really cannot tell you how repulsed I am by this state, nor how fervently I think something has to be done down here. I cannot describe the fears, the tensions and the uncertainties of living here. When I walk, I am always looking at cars and people: if Negro, they are my friends; if white, I am frightened and walk faster. When driving and a car approaches, I am always asking: black? white?

Laurel

We feel safe here surrounded by the Negro community. The feeling of security evaporates when we go downtown ... They all look like Snopes family to me....

Meridian, Mid-summer

We live so completely within the Negro community that there is little confrontation of the white community. I noticed the other day that some white kids I passed looked to me as though they'd been washed too hard.

Dear people,   Batesville, July 26

Coming down from Crenshaw yesterday evening, I was in Reverend John's station wagon (with Jersey tags). We stopped in Batesville for gas at a white station, and two Negro workers there moved over to work on the car while the white proprietor collected the money from the Reverend. The young fellow (younger than I) who started cleaning the windshield kept giving me a beautifully friendly half-smile as he wiped the glass, a smile that seemed to be keeping a secret from the white proprietor. Every time he caught my eye, he smiled, and I was laughing back; it was wonderful communication. I said yes, please. As he bent under the hood to check the oil, I got out of the car and stood next to him as if mentioning something about the innards of the car. I asked him quietly (while the white man stood a ways away) if he smiled that way for all his white customers, or just for civil rights workers. We communicated in a stifled laugh for a minute, then he answered, "Just civil rights." It's getting harder and harder for me to listen with a straight face when a cracker tells me that "our niggers don't want you here."

Love,
Jim

But this new identity wasn't always so simple ...

Batesville

Before coming to Mississippi, we had been told that whites considered all civil rights workers not only "nigger lovers" but white Negroes as well. We had also been told that in the colored community you may soon be considered black.

But a white man never turns black in Mississippi. Sometimes you feel you've crossed the color line when a woman tells you about her fears and how she lies to the white folks but secretly hates them. She has probably never talked like this to a white man before; for a moment you believe you are turning black. Yet there are still the long silences and the incomprehensible phrases. Women still call me Mr. Geoff instead of Geoff, and old men offer their chairs. That doesn't disappear when they start to talk about their fear. And neither does your secret belief — which the old men and women encourage — that you are, after all, superior. Maybe this will all change when you've been here longer and when you visit a family for the fifth time. Maybe; but you're still college educated, still play acting, and still white ... You're still amused when in sorting out books for the Freedom library one Negro worker insists on discarding *Black Beauty* and a young local dark girl parades about with her recently discovered copy of *Pride and Prejudice*. It helps only slightly when you watch one of your fellow white volunteers throw away a copy of *Nigger of the Narcissus*. Following a marvelous dinner at the house of your local landlord, you hear yourself say "*Boy*, was that a great dinner" and you choke involuntarily on the expletive. You can't forget that you're still white ...

Ruleville

I am staying with one other project worker at the home of an elderly midwife widow. Last night we met two of her neighbors and spoke a limited amount with others young and old.... I felt that at any moment they would be willing to say "Ma'am" to me if I should raise my voice. How can I help create an honest relationship after years of lies, of words that came from the lips and not the heart?

Columbus

When the men from town here are drunk, they come up to the house saying "shit, I'm not scared of anything, hear." By the next day they are crawling again. The fear in their faces is pathetic. Last night a drunk man latched on to us. He kept talking about two things: he fought hard in Korea (shell shock and lost two toes, he has) and when he returned, the same people he was fighting for treated him like a dog; his wife died three months before. He took us to see his home ("it's open to you anytime"). There were three people there, his child, his mother-in-law, and her husband. The adults were all staggering drunk. There's not much recreation for Negroes except drinking and screwing, empty as life can be. The father-in-law was drunk but he was still terrified. You should see the faces, the eyes, of the men who are broken. The mother-in-law started talking: "sit down god-darned it, I want to talk to you. The white people treat us colored folk so bad. There's nothing we can do. They killed those three boys, they'll kill us all. What can we do?" I wish I could remember what all she said. She was so drunk she didn't "Yasuh" us and she swore at us. That was good, because she told the truth (what she really felt) and for a white man to get this from a Mississippi Negro is exceptional ...

Some of the proud Negroes among us say we are trying to save the black man's body and the white man's soul. But we have to save both souls. Many of these people are so smashed and whiplashed by the treatment they've gotten that they're lost ... This is the worst thing about segregation, it breaks people, it makes boys ("hey, boy, come here") out of men. The men are often so pitifully weak — unable to decide anything or to do anything. Another problem is that when the people get stronger, they often release against whites all the anger which they've repressed ...

We are frustrated by the dozens of beaten down people we meet every day. Yesterday when we were in the rural areas of Lowndes County, we talked about Freedom registration to one woman in a terrible house who said "I can't sign no paper." Lester then asked her "How will the pay for jobs and the homes ever get better unless we get together. Negroes have to do something to get something." She said, "I ain't no Negro, I'm a nigger. The Boss Man, he don't say nothing but nigger girl to me. I'm just a nigger, I can't sign no paper."

Meridian, Mid-summer

Last night, one of the boys said to his 6 year old brother, shortly after we had asked them why they didn't go home for supper: "Hey, Lance, tonite she'll be drunk & tomorrow he'll be drunk all day and we can get a lot of money out of them." (He & she being father & mother) ... One day I watched a boy about 12 pick out very slowly and without a single mistake, on the old typewriter at the community center:

The freedom we fight is for undrunks.

Indianola

... The interesting and horrible part of Negro life here is the absolute castration of the Negro male. He is trained to be nothing more than a child, with his ... sheepish expression and "Yessir, yessir" to everything the white man says. Children must then emulate the mother who usually takes the aggressive, stronger role in the family. Few Negro boys can look to their fathers as a strong figure with which to identify ...

Ruleville, July 2

The women make up the lion's share of the movement. This may be partially because they aren't as vulnerable economically but I don't think that factor is very important. Too many women work and oftentimes a man will get fired for the sins of his wife. Perhaps the major reason is that the women have the calm courage necessary for a nonviolent campaign.

On July 2, the Civil Rights Act was signed by President Johnson. The volunteers regarded it with their new eyes and new knowledge. For this was the South, where 98.8 per cent of the Negroes were still in segregated schools ten years after a Supreme Court ruling; this was Mississippi, where 100 per cent of the Negroes still attended separate schools. This was also the state, one volunteer noted, where, when President Kennedy was shot, a police chief declared a holiday and served fried chicken in the jail.

Dear Mom and Dad,   Clarksdale, July 3

Emotions in me are mixed now — watching that man who looks enough like Harry S. Truman to be his twin brother sign the civil rights bill — pride, joy, fear, disbelief, a wait-and-see streak. Thoughts of the thousands of Negroes, hundreds of thousands who will be helped by the bill, and the millions of poor to whom it will give dignity but no bread.

Watching the signing was a moment of happiness and a pain of hurt: people here in Clarksdale all know about that bill but tomorrow and Saturday, the 4th of July, they will still be in the cotton fields making three dollars a day. They'll still be in white homes working as maids, making three dollars a day. They'll still be starving and afraid.

I hurt more than I'm happy.... I know these people now and all I can say to them is vote, organize, starve.

Love,
Bob

Outside the COFO office in Greenwood

Dear friends,   Greenwood, July

It was rumored that some people would try to test the new bill. As most of you know, the Summer Project and SNCC decided not to test the bill. Mississippi is already a powder keg and it seemed foolish and dangerous to ignite it. We decided that the long range objectives of the project were more important than the short range objective of eating a hamburger in a white grease joint....*

That next day we received a call from a local Negro, who said with such pride, even a little as if here had come her chance to be vindicated, "Ah'm going swimmin' in that pool; ah've waited a

---

This decision was also based on the fact that testing would tie up too many summer workers and staff, both in general terms of time and personnel and because it might easily land people in jail. However, at least one project headquarters (in Clarksdale) did some unsuccessful testing with local people, mostly NAACP members.

long time." We worked hard to convince her that a swim in the pool wasn't worth it, but it wasn't easy. How do you tell them to wait, if the law says they can? How do you convince them that the vote, education, and community awareness are more important than a lousy hamburger which to them symbolizes freedom? Yet somehow most of the local Negroes did become convinced and once again agreed to wait some more, a little longer. Where does their patience and faith come from? How much longer will it last?...

Best regards,
Phil

On the Fourth of July the volunteers had a holiday — but not to celebrate Independence Day nor the passing of the Civil Rights Bill. The project feared that antagonistic whites might take the occasion to demonstrate their "independence," so no work of any kind was attempted outside the offices that day. In several towns the local women cooked great quantities of food; there was picnicking and softball and the day became a feast for new friends.

Ruleville, July

We ate from two until five-thirty and every time we said we could eat no more we were served again with spicy chicken and this woman's or that woman's special ham and potato salad and sweetbread and corn bread and hot muffins and peas cooked in bacon and onion sauce and home-made applesauce and sodas and punches and grape juice and potato casseroles and more and more and more until the pies and the cakes and the ice cream came and we could not refuse. But the real part of this which makes it unforgettable for me were the many people who spoke of their gratitude for what we were doing. One woman said, "Most of all, these young white folks who are already free, they come here only to help us. They is proving to us that black and white can do it together, that it ain't true what we always thought, that all white folks is booger men, 'cause they sure is not." And people wonder why we came....

HOLLY SPRINGS

BATESVILLE   TUPELO

CLARKSDALE

CHARLESTON   **1**   ABERDEEN

CLEVELAND

SHAW   RULEVILLE   **2**

INDIANOLA   GREENWOOD   COLUMBUS

GREENVILLE   ITTA BENA   STARKVILLE

TCHULA

BELZONI

                        CARTHAGE

                CANTON   PHILADELPHIA

            FLORA

                                MERIDIAN

VICKSBURG   **4**

JACKSON

            3

                                LAUREL

NATCHEZ

                                HATTIESBURG

        McCOMB

                                5

• LOCATION OF MISSISSIPPI PROJECTS

GULFPORT   BILOXI   MOSS POINT
                    PASCAGOULA

CONGRESSIONAL DISTRICTS OF MISSISSIPPI

They say in Mississippi
There are no neutrals found
You either Tom for Ross Barnett
Or else you are a man.
Oh, which side are you on, boy?
Which side are you on?...

Freedom Song

That Long Walk
to the Courthouse

Oxford, June 24

Howard Zinn says that Mississippi is not just a closed so-ciety, like the rest of the South. It is a locked society for which we must find the key. Many feel that the vote is the key and the number of votes the pressure on that key. All I can say is that I hope so....

The Summer project was a five-pronged assault on the status quo: 1) voter registration and organization of the new Mississippi Freedom Democratic party; 2) the Freedom Schools; 3) community centers; 4) the white community project; 5) Federal programs research (to see how Negroes might obtain aid under existing or potential govern-

ment arrangements). The volunteers worked on one or sometimes two of these programs; a small number were assigned to man the Project offices.

The first three programs formed the heart of the Project. They were interrelated, for the success of each depended on getting the Negro community organized and moving. The Project's basic idea was that, in the absence of federal action in Mississippi, the Negro had to lead his struggle for salvation himself; that to do so, he must find his own strength — and that the volunteers would aid him in this.

The largest number of volunteers were assigned to what they called VR — voter registration. They had two simultaneous tasks: to help Negroes register in the conventional way, and to help build up the Freedom Democratic Party, a new political organization designed to give a voice to the disenfranchised Negro voters. The Freedom party is described in Chapter X. Regular VR meant, of course, registering in the way prescribed by Mississippi law to vote for federal, state and local officials. At the beginning of the summer, the volunteers concentrated on this aspect of political work.

They had been briefed at Oxford.

Dear people,   Oxford, June 25

Mississippi's eighty-two counties are divided in five congressional districts, and these districts serve as the frame for our work. The first district is the northeastern part of the state; Bob Moses describes this region geographically with the three letters, TVA. The TVA has had some liberalizing influence here. Also, the proportion of Negroes in the area rarely goes over 30% in any county and is under 5% in one county. The Negro farmers here are isolated from the mainstream of thought and action and the problem of registration workers is not so much the hostility of the local white citizens as it is the difficulty of finding, educating, and bringing the unregistered to the court-house.

The Second Congressional district is the delta area, the land of extensive plantations, and poor, dependent sharecroppers. The Negro population here runs well over 60%. In the Second district, the principal opposition to registration work comes from the White Citizens Councils, and their main weapons are economic here: one way or another, the majority of Negroes depends on the plantations for jobs and homes. Senator Eastland's plantation in Sunflower County is in this region.

The Third Congressional district runs from the Second south to Louisiana. This is mainly hill country, and our work here is centered in five areas. Jackson, the capital; Vicksburg, which has had an indigenous voter registration drive since the late forties and is generally considered "open"; Natchez on the Mississippi, which has a large Armstrong tire and rubber plant, and the whites there feel definitely threatened by Negro labor (terrorism and brutality are believed to be the work of white industrial workers in this area); McComb, the capital of Pike County, with a long record of brutality and terrorism. Most Negroes in the Third district are small farmers, and a high percentage own land. The danger in the Third district, which is 40-50% Negro, comes from the revived Ku Klux Klan.

The Fourth district, directly east of Jackson, is generally considered the "easiest" in the state, but what happened in Philadelphia shows how relative that is. Negro population here runs under 50%.

The Fifth district runs south from Laurel to the coast. This area includes Hattiesburg and the Gulf Coast which has a large shipbuilding industry and tourism and is generally exposed to the outside world. The Negro population is under 33% and they don't have much trouble registering to vote on the coast....

Jim

The voter registration workers learned that some of the places they would be going already had an active local movement while others would have to be "opened up." This meant first visiting the town from a nearby base; talking to the people to see who would go down to the courthouse to register; locating a place for meetings and if

White Citizens Council Office

possible Negro homes in which to stay. The main goal was to find a few local Negroes willing to organize their neighbors and then carry on the struggle by themselves.

It was a large order: according to the most reliable statistics, some 94 per cent of the eligible Negro voters in Mississippi weren't registered.

Valley View, August 25

The right to vote is completely controlled by the registrars —one to each of 82 counties. They alone decide whether an applicant has passed the test, they inform him only after a 30-day wait, and they don't have to tell him why he failed the test.

The registrar could always find a reason for flunking a Negro applicant: the undotted "i," a misspelling, or especially an error in question 19 which required the applicant to copy out and then interpret any one of the 286 sections of the Mississippi Constitution specified by the registrar. Some of the sections run as long as two pages, all in legalese. Negroes with Ph.D.'s were flunked, while white men with only a grammar school education were passed.

But more discouraging to the Negro than these technical traps was the fact that the names of all applicants were published in the newspaper for two weeks or more. It wasn't difficult to tell white and Negro names apart, as the white names were dignified by Mr., Miss, Mrs. And once identified ...

Batesville

... Fear of The Man, fear of Mr. Charlie ... Occasionally it is the irrational fear of something new and untested. But usually it is a highly rational emotion, the economic fear of losing your job, the physical fear of being shot at. Domestic servants know that they will be fired if they register to vote; so will factory workers, so will Negroes who live on plantations. In Mississippi, registration is no private affair ...

Dear Mom,   Holly Springs

When we walk up to a house there are always children out front. They look up and see white men in the car, and fear and caution cover their expressions. Those terrified eyes are never quite out of my mind; they drive me as little else could. The children run to their parents, hide behind them. We walk up, smile, say howdy, and hold out our hands. As we shake hands I tell them my name. They tell me their names and I say Mr.—, how do you do. It is likely the first time in the life of this farmer or housewife that a white man has shaken hands with them like that. This does not necessarily bode well to them. They think, if Mr. Charlie knew ... Many are sharecroppers, who must turn over a third to a half of the year's harvest to a man who does no work at all, but who owns the land they till. They may be evicted, and have often been for far less serious offenses. Nearly everyone black in Mississippi is at least a year in debt. The threat of suspended credit and foreclosure is a tremendous burden....

Love,
Bob

Greenwood, July 15

We are trying to get people to go down to the courthouse to register. In Mississippi there are no deputy registrars, the only place that people can register is at the Courthouse at the County Seat. The county seat for Leflore County is Greenwood. This in itself restrains Negroes from voting because they don't like to go to the courthouse, which has bad connotations for them. Behind the courthouse is the Yazoo River. The river also has bad connotations; as Albert Darner said, it's "Dat river where dey floats them bodies in."

Gulfport, July 8

Canvassing, the main technique in voter registration, is an art, and like an art, it is not a scheduled thing. You don't work from 9 to 5. There is no such thing as a completed job until *everyone* is registered. When you cheat and take a lunch hour (and it feels like cheating) you suddenly find yourself reviewing a failure or a success to discover the whys: maybe I should have bullied him slightly, or maybe I should have talked less — and relied on silences. Did I rush him? Should I never have mentioned registering at all, and just tried to make friends and set him at ease? It goes on and on....

Techniques and approaches vary. Mine is often like this:

Hi. My name is Steve M. (shake hands, having gotten name, address from a mailbox). I'm with COFO. There are a lot of us working in this area, going from house to house trying to encourage people to go down and register to vote. (Pause).

Are you a registered voter? (This is the direct technique. Often people, being afraid, will lie and say yes, but you can usually tell, because they will be very proud.) Are you planning on going down soon? (This makes them declare themselves. Usually they say "yes" or "I hadn't thought about it much." The other answer is "No, I ain't going down at all.") "Well, I have a sample of the registration form." (Take it out and hand it to them.) "You know, some people are a little afraid to go down because they don't quite know what they're getting into. It's something new and different, and they're not sure about it."

Then I go on, "You know, it is so important that everyone get the vote. As it stands now, that man downtown in charge of roads doesn't have to listen to the Negroes. They can't put him out of office. He should be working *for* you." (Much gossip, chatter, mutual questions through all this).

Then pull out the Freedom Democratic Party application.

"This is a protest party. Anyone can join to protest the laws about voter registration and the way elections are carried out."

You get the picture. It goes on, 10 hours a day, 6 days a week. On Sundays we rest by working at other things. We go to church. Since all visitors are allotted time to speak, I relate voter registration to God. I have become a pretty good preacher....

Few volunteers worked on canvassing the plantation workers; this perilous task was usually left to experienced staff members if attempted at all. But in Holmes County, a small group of volunteers developed a technique for doing it with the assistance of local Negro youths.

Dear folks,   Mileston, August 18

One can't move onto a plantation cold; or canvas a plantation in the same manner as the Negro ghetto in town. It's far too dangerous. Many plantations — homes included — are posted, meaning that no trespassing is permitted, and the owner feels that he has the prerogative to shoot us on sight when we are in the house of one of *his* Negroes.

Before we canvas a plantation, our preparation includes finding out whether the houses are posted, driving through or around the plantation without stopping, meanwhile making a detailed map of the plantation.

We're especially concerned with the number of roads in and out of the plantation. For instance, some houses could be too dangerous to canvas because of their location near the boss man's house and on a dead end road.

In addition to mapping, we attempt to talk to some of the tenants when they are off the plantation, and ask them about conditions. The kids often have contacts, and can get on the plantation unnoticed by the boss man, with the pretense of just visiting friends.

Our canvassing includes not only voter registration, but also extensive reports on conditions — wages, treatment by the boss man, condition of the houses, number of acres of cotton, etc. Much more such work needs to be done. The plantation system is crucial in Delta politics and economics, and the plantation system must be brought to an end if democracy is to be brought to the Delta....

Love,
Joel

Sometimes people said "yes sir," they'd go down to the courthouse — and the volunteer felt they would have as easily said "no sir" if asked not to go down. It made no difference: they didn't go anyway. At the mass meetings, many would get all worked up with shouts of Freedom NOW, but do nothing when the time came. The fact that black Mississippi had become a land of children and old people — so many in between had gone north to escape — was a problem in many areas: "Senator Eastland needn't complain about all us idealists coming here, he's exiled all his in-state leaders." But there were Negroes of all ages who slammed the door in a volunteer's face when they heard the word "vote." And who could really blame them, when a police car was driving slowly by or the boss's brother was watching from the road — or an Uncle Tom?

Canton

The hardest of all to take are the "Uncle Toms," who sit in on our mass meetings, visit the homes we're staying in, gathering all the information they can to sell to the White Citizens Council....

Clarksdale, July 9

One of the small Negro kids is a spy for Ben Collins, chief of police. He goes around listening to our talk all day, finds out where we live, and reports all we do every night. He calls himself Superman, and rumor has it that he is paid $3 a day for his services. He is only 12 years old.

Some of the "Toms" could be found among the Negro cops — a handful of men who were not permitted to arrest whites, weren't paid (except by the head, for each fellow Negro arrested) and had to buy their own uniforms.

Gulfport, June 24

While at the bar, we started taking down names of local people who wanted to help us. One was a big lugubrious Negro man who said he was visiting from Chicago because he was bringing home the body of his dead wife. He was so dejected that I kept murmuring sympathetic phrases. Well — It turns out that he was a policeman who was following us. We're wondering whether to take him down to register ...

And sometimes the volunteers ran into a very different sort of problem while trying to get the local people involved.

Ruleville, July 2

Mass meeting in the evening; Freedom songs, etc. Walking home in the dark, I was stopped by a young Negro man who began a conversation by asking me what went on in the mass meetings; he wanted precise details, where the money went, why do we sing so much? what do the people say? and so forth. He was persistent, forceful, and asking the most difficult questions. It came out that he wanted to join the Movement, but he couldn't understand non-violence. "I seen a picture in one of the books of this guy sitting on the ground, with his head down and his arms up, and this other fella was running and hit him on the ear like that. Just hit him. I don't get it. I couldn't do that." His voice was soft. I didn't see his face, it was dark, but we talked for almost two hours, walking …

Mass meetings were one of the main ways to get a community moving. People could then see that there were others who wanted their rights. But sometimes the fear in a community made it difficult just to get a church or hall for the gathering — and with some reason. Thirty-seven Negro churches were bombed or burned during the summer.

Como, August 18

"Good evening, Mr. Wallace."

"Good evenin'. Won't you come up and have a seat on the porch?"

"Don't mind if I do. That heat's something, isn't it?"

"Sure is. Water?"

"No, no thank you, sir. This shade is just fine. I didn't see you at the mass meeting last Thursday night."

"Well, I reckon you didn't. I *meant* to get out there, but Mrs. Wallace, you know, wasn't up to it. I hear it was a pretty good meetin', though."

"Well, you know, we had a lot of spirit there, but not too many people. Lots of young folks, but the adults just didn't turn out."

"That's the way it is — the young folks is always right out there runnin', and the older folks just sort of trot on behind."

"Well, we missed you, Mr. Wallace."

"I planned on bein' there. You countin' on having another meetin' soon?"

"That's one of the things I wanted to talk to you about, Mr. Wallace. I understand you're a deacon right here at the Baptist Church in town."

"That's right. Been a deacon there thirty-four years. My brother, George — you know — he's a deacon, too."

"Yes, sir. I've talked with him. How many deacons does your Church have?"

"There's seven now, I think. There's me, and there's George. And then there's Henry Eastland, and Jimmy Stennis, and Mr. Howard out there east of town. Will Barnett lives down in Sardis, you know. Then H. K. Williams and Mr. Robertson right here in town."

"Yes. I've already spoken with Mr. Robertson. He said it would be all right with him if we organized a meeting up at your Church next week; but, of course, I'd have to speak to all the deacons first."

"Jack Robertson told you that?"

"Yes, sir, so I thought I'd come and see you, Mr. Wallace."

"Well, I'll give it to you just like it is. I'm with you one hundred per cent, and I'm plannin' on goin' down to the court-house soon, you know. But speakin' for the Church, I'm not so sure about that."

"Why's that, sir?"

"Well, I guess just not yet. We're not ready for that yet, right here. But I'm with you one hundred per cent, and I think you're fine fellows doin' a fine job with our folks. The colored people around here have needed this for a long time."

"We're not really *doing* anything here, Mr. Wallace; it's you local people who have to do things, right here in Como, before the white man stomps you down. We're just here to let you know what we think can be done — by you."

"That's right!"

"And that's why we need to hold meetings, so we can talk to the people."

"That's right. What our people here need is education, and I think you're doing a fine job. That's what I tell all the folks around here when they talk against you. You're here to help us and we should do all we can."

"That's why we need your Church for a meeting, Mr. Wallace. We've held two meetings out of town now at Mountain Hill, and we'd like to talk to the people right here in town."

"I'm telling you now just the way it is; some of the white folks have been talkin' up against you all and your meetings now, and I don't want any trouble. I've been readin' about all them churches bein' burned and bombed …"

"But none of that has been here in Panola County, or anywhere around here. We've got the FBI watching here and Sheriff Hubbard has helped us out a couple of times."

"Well, I just don't want any trouble. You've been havin' your meetin's out at Mountain Hill — why can't you keep on havin''em there?"

"That's two miles out of town, Mr. Wallace, and we'd like to move into town, now, for our meetings. It's easier for the people who live here."

"Well, I just can't say yes."

"All right, Mr. Wallace. But Mr. Robertson said it was okay. So I think I'll talk to the other deacons. You haven't been down to the courthouse yet, sir?"

"No, but I'm plannin' on goin' down right soon now,"

"Lots of people are going down this week. Maybe you could get a ride with Mr. Rice tomorrow."

"Well, not this week — but I'll be goin' down soon."

"All right, Mr. Wallace; I'll be back to talk to you again soon. I've got to be getting along now. I'll talk to the other deacons, and I hope to see you down at the courthouse soon, sir!"

"That's right! I'm with you one hundred per cent now. Good

luck! And come on back."

Mr. Wallace represents a large number of people here in Como. Not everyone — far from it — but enough people think like him to make work occasionally exasperating, especially for the local people who are not "one hundred per cent *with us*" but who are working like hell to build a better Como for themselves ... That "one hundred per cent with you" has become a joke with us. So much so that Mr. Howard, who went down with us to Batesville to register this morning, and who is going to be one of the stars of our mass meeting, said, as he left us this noon: "If I've passed that test, I'm with you *two* hundred per cent!"

In Indianola, the seat of Sunflower County (number of eligible Negroes registered: 2%), the ministers refused to lend their churches but a Negro Baptist Convention in the area voted unanimously to let the project use a three-room brick schoolhouse. A mass meeting was called for July 23; no more than 100 local people were expected.

Dear Folks,   July 24

Last night was one of those times that are so encouraging and inspiring. We had a mass meeting in Indianola. Three weeks ago, there was no movement at all in that community. A few Project workers went in and began canvassing for registration. It was decided to set up a Freedom School. Another few workers went in as staff. In that short time they had generated enough interest and enthusiasm to bring out 350 people to the meeting!

I sat and watched faces that had been transformed with hope and courage. They were so beautiful, those faces. It is hard to put into words an experience like this. That sense of hope was so strong, so pervasive, each of us there felt with complete certainty that there can, there will, be a better world and a good life if we work for it. When James Forman speaks, he talks "soul-talk," reaching out to that part of us that is vital, that is creative, and the people respond with a radiance and a sure-

ness that is so new to them. The word "new" is very significant
— it not only means a change in the externals of their lives
... the greatest import of "new" is the emerging "new value of
themselves as human beings, with the right and will to act, to
move, to shape their lives ...

Love,
Ellen

There were other times, other places, when all the long hours of
walking and talking seemed worthwhile.

McComb, August 20

The voter registration program, despite its shortcomings,
is a beautiful thing to watch. Such a big step for these people!
The voter registration classes are slightly tense, but what is more
present is hope, positiveness. The people dress up carefully. They
shake each other's hands, await eagerly the return of those who
have gone down to the courthouse already. Two functional il-
literates have come, and so many others have so much trouble
filling out the form. But they're going down — a cemetery
caretaker, a blind man, a cafe owner, a domestic ...

Not only did people in a single town range from the fearful to the
militant, but Negro communities as a whole varied from one part
of the state to another. There was Greenville, for example, located
on the Mississippi River; once a major port, it had been opened to
the outside world ...

Dad,   Greenville, August 9

Greenville is certainly a liberal city by Mississippi standards.
It has three Negroes on its police force. The town appropria-
tions to white and colored schools have each year come closer
to being equal, and the police force watches the Klan as closely
as COFO.... The public library is integrated (after a small
group of Negro high school students last year demonstrated

and spent months in jail.) The Negro and white swimming pools are exactly alike. One of the town's leading newspapers, Hodding Carter's *The Delta-Democratic Times*, urges moderation and compliance with the law. In other words, Greenville does not use terror tactics to maintain segregation and it has come a bit closer than other cities in Mississippi to making the separate but equal policy a reality. In Illinois, a city like Greenville would be ultra-conservative and would make even Winthrop Harbor seem a haven for fanatic revolutionists. In Mississippi, it's liberal....

Buzz

Greenville, unlike the rest of the Delta, had a sizable Negro middle class.

Greenville, July 9

The whites here are darker than the colored sometimes, making you wonder who should swim with whom. As for the colored, I heard a little Negro girl saying scornfully to her friend while touching her neck, "Oh Honey, you sure is black."

July 14

The Negro leaders are of course the rich Negroes in town. Many of them are afraid of their own position in the white community and they don't want to move now that there are a lot of people who want to move.... A lot of kids here take a very cynical attitude toward the NAACP and even Martin Luther King.

Hi,   Greenville, July 3

There is a group of approximately 150 high school boys called the Mississippi Student Union. They've had a couple of demonstrations and are eager to do something and pretty informed. This is where our big problem comes in. COFO told us absolutely no demonstrating. Now we're faced with the problem that if we don't support these kids in their demonstrations, we're not going to get the respect and cooperation we need from them …

The old Negro leaders threatened to put an ad in the papers branding us as Communists. It's a bad situation. A lot of the poor Negroes who are just beginning to get active accuse the old leaders of being directly under the thumb of the white power structure (receiving bribes, etc.) … Your point in one of your letters is certainly right, mom. They are as much victims as others. But it seems they are in positions, and have been, where they *could* work changes instead of blocking them. I hope we can reconcile …

Love,
Barb

Mileston, on the other hand, had a long tradition of violence; yet the situation in that little rural community was very different from most of Mississippi — for an unusual reason.

Dear Mom and Dad,   Mileston, July 6

Mileston, where I'm staying, is in the flat Delta section of Holmes County. The Negro farmers here were once part of huge plantations. In 1939 the federal government confiscated the land when the plantation owners failed to pay back taxes, and the land was divided up among Negro families who had applied for it. Land reform (on a minuscule scale) has had an enormous effect on the people …

Last year Hollis Watkins, a SNCC staff member, began a voter registration drive here. He got about 14 Negroes to go to the court house with the intention of registering to vote. Sheriff Smith greeted the party with a six shooter drawn from his pocket, and said "Okay, who's first?" Most of the Negroes remained cautiously quiet. After several seconds a man who had never before been a leader stepped up to the Sheriff, smiled and said, "I'm first, Hartman Turnbow." All registration applications were permitted to be filled out and all were judged illiterate. The next week, Turnbow's house was bombed with Molotov cocktails. When the Turnbows left the burning house, they were shot at, and they shot back until the attackers fled. A couple of days later, Mr. Turnbow, Hollis Watkins, Robert Moses and a couple of other people were arrested for arson; Turnbow was accused of having bombed his own house which wasn't insured. Sheriff Smith was the one witness against them. Mr. Turnbow was convicted in a Justice of Peace Court, but the conviction was overruled in a federal district court ...

The Negro people we are living with have enormous hope and are extremely practical about achieving their goals. This community is an oasis of hope in a desert of broken minds: the plantation sharecroppers who have little reason for hope ...

Love,

Joel

Both Greenville and Mileston had some history of civil rights action. The town of Drew, also in the Delta, was a new experience: volunteers had to "open it up," commuting there from nearby Ruleville where Mrs. Fannie Lou Hamer lived.

A 24-year-old white volunteer from Philadelphia who had been a youth worker with the Quakers tells part of the story of Drew in a series of letters.

Dear friends   Ruleville, June 24

Last evening we went up to Drew, the tough little town north of here to do some canvassing. Whites streamed through the area ... sometimes they would call a Negro over to their car and send him scampering back to his house. The police kept talking into their mikes as they cruised by. Most of the [Negro] people were not at all receptive. I talked for a while to some kids who may be willing to start a group. We talked about the whole movement and about how you were safer if the community was united. This evening we will go back again and talk to the people a bit, just to show them we are still around....

July 2

There were still a lot of folks who didn't want to have anything to do with it all because it meant trouble. I met a very tall freshman at the local high school who said he wasn't afraid of the "man." As I walked down the road with him, his mother came to warn him not to get mixed up with us. She said they probably wouldn't hurt us but would beat *him* as soon as we had left. She told me she was afraid for her boys. She wants to raise them safely and get them out of here ... There was an old couple, married 62 years, who said they couldn't pull much any more but could still push. This seems to be the sentiment of many of the people in this town. They would be willing to take a step but they don't want to be first. We are gradually getting a list of about half a dozen people who say they are now willing to go down to the courthouse....

July 11

I drove up to Drew to see if the one-legged WWI veteran was ready to go to the courthouse to register. He said he was ready at any time, though he had lost his glasses and so couldn't read very well. I assured him that the important thing was to take the stand of going down ... It will help the Justice Dept. case against this registrar to have as many people attempt to register as possible. I accompanied Mr. K., a proud 70-year-old, into the courthouse. We were informed that the registrar was out for a while and that I would have to leave as soon as he came back. I suggested that Mr. K. take the empty seat but he was reluctant to risk a rebuke by sitting "out of bounds." We stood there for ten minutes. Finally the registrar came in and asked me if I intended to help Mr. K. register. I said, "no," and asked him if Mr. K. could have a seat. He said "of course." Our hesitancy in this instance had not been warranted, but what about next time?

I sat out on the porch of the columned courthouse and waited. It didn't take long. The print was so fine that Mr. K. couldn't make much out of it. We went over to a Negro cafe for a pop and then I left to do some canvassing. Mr. K. assured me that the 2 hour wait [to ride back with me] wouldn't bother him. The fight for freedom needs a lot of patience, he thought, and that was one thing he was strong on.

I also met a guy who said that the preacher told the people not to mess with us. We got into a long biblical argument about whether people should sit around and get along as best they could while waiting on the Lord or try to change things to more nearly meet his design. I think I got the best of the argument, but then he talked about how well he got on with the white folks. He said, "Why it was just the other day that Mayor Williford congratulated me for being a good Negro." I could see that he had so deeply identified with the present system and the ways it left open for Negroes to get ahead that he wasn't open to ideas of change. The Negro kids I was canvassing with were disgusted. The man's wife gave me a sort of whimsical smile from the door. I read it (maybe wishfully) to mean "You can't talk any sense into that old man." A number of people in Drew seem to resent our forays. It is crucial that we get a place for meetings there and have some people stay there for a week or two. Now we are planning an open-air meeting for next week. I hope it will get things off the ground.

The day of the first mass meeting in Drew arrived: Tuesday, July 14.

July 18

... Four of us went to distribute flyers announcing the meeting. I talked to a woman who had been down to register a week before. She was afraid. Her husband had lost his job. Even before we got there a couple of her sons had been manhandled by the police. She was now full of wild rumors about shootings and beatings, etc. I checked out two of them later. They were groundless. This sort of rumor-spreading is quite prevalent when people get really scared ...

At 6 p.m. we returned to Drew for the meeting, to be held in front of a church (they wouldn't let us meet inside, but hadn't told us not to meet outside). A number of kids collected and stood around in a circle with about 15 of us to sing freedom songs. Across the street perhaps 100 adults stood watching. Since this was the first meeting in town, we passed out mimeoed song sheets. Fred Miller, Negro from Mobile, stepped out to the edge of the street to give somebody a sheet. The cops nabbed him. I was about to follow suit so he wouldn't be alone, but Mac's policy [Charles McLaurin, SNCC project director] was to ignore the arrest. We sang on mightily "Ain't going to let no jailing turn me around." A group of girls was sort of leaning against the cars on the periphery of the meeting. Mac went over to encourage them to join us. I gave a couple of song sheets to the girls. A cop rushed across the street and told me to come along. I guess I was sort of aware that my actions would get me arrested, but felt that we had to show these girls that we were not afraid. I was also concerned with what might happen to Fred if he was the only one.

... The cop at the station was quite scrupulous about letting me make a phone call. I was then driven to a little concrete structure which looked like a power house. I could hear Fred's courageous, off-key rendition of a freedom song from inside and joined him as we approached. He was very happy to see me. Not long thereafter, four more of our group were driven up to make their calls ...

The Drew jail consists of three small cells off a wide hall. It was filthy, hot and stuffy. A cop came back to give us some toilet paper. We sang songs for a while, and yelled greetings to Negroes who drove by curiously. One of the staff workers had been in jail 106 times. I asked the cop if he could open another cell as there were not enough beds accessible to us. He mumbled something about how that would be impossible and left. They hadn't confiscated anything and one of the guys had a battered copy of *The Other America*, so we divided up the chapters. I got the dismal one on the problems of the aged ... To be old and forgotten is certainly a worse sentence than mine (I wouldn't recommend that book for those planning to do time) ...

Well, the night was spent swatting mosquitoes. An old Negro couple walked by in front of the jail and asked how we were doing. They said they supported us and the old lady said, "God bless you all." This, in the context of a tense town with a pretty constant stream of whites in cars driving by....

The group was released the next day after paying $100 bail apiece on a charge of unlawful distribution of literature. In order that the black people of Drew would not think the arrest of seven workers could stop the Movement in their town, a second mass meeting had been called for that same night. At 4:30 a.m., while the seven were still in jail, volunteers distributed announcements to the Drew plantation workers before they went to the fields for the day.

The meeting began to roll about 6 p.m. on July 15.

July 27

... When we got there we found the group, a much larger group that the night before, with a considerable number of adults, singing on the lot next to the church grounds. (The police had put pressure on the deacons to deny us the use of the church grounds.) There were deputies in great profusion this time, in their white helmets. The street had been barricaded off, but there was still a large crowd watching from the other side of the street. Mac was making a forceful speech … Just then the cop came up with an old lady who said she owned the lot we were meeting on. The chief called Mac over to the car and the lady told him the niggers didn't want us around. Mac said that all who wanted to stand for freedom should meet in the street. I held back, but when I saw so many local people taking that courageous step, I was drawn to support them. The deputies marched us off to the little jail we had left just that morning.

This time the place was pretty crowded. There were about ten of us plus 5 kids from the Ruleville Student Movement and ten local people. There was one high school boy from Drew who had been on his way to football practice, about 6 ladies in their thirties who were worried a bit about their families but were generally quite solid.…

Well, it took them over an hour to decide where to send us all and how to get us there but finally we set out in a long convoy, first to the county farm to let off the Negro men and women, and then on to the county jail to let off the whites. We were a bit scared about the prospects of landing in a cell with a bunch of whites, so we ditched our SNCC pins.

We were marched up to the second floor by a Negro jailer and put in a cell with one white prisoner. The cell was very small with three double bunks, one of the beds had no mattress and was strewn with the refuse of past boarders. We told the guy that we had been picked up for standing in the street and bitched profusely about the injustice. He had been there a week. Was picked up, he said, for drinking two beers, charged with disturbing the peace and sentenced to a month at the county farm. He was endowed with this typical attitude toward Negroes but had some very healthy grievances against the system down here and I think we might have made some progress with him if we hadn't been so cautious about revealing our identity.…

Best,
Mike

Again they were released the next day. By now, bail for those arrested had mounted to almost $4000. More dollars were being put in the town coffers than new voters on the rolls. And so it went in most parts of the state.

In some counties, suits had been brought against the registrar to stop discriminating against Negro applicants. The federal injunctions or court orders which followed promised to give the potential Negro voter a real chance. One of these had been issued in Panola County, in northern Mississippi, which has a 56 per cent Negro population. There were two county seats there instead of the usual one—Sardis and Batesville—and after the court order, the registrar's office in Sardis closed. So Batesville became a center of activity. It had a twenty-year-old tradition of local people taking the initiative; their Voters' League had filed the suit which led to the court order of 1964. Two of Batesville's leaders were Robert J. Miles and his wife.

June 30

... He is a Negro farmer who owns his own land (about 600 acres as I understand). He has a college education as do all his children. A quiet, humble fellow with a great sense of humor. He thinks out his moves carefully and doesn't take any crap from the white man ...

... Mrs. Miles had a great comment on the town swimming pool which is, of course, not integrated. She said, "I don't see why they won't let us swim in the pool. It's been proven we don't fade."

The volunters started working the town. One of the first targets was the teachers, always the hardest group to get moving. As county employees, they had to take an oath swearing that they did not belong to the NAACP — among other "subversive" organizations.

Dear people,   Batesville, July 9

The good colored people of Panola County support five high schools, with a total faculty of a few over one hundred. Of all the people who have already registered to vote in the county, there have been no teachers. We are trying to get the teachers to register in a special campaign. Everyone is willing to go to the courthouse — after someone else …

Just before COFO moved into Batesville the county colored teachers were given a slight raise in salary. The contracts are to be signed this week — maybe. We have finally assembled a group of twelve to fifteen teachers who promised to go to the courthouse next Saturday, contract or no contract …

                                    Jim

The principal of the Negro school (1 through 12 in the same building) here in Batesville is no help. We are going to get a group of teachers together without him, and have them go down in a group. If any one is fired, all will be, and we are told by the local Justice Dept. man that we could have a quick suit. I interviewed the principal myself. He sat in his air-conditioned house and talked about how he didn't want any "fanfare." Next door a family of 8 or 10 sat in front of one of the worst looking shacks I've seen down here …

                                            July 23

… Finally last Saturday, having studied their strategy carefully, five teachers went to register together. Four of them are young and energetic and certain that they could find a job elsewhere. One of them is a dynamic widow with ten children and a patch of land. She could not possibly afford to lose her job. Their courage has paid off. In the five days since the group went, teachers have been going to the courthouse at the rate of three a day. Yesterday, to the surprise and delight of the entire community, the Principal registered.

The teachers did not lose their contracts. And the Negroes of Panola ceased to dread the publication of their names in the newspaper.

... In Panola county now the Negro citizens look with pride at their names in the *Panolian*; they point out the names of friends and neighbors and hurry to the courthouse to be enlisted on the honor roll.

Meanwhile, voter registration workers had spread out into other towns of Panola County like Como and Crenshaw. Registration was going well. Too well, for the white folk of Batesville.

Batesville, August 1

We're all a little nervous. Four COFO workers — including me — are staying with the Robert Miles' on their farm just outside of Batesville. Mrs. Miles' 25 yr. old son Robert Jr. is stationed out in the yard with a gun. (Yes, the Movement is still non-violent; but every farmer — white and black — in the Delta has a gun. Mr. Miles has seven, all loaded.)

Things are getting very tense around here. Last night, while I was eating a peanut butter sandwich in the kitchen and talking to the other white girl staying here, two shots whizzed right by the kitchen window — I could even see a flash of light from the gun.

Since last Saturday night when the Miles' house was bombed with a tear gas grenade, several other Negroes in town have received bomb threats....

We think that the heightened tension is pretty much a testimonial to the success of our voter registration drive. About 500 Negroes have registered since the summer volunteers arrived in Batesville — this in a county where until recently only two Negroes had been able to register in seventy years ...

Robert Miles, President of the Panola County Voters League

But the Panola story was unique. Tallahatchie county also had an injunction; two Negroes attempted to register that summer for the first time since Reconstruction — with five carloads of F.B.I. men standing by for the occasion. In Madison County volunteers found that economic intimidation made the injunction virtually worthless.

There are 82 counties in the state of Mississippi; rulings against the registrar would have to be obtained in 82 separate suits — and that was only a first step. An omnibus ruling against all registrars had been rejected by a federal court in Mississippi.*

---

*In March, 1965, the Supreme Court overruled the decision and upheld the power of the Justice Department to sue a state in order to enforce voting rights.

As Martin Luther King pointed out in a speech, even at slightly better than the present rate, it would take a hundred and thirty-five years to register half of the eligible Negroes.

Jackson, August 14

Until I got here, I didn't fully realize how much is needed and how long and slow everything goes. The one complaint that is most often heard is, "Where is the Justice Department?"

At work in a Freedom School

If you can't go, let your children go —
I'm on my way, great God, I'm on my way

Freedom Song

School for Freedom

Greenwood, July

All day long the older people sit stilly on their porches. The hand that occasionally moves to fan is almost accidental, even miraculous. When we walk down the street we walk a kind of gauntlet between these porch-sitters. Out of the dull resentment and the weary suspicion that is directed not so much at us (for they all seem to know our mission) as at the railroad tracks, at the street itself, come the words and the tone that are always shocking: "How you all?... Jes' fine, thanky', jes'fine!" Always an artificial, pious enthusiasm, until it seems a ventriloquist's trick. And I always find it a parody of the behavior that white supremacy has enforced on the Negro.

But lo, brown and black and cream-colored children fill the street with a marvelous vitality. The smallest of them has an air of authority and self-reliance about him, has a sure knowledge of the game at hand; and he always, always stands up for his rights. If you view the scene of porch and street as a timeless version of the range of a single generation, then that boy, free, running, yelling, is simultaneously that old man fading into death, submitting to it, on the shaded porch. Because between the street and the house something important has died, something has been killed.

I think this kind of image, and the possibility of a variation on it, is at the heart of the momentousness that all of us teaching in the Freedom School are beginning to feel.... Our purpose is to expand awareness, to fortify what the student already knows —although inarticulately — that he is a human being and deserving of respect ...

Dear people,   Ruleville, July

Mississippians often boast that more money has been spent on Negro schools in the last ten years than on white schools. This is true, at least with one qualification: *capital expenditures* on Negro schools have exceeded those on white schools. On annual per pupil operating expenditures, the white schools are still way ahead. The reason for this tremendous increase in capital expenditure is simple: they are starting from scratch because there were hardly any Negro schools before. Every Negro school you see is new, but that is not because of the white Mississippian's generosity towards "his Nigras." It is because of the Supreme Court decisions of 1954 and 1955. The South is finally trying to carry out the letter of the Plessy vs. Ferguson, "separate but equal" decision of 1896.

However, with this "step forward" came what is perhaps an even more vast step backward: the abolition of compulsory education in 1956, still in effect. That was done to prepare for the setting up of private schools, as in Prince Edward County, Virginia. It has already hurt one generation of Negroes, who, just as schools were finally being set up, have in many cases been enticed away from the schools to work in the fields.

But let's see what kind of schools they have been enticed away from. After lengthy talks with several teachers and many students, I feel able to reach some conclusions. First of all, those brand new buildings are shells. In Shaw, for instance the following things found in the white school are missing from the Negro school: lockers of any kind (even for the football team), ventilators, central heating (they have those electric fan units in the ceiling such as you see in garages), water coolers (there is one cooler for 1800 students), bleachers for the football games, a school car of any kind, landscaping or anything else to make the school pleasant. Children get textbooks discarded by the white schools. Shop equipment and typewriters for business courses come the same way. Perhaps it is what Aaron Henry called "Mississippi's affinity for the bottom" that we are fighting …

Charles

Greenville

The training of teachers in Mississippi is, to make a crude understatement, inadequate. To begin with, these teachers are themselves products of Mississippi grade schools and high schools. The qualifications for teachers are low at all levels, including college. The Negro colleges are understaffed, underequipped, underpaid, under everything. Many of the Negro teachers in Greenville went to college at MVC (Mississippi Vocational College), which isn't even accredited outside of Mississippi … The schools of Greenville are all segregated, and Greenville just can't afford to operate two school systems on an equal basis …

Carthage, August 9

… I couldn't begin to describe the condition of their 25¢ school bus. Last year the bus had no heat and no windows. If children are picked up at 7:30 a.m. they often didn't make it to school until after 12:30 p.m. Several times when the bus broke down the children would have to walk to a farmhouse to warm up. Then when they get to school they are supposed to get an equal education.

Some of the Negro high schools weren't even dignified with the name, but called Attendance Centers. "And I gather that attendance is indeed the major content of the school day," *wrote one volunteer.*

Canton

Yesterday I decided to find out just how much they, (mostly 6th and 7th graders), knew about our federal government. When I got discouraged by the blank looks on their faces, I asked, "What is the capital of the United States?" "Jackson?" ... "How many states are there in the U.S.?" "??... 82?" (82 counties in Miss.) Is this symbolic?

Hattiesburg

The students are taught nothing of their heritage. The only outstanding Negroes they are told about are Booker T. Washington and George Washington Carver. They learn nothing of the contributions Negroes have made to our culture or anything else which could give them any reason to disbelieve the lies they are told about Negroes being unable to do anything worthwhile ...

Mound Bayou

The county superintendent of schools ordered that neither foreign languages nor civics shall be taught in any Negro schools, nor shall American history from 1860 to 1875 be taught ...

Hattiesburg, July 8

My students are from 13 to 17 years old, and not one of them had heard about the Supreme Court decision of 1954. I don't need to tell them that segregation is wrong, and that separate-but-equal is a myth; but they are surprised to hear that the law is on their side, because they hear only about the laws of Mississippi in their schools....

The Negro response to the opening of the Freedom Schools was dramatic: by midsummer, 41 schools with 2165 pupils had been established. In Hattiesburg, it wasn't a response but an onslaught.

Saturday, July 4

... all this week we have been working on curriculum, schedules, registration of students and assembling materials for the Freedom Schools at Hattiesburg. It became evident quite early that we were going to have many more than the expected 75 students. We called Jackson and got a promise of more teachers — at full strength we will have 23. This was when we expected 150 students. On registration day, however, we had a totally unexpected deluge: 600 students! They were expecting only 700 for the whole state. After a while, as they were coming in, it changed from a celebration to a crisis. This is 26 students per teacher — much better than the local or usual ratios, but still not enough (like 5 to 1) to do all we want to in six weeks. Somehow we must set up a complete school system: 6 churches as schools spread around the city (which makes a huge transportation problem for teachers); next to nothing in materials; and age range from 8 to 82....

We have been here only a week and we must set up this system before Monday when school starts, but we will do it; in fact the thought that we might not make it hasn't even occurred to us. The point here, as I told a curious white Baptist minister on registration day, is that the Negroes of Hattiesburg *do* want to study and learn....

The Freedom Schools stood for everything which the regular schools had discouraged. They were a sort of mental revolution, requiring special tactics: a "citizenship curriculum" in which reading, writing and speaking skills would be developed through discussion of Negro history, literature, the Movement, and the Mississippi power structure. All the pupils had a session of this course, which went by different names at different projects, and then they chose from more academic subjects for the rest of their time in school — algebra, chemistry, biology, whatever they asked to have taught. The evening classes for adults offered health, literacy, and typing classes, again with an emphasis on life as the Negroes knew it.

Dear Mom and Dad;   Holly Springs

The atmosphere in class is unbelievable. It is what every teacher dreams about — real, honest enthusiasm and desire to learn anything and everything. The girls come to class of their own free will. They respond to everything that is said. They are excited about learning. They drain me of everything that I have to offer so that I go home at night completely exhausted but very happy....

I start out at 10:30 teaching what we call the Core Curriculum, which is Negro History and the History and Philosophy of the Movement, to about fifteen girls ranging from 15 to 25 years of age. I have one girl who is married with four children, another who is 23 and a graduate from a white college in Tennessee, also very poorly educated. The majority go to a Roman Catholic High School in Holly Springs and have therefore received a fairly decent education by Mississippi standards. They can, for the most part, express themselves on paper but their skills in no way compare to juniors and seniors in northern suburban schools.

In one of my first classes, I gave a talk on Haiti and the slave revolt which took place there at the end of the eighteenth century. I told them how the French government (during the French Revolution) abolished slavery all over the French Empire. And then I told them that the English decided to invade the island and take it over for a colony of their own. I watched faces fall all around me. They knew that a small island, run by former slaves, could not defeat England. And then I told that the people of Haiti succeeded in keeping the English out. I watched a smile spread slowly over a girl's face. And I felt girls sit up and look at me intently. Then I told them that Napoleon came to power, reinstated slavery, and sent an expedition to reconquer Haiti. Their faces began to fall again. They waited for me to tell them that France defeated the former slaves, hoping against hope that I would say that they didn't. But when I told them that the French generals tricked the Haitian leader Toussaint to come aboard their ship, captured him and sent him back to France to die, they knew that there was no hope. They waited for me to spell out the defeat. And when I told them that Haiti did succeed in keeping out the European powers and was recognized finally as an independent republic, they just looked at me and smiled. The room stirred with a gladness and a pride that this could have happened. And I felt so happy and so humble that I could have told them this little story and it could have meant so much.

We have also talked about what it means to be a Southern white who wants to stand up but who is alone, rejected by other whites and not fully accepted by the Negroes. We have talked about their feelings about Southern whites. One day three little white girls came to our school and I asked them to understand how the three girls felt by remembering how it feels when they are around a lot of whites. We agreed that we would not stare at the girls but try to make them feel as normal as possible.

Along with my Core class I teach a religion class at one every afternoon and a class on non-violence at four-fifteen. All my classes are approximately an hour. Both these classes are made up of four to six girls from my morning class and about four boys of the same age group. In religion they are being confronted for the first time with people whom they respect who do not believe in God and with people who believe in

God but do not take the Bible literally. It's a challenging class because I have no desire to destroy their belief, whether Roman Catholic or Baptist, but I want them to learn to look at all things critically and to learn to separate fact from interpretation and myth in all areas, not just religion.

Every class is beautiful. The girls respond, respond, respond. And they disagree among themselves. I have no doubt that soon they will be disagreeing with me. At least this is one thing that I am working towards. They are a sharp group. But they are under-educated and starved for knowledge. They know that they have been cheated and they want anything and everything that we can give them.

I have a great deal of faith in these students. They are very mature and very concerned about other people. I really think that they will be able to carry on without us. At least this is my dream ...

Love,
Pam

Indianola, August 17

I can see the change. The 16-year old's discovery of poetry, of Whitman and Cummings and above all, the struggle to express thoughts in words, to translate ideas into concrete written words. After two weeks a child finally looks me in the eye, unafraid, acknowledging a bond of trust which 300 years of Mississippians said should never, could never exist. I can feel the growth of self-confidence ...

Biloxi, August 16

In the Freedom School one day during poetry writing, a 12-year-old girl handed in this poem to her teacher:

What Is Wrong?

What is wrong with me everywhere I go
No one seems to look at me.
  Sometimes I cry.

I walk through woods and sit on a stone.
I look at the stars and I sometimes wish.

Probably if my wish ever comes true,
Everyone will look at me.

Then she broke down crying in her sister's arms. The Freedom School here had given this girl the opportunity of meeting someone she felt she could express her problems to ...

Dear Mom and Dad,   Meridian, Midsummer

The Freedom School is an old Baptist Seminary, which was supposed to be condemned last year. We are thankful for it. We are one of the few Freedom Schools with a building of our own and classrooms and desks and blackboards. I teach two sections of a course called Freedom and the Negro in America — we talk about things like "What do we mean when we say, 'Things are bad in Mississippi?'" "What do white people have that we want?" "What do they have that we don't want?" And I am teaching French to the younger kids — mostly 11 to 14. I never expected to come to Mississippi to teach French, but they love it. As it is not taught at all in the Negroes' school, and is taught in the white schools, it is a symbol of what they do not receive in school. And it turns out to be a good way to develop grammar and phonetic skills that would bore them in English, and to do some desperately needed broadening of cultural horizons ...

Love,
Gail

A Freedom School meeting in the Batesville COFO office

Meridian, July 15

… One thing that I've found here is that the students are on a much higher level than I had been led to expect. A lot of books which I wouldn't think of bringing because they would be "on too high a level" or "too intellectual" are being used very successfully. If reading levels are not always the highest, the "philosophical" understanding is almost alarming: some of the things that our 11 and 12 year olds will come out with would never be expected from someone of that age in the North.…

Harmony, July 20

… My History of Religion course is going fine — they are extremely interested in Judaism, in the fact that I am a Jew, in the rituals and beliefs of Judaism, etc. By this week, I hope to get into the origins of Christianity in Judaism so that they can all (about 12) get a deeper feeling for the roots of Catholicism, and in turn the roots of their *own* faith, Southern Baptist.…

August 19

Wednesday I went with a bunch of Freedom School kids to Biloxi where we saw *In White America*. A touring company has been formed this summer to play all over the state.

I guess you know what the play is about — a symposium on the Negro in America. It is pretty strong stuff — what the slave ships were like, what being a slave was like, the lynchings, Father Divine in the 30s, Little Rock, and an added scene: a speech by Rita Schwerner.

This was the first theater most of these people had ever seen. They didn't have theater manners yet and it was great. They shouted "Sho nuff" and "You said it" when they agreed with something and joined in singing the songs. One of the actresses said, "You can't imagine what it was like under slavery" and a 15-year-old girl next to me said, "Oh, yes I can."

Clarksdale, August 3

Most of last week was spent working on the "Clarksdale Freedom Press." Getting all the interested kids in the basement of Haven Methodist Church, examining possible articles, editing them, typing them, etc., was great! The place looked just like a newspaper office with people running in and out, with typewriters going, and newsprint everywhere. It was excellent experience for the kids too ... They did most of the work and made most of the decisions....

Many of the schools mimeographed such newspapers, using material written by the students: reportage, political essays, poetry — always about themselves and their feelings as Negroes and how to change things for the better. But along with this kind of success, each Freedom School had its own problems and each teacher his discouraging experiences.

Dear John and Cleo,   Canton, July 10-16

I'm sitting in what we've turned into a Freedom School — a one room wooden church ... Most of the windows are half paneless. The only seats resemble picnic benches. One lamp, hung from the ceiling ... A colored U.S. map, a few freedom posters, some prints torn from an old calendar have brightened the room a little since we came. A broom and a scrub brush helped, too, to dispel the terrible depression that fell over my two fellow teachers and me when we first saw the place. That depression got heavier before it became lighter, though. On registration day nobody came and we had our scrubbed benches, clean floors and brightened walls all to ourselves. For several days after, we combed the area for students. Some were holding back out of fear — their own and/or their parents' (this building was bombed a month ago; the police have been circling it almost hourly since we moved into it); many distrusted us; some simply didn't care. But by some mysterious force which I really don't understand, a few people began appearing for classes, averaging about 20 a day now — never the same 20. I don't know how meaningful or lasting a response we're getting overall. Somedays I'm kind of thrilled; other days bring bitter discouragement....

Love,
Jo

Indianola

Naturally they hardly trust whites and there is a lot of 'Yes Ma'am' and constant agreement with what you say. Until a week and a half ago, these children had never seen a white woman get down on her hands and knees and scrub a floor....

Hattiesburg, August 1

The Summer project has two Freedom Schools in Palmer's Crossing, a rural community about two miles outside of Hattiesburg. The two schools have nine teachers, five of them (including myself) professionals. It has been rough. Much of what we know about teaching must be unlearned or relearned here. The standard academic approach has not worked at all well, even when material has been simplified ... The kids we are dealing with are not trained to listen to, and absorb information presented in an organized, "logical," manner ... The students do not seem to be able to follow a point-by-point presentation at all, whether simple or complex. They learn by talking, by conversation, by rambling around and beating the nearby bushes. And they learn by acting things out.

We have rather small children (aged 8 and up), and these are our worst problems. Once when it was my turn to babysit I tried to hold a lesson on politics. None of the little kids knew what politics or government were, so I asked them if they knew what the mayor is. Someone volunteered that the mayor is sort of like a horse. (This led to a spelling lesson on "mayor" and "mare"). In order to get down to real basics, I asked if anyone had ever seen a street or road. Yes, they had. How, I asked, did they think streets and roads got there? Who made them? Here the civics lesson came to an end. "God," a little girl replied. A lengthy theological discussion followed. "Does God make trees?" "Yes." "Do people make trees?" "No." "Does God make houses?" "Yes." "Do people make houses?" "No. God makes everything." This position seemed unassailable by logic alone, so, thinking that something massive must be done at once, I asked a few of the more sober-minded boys if they had ever seen someone build a house. Indeed they had, and I launched them on a long description of how this is done, making sure that real people figured prominently in the description. It was not without interest, but it wasn't a civics lesson.

One day we listened to the recording of "In White America" … The kids were struck by the incident in the Little Rock integration riots, in which a small Negro girl describes movingly how she was spit on and cursed as she tried to go to the previously all white school. Our discussion soon came to examine the purposes of school integration. All the kids were totally convinced that integration will mean that they would get schooling as good as the whites. It was, for them, a very simple point: Negro schools, in hundreds of little ways, are not so good as white schools.

I tried to make the question more theoretical. Suppose Mississippi should decide to spend as much money on Negro education as it does on white, so that the two schools would really be equal. Would they still favor integrated schools? For some of the kids this possibility was too incredible to accept seriously. They could not imagine Mississippi making Negro schools equal. But others saw that the point of the question was whether integration has a value in itself, apart from the equality it would bring. Few kids seemed ever to have thought of it just that way, but a little prompting gave them an idea. Did they think that Negroes and whites in Mississippi really understood each other? There was a chorus of deeply felt Noes.

They quite frankly admitted not understanding white people any better than white people understood them. Did they think this would be true if whites and Negroes had been going to school together all their lives? Probably not. I was then able to get in a philosophic point about education. Education, I said, is supposed to give people an understanding of what the world is really like. A school system that closes students off to half the people in their world cannot do this. And so segregation deprives whites equally with Negroes....

Dear Friends: Meridian, July 7 & 15

Today was the second day of full operation at the Meridian Freedom School. In one way, it has been a tremendous success; so far, we have probably had about a hundred and twenty students register (we were only expecting about 50 or so), and that only includes students over 12 years of age. Partially because the school is entirely voluntary, and partially because there is no punishment or even threat arising from lateness or absence or noise, there is no discipline problem. Everyone seems to be having a good time (except, of course, the teachers).

The unfortunate results are that we have tended to set up a somewhat formal structure (with, malheureusement, even bells between classes). The classes tend to be larger than the five or six students that were originally planned: yesterday there were 38 students in my math class and 41 in my French class. The result is a slowly emerging super-bureaucracy, and a tendency toward more "conventional" methods of teaching (this latter being helped along somewhat by some of our "professional" teachers, who have a condescending attitude toward the rest of us; the remark, "Well, you don't know because you're not a *professional*" has more than once wafted from their lips.) …

Best,
Pete

Teachers in the Delta and other cotton-growing areas faced a special problem: the split shift.

Indianola, August 9

The Negro schools in the delta are open from early Nov. until late May. Then the schools close so the kids can chop cotton for Mr. Charley. In the middle of June, they open again and the kids go to school from 8 until 2:30. Then in Sept., when all the whites go back to school, the Negro schools close so that the children can pick cotton until November. Talk about King Cotton!

Since it wasn't chopping or picking time, the regular schools were open and Freedom School classes could start only after three o'clock. For this and other reasons, a crisis evolved in Shaw (Bolivar County) shortly after volunteers went there from nearby Ruleville to set up a school. "Shaw," a SNCC report had told the volunteers, "is a depressing little town uselessly and stupidly stuck in the middle of the cotton fields ..."

July

... We aren't teaching the kids. They go to school now from seven until one o'clock and they want to sleep, not to have more study in the blazing heat of the Mississippi sun and dust. So would I in their place. Furthermore, they don't see how we can help them to be free. At this point, neither do we. Slow change is unthinkable when so much change is needed, when there is so much hurt ...

We have cast about for a way to allow the Freedom School to express this feeling and to attract the students; we read jealously the reports of other Freedom Schools in the cities, where it is much easier and where students are much more deeply involved as well as being more literate: Hattiesburg, 600 students, desperate shortage of teachers, ten more New York school teachers coming specially; Gulfport, 250 students; Moss Point,

200 students; Vicksburg, 300 students; McComb, 75 students on the lawn in front of the second church bombed in two days, while the young children play in the ruins. Everywhere there is enthusiasm, and everywhere students — on vacation — had eagerly awaited the Freedom Schools to end their boredom. Everywhere, that is, except Shaw ...

The Freedom School coordinator in Shaw wrote to the statewide director, Staughton Lynd.

Dear Staughton   Shaw, July 11

I think I am rapid losing whatever effectiveness I may have had as a coordinator, or even as a rights worker. Part of it is family trouble. Virtually all letters and calls from my wife are depressing. She is frightened and also very concerned about our little boy who is lonely and quite upset by my absence. Because of this, I have in the last two or three days found it difficult to concentrate on my job here.

I could probably straighten this problem out and remain here, if it were not from something else even more important. I realize things are bad with us here because all we have been able to do is fix up the school and community center and attend a few mass meetings. But during this time the depressing reality that surrounds me has been gnawing at my emotions until now I am completely frustrated. Living conditions here are so terrible, the Negroes are so completely oppressed, so completely without hope, that I want to change it all NOW. I mean this as sincerely as I can. Running a freedom school is an absurd waste of time. I don't want to sit around in a classroom; I want to go out and throw a few office buildings, not to injure people but to shake them up, destroy their stolen property, convince them we mean business ... I really can't stand it here ...

Wally

Staughton Lynd came to Shaw three days later. He and the coordina-
tor had a long talk that night; the volunteers discussed their problem
the next day, July 15.

July 16

The answer to our questions came as a result of the voter
registration work. We held a Freedom Day today at the court-
house of Bolivar county at Cleveland. We brought some 40
Negroes down to register, and 25 were allowed to take the test,
an incredible success, and perhaps a record for any courthouse
registration ever in Mississippi. For the younger people we held
a picket line complete with freedom songs ... Yesterday we had
prepared the students for the picketing by special workshops in
non-violence and picketing discipline. They had enjoyed them
because they understood and valued the end to which we were
directing them, and ever since they have been begging to go
picketing again. It suddenly became clear to us that what we
should do was to have special tutoring in anything the students
desired.

Now we have something the students want, and over a third
of the high school students — about 35 — are coming here in
the afternoon. Not only are they having special workshops in
leadership and non-violence, but we are sneaking in all kinds
of citizenship education, and they are enjoying it. We even have
several who are interested in straight Negro history, and not
too few who want academics, the normal type. So to this more
limited, but under the circumstances healthier extent, we are
underway as a Freedom School, the last in the state to do so.

Classes in voter registration work and political play-acting were
a success everywhere. With innate sophistication about their own
plight, the kids pretended to be a Congressional Committee discuss-
ing the pro's and con's of a bill to raise Negro wages, and the "con's"
would discover neat parliamentary tricks for tabling it. Or they'd act
out Senator Stennis and his wife having cocktails with Senator and

Staughton Lynd addressing volunteers

Mrs. Eastland, all talking about their "uppity niggers." Sometimes they played white cops at the courthouse, clobbering applicants with rolled-up newspapers....

Hattiesburg, July 24

We had a marvelous time at school today with a mock demonstration as a role-playing device designed to illustrate what Negroes have done to fight for their rights. A Volkswagen bus served as a "white only" restaurant complete with sign. The younger children, carrying and wearing signs, picketed in an orderly and very professional way, first in silence and then singing, according to the directions of their leader. They even held firm when at one point "a segregationist" poured water on them as they went by from a jug held over their heads. Along with some of the older girls, who played members of the Citizens Council, the white teachers played segregationists. This was a sort of test for both children and teachers: it took courage for us to assume this role and know the children might become frightened and more unsure than they are already of our feelings, and it took courage for the children to accept our position as temporary. It appeared that we all passed. The police, played with a vengeance by some of the older boys, came and hauled the picketers off to jail when they refused to disperse. The whole thing went off beautifully, with enthusiasm and spontaneous creativity displayed on all sides. Tomorrow we will hold a trial (something for which I am well prepared)....

Hattiesburg, August 1

We have an 11-year-old girl named Rita Mae who is the equal of the best of us. At one role-playing session, when I took the part of a Negro unwilling to register, I found myself unable to hold up the argument in the face of Rita Mae's logic, common sense, and determination. I could find no good reason why I should not register, and was ashamed to admit that I was scared, so I tried a dirty trick: I promised to go down, but said I needed a ride to the courthouse. This Rita Mae said she would provide; but when she came around with a friend in a car, I had skipped out and couldn't be found. Rita Mae ruefully admitted that the dramatization had a most realistic ending ...

Hattiesburg, August 7

Today I went to Palmer's Crossing — a rural community outside Hattiesburg. There is a community center there and 2 Freedom schools. The student we talked to was a slim pretty girl who looked as if she'd just stepped out of the library at Willamette University where she'd graduated. Now she's living in a house where 4 families share a pump and an outhouse. She's a music major but her specialty here is literacy. She teaches individually at night and also has passed on to 6 high school students the literacy technics [the Laubach "Each one teach one" method] she learned at Oxford. Some of her students are over 75.

The Center was decorated from a teenage dance the night before for 135 youngsters. They called it "Swinging into Freedom" and had decorated with black and white hands of welcome on the front door. The two Freedom Schools were having a debate on the church lawn.

Resolved: that violence is necessary to obtain civil rights. The points are outlined below. (The debaters were 12-16 years old.)

Affirmative:

1. It's too late for non-violence. (NV can only work if it can reach the conscience (e.g. Gandhi and the British). The white conscience is dead. The Jews practiced NV against the Nazis and were exterminated.

2. Violence has been successful in Africa — we must show the white man we aren't afraid. Haiti got freedom by violence — Joseph Saint led slaves to freedom after a revolt.

3. Violence shows people you aren't happy even if you don't win.

Negative:

1. Negroes should not stoop as low as whites.
2. We're out-numbered — life is a very precious thing — we can save lives by NV.
3. Love creates community between brother and sister.
4. Negroes have come a long way through NV. (e.g. the Civil Rights Bill.)

Rebuttal Negative: White man's conscience isn't dead — I don't believe it and neither do you. Frederick Douglass may have fought but he fought harder with words. U.S. isn't 100% against us or how would Civil Rights Bill have passed?

Rebuttal Affirmative: People are afraid to use Civil Rights Bill — if you really believed it, you'd all enroll at Hattiesburg High (white). (This caused shouts of laughter.) People pick on you if you're NV — what good did it do Medgar Evers?

I regret to say the Affirmative won. The debaters were older and spoke better. Then there was the most spine-tingling singing of Freedom songs, led by a 15-year-old girl who had been in jail several times. Every time a car with a white face passed, the children sang louder and waved. The cars slowed down but all summer no one has ever waved back. "Maybe someday they will," the children say ...

Interaction between the classroom and life, education and politics came to a climax at the Freedom School Convention in Meridian on August 7-9.

Dear Mom, Dad, and kids ...   Biloxi, August 16

The purpose of the convention was to formulate a youth platform for the Freedom Democratic Party, and the kids did a fantastic job of it. Each school sent three student representatives — about 120 in all — and a coordinator. There were eight different committees, each concerning a different area of legislation: jobs, schools, federal aid, foreign affairs, voting, housing, public accommodations, health. Sometimes the committee discussions were long and even bitter, particularly on foreign aid where a demand to boycott Cuba and all countries that trade with Cuba was adopted but then finally voted out in the general session. Resolutions in favor of land reform were voted down because they were considered too socialistic, but there is a history of Negroes' land being taken away from them here that was the basis of these vetoes. The kids really learned something from the convention; for the first time, Negro students from all over the state came together to discuss their common aims ...

Love to all,
Al

White Mississippians didn't like the Freedom Schools any better than the rest of the Summer Project. It wouldn't have made any difference if the schools had offered only typing classes; the whole idea was dangerous. So they threatened parents who let their children go and they harassed the teachers and sometimes they destroyed the schools.

In rural Madison County, at a settlement called Gluckstadt, the Freedom School had been set up in a church known as Mt. Pleasant Society Hall. It opened later than most, but went very well ...

Monday, July 20. The first day of school — 14 students, ages 12 to 47. A student was assigned to report on civil rights news for the next few days ... We gathered on benches under the trees. I asked one of the students to read an excerpt from a speech by Frederick Douglass. Asked three others to read aloud poems by Langston Hughes. When we finished, Arthur asked if he could take the Langston Hughes book home overnight.

Tuesday, July 21. Six students took turns standing and reading a play called "Protest," about a Japanese family confronted with change in the form of an alien, a chair. They seemed to enjoy it and three of them were quite good. Several of the boys went off by themselves and read Hughes' poetry aloud. I spoke to Mrs.____ about the possibility of building book shelves so the building could be used as a permanent library for the community (a library that could be increased by books solicited after I go home). I asked if she would be willing to act as librarian. She said she would think it over.

Wednesday, July 22. Discussed origin of slavery in America —slave revolts — Negroes in the American Revolution — mutiny on the *Amistad*. It would be fine if we had a Pictorial History of The Negro for every student — less lecturing and more discussion. Two students and I read 3 of James Thurber's *Fables For Our Time*. Well received. Summaries written. Books signed out. Mrs.____ said she would act as librarian if we could get permission to use the building.

Thursday, July 23. Reviewed some myths about Negroes, asking students to give reasons why each was false. Some tried to defend them! Indoctrination has been well done ...Walter reported on "The Harlem Rent Strike"— without using notes. Summaries of the day's work or essays on any subject were written.

Friday, July 24. 'Lectured' on the Reconstruction period. Discussed the Civil Rights Act of 1875. The big hit of the week was the poetry of Langston Hughes. There was hardly a time during the day when some one wasn't reading our one copy of *Selected Poems.*

Sunday, July 26. At church today the congregation agreed to have the library. Everyone seemed pleased at the idea because there has never been any library available to the Negroes here.

So it went for another week. More plans for the library. Poetry, plays, oral reports, written reports, study of political and power structure of Mississippi, classes in typing, Spanish, French, Drawing, History. Students driving *themselves* on in a hot, faded wooden building. "I didn't do so good on that report (an oral report). Could you give me another one?" (Ernest, age 18)

Tuesday, August 11. Gluckstadt Freedom School burned to the ground late last night. There is little doubt of the cause of the fire. There have been too many others like it in Mississippi. We start tomorrow to raise money to rebuild the building.

Complementing the Freedom Schools were the Community Centers, which aimed to provide recreation and sports facilities, arts, handicrafts and libraries for a people who had little or nothing like that in their lives. They also offered sewing classes and sometimes a teen-age dance — but above all books, books, books ...

Greenville, July 21

I was overwhelmed at the idea of setting up a library all by myself. I had memorized the history of printing last summer session for the final exam, yet I did not know what the basic steps were for setting up a library and what the minimum essentials were. Then can you imagine how I felt when at Oxford, while I was learning how to drop on the ground to protect my face, my ears, and my breasts, I was asked to *coordinate* the libraries in the entire project's community centers. I wanted to cry "HELP" in a number of ways....

We've done a lot of sorting of the 20,000 books that were dumped in our nice little community center, filling all the rooms. The temperature in those upstairs rooms was 110°...We've spent three days working to get to the windows. We sorted the books in the broken boxes (about 5,000), took the others to an old deserted house (the key to the house was immediately lost). Now I'm sorting the books on the newly built shelves into subject categories....

Dear Mom and Dad,   Hattiesburg, August 7

Nancy is now a full-time librarian, which she enjoys very much. She keeps the library open 8 hours a day (9-12, 3-6, 7:30-9:30) and it's very heavily used. She already has a thick file of names of borrowers. We have about 6,000 books in the library, main branch, and are opening new branches in several places in town and at Palmer's. (The Negro library supplied by the city has about 2,000 books or so. Negroes can also use books in the main library downtown but can't get a card or take anything out). What will happen to these libraries after we leave, heavens knows; finding people to continue the programs is number one problem now ...

Love,
Joe

The most unusual Community Center of the summer was the one built in Mileston by a white man from California, who raised $10,000 for it himself and did much of the actual construction work. But the center in Harmony, a small rural community in Leake County, had its own special history; it was one case where getting the local people to assume responsibility for their center presented no problem.

The story began when the Freedom School teachers ran into difficulties shortly after their arrival ...

Dear parents and sister and dog-sister,   Carthage, July 1

...We are not actually in Carthage — that's a hot box. About 12 miles away is Harmony (pronounced Hominy), a Negro farm community of about 300-400 population. The people have been active for a long time in the NAACP. They were the first in Mississippi to file suit for integration of schools and consequently there was terrorism last year. Their hero is Medgar Evers, with whom they had a close relationship. Although few of the people have had much education themselves, they know the value of it. They speak intelligently and articulately. The first time I began to get excited and optimistic about our task here was when we arrived in Harmony. There was a welcoming committee of about 40 people out at the school to greet us. We didn't arrive until near noon, but the people had been there waiting since eight. All kinds of speeches were made to tell us how much we were welcome. It was great.

We are on a farm — 180 acres — very prosperous by Mississippi standards ... The farm is the most beautiful you could imagine — red, red dirt. Pines and other trees, hills, birds galore. The mockingbirds just won't shut up. To show how much of a country place this is, here is this morning's menu (breakfast at 7:00):

> homemade biscuits
> homemade jelly and syrup
> fried eggs and bacon

grits
coffee with chicory
fresh milk (i.e., straight from the cow.)

They hardly buy any food — even their lard is home made. Choctaw Indians are all over. The women all wear long ruffled dresses with long sleeves and have aprons and sunbonnets. Hair down to their legs. Choctaws are pretty much classed with Negroes, who have a good feeling for them — a feeling of kinship. All Choctaws live on the reservation controlled by the federal government. There is some question as to their status under the civil rights bill. Seems to me they are included except that their school will not be integrated, as I now understand it. Why not?

We have four old school buildings — run down, wooden frame, few windows left — filthy. They are old for one reason. There has been no school in Harmony since 1961 [when the schools for the area were consolidated elsewhere]. But the people had entirely cleaned out one building, put in homemade chairs and tables and arranged the library — there are probably over a thousand books already. Today we worked cleaning out what will be our building …

Love,
Judy

… About 20 adults, teens and young kids began to come to help clean out this gigantic school house, abandoned for over 6 years. The dust in each was inches thick; books were ripped in shreds and all over the floors and closets; loose glass was everywhere. It was a miracle — just like in *Lilies of the Field.* We sorted good and usable books from others, knocked all the loose glass out of the windows, 3 & 4 year olds were sweeping out rooms and carrying books to a huge fire where we were burning all the trash. In less than two hours, we were even pouring water over the floors and scrubbing them clean.

Then the sheriff came with about six white men, who were introduced as the "Board of Education." If they weren't Klan men, then they were at least Citizens Council people. God, they hated us. After we had finished cleaning the school, they told us we should not use it; it is county property. We told them it is private property [it did belong to the Negroes once but apparently had been deeded over later under complicated circumstances]. We are getting a lawyer and will fight in court. Meanwhile, tomorrow, Thursday, we will teach in a nearby church and outside. I fear that they will burn the school, and our library of 2 encyclopedias, *hundreds* of textbooks and actually *thousands* of hard-and-soft-covered books, donated from all across the U.S.A....

The case was lost. Grassroots enterprise went into action.

July 29

Every day this week — the 22nd to the 29th — the men of the community hammered and poured cement. At noon, about 7 or 8 women all gathered at the center with fried chicken, fish, salad, gallons of Kool-Aid and apple turnovers, and served them to the men, we teachers, and each other. It is a thing of beauty to see us all work together. Tuesday and Wednesday was the laying of the sub-floor. Two men cut the wood, two or three teenage boys and girls lay the wood down and hammered it in, a few more are bringing more wood. We are a living repudiation of the "too many cooks" theory. It should be up by Saturday, or at latest Tuesday. The land was given by a local man for "the sum of one dollar," and deeds were drawn up. The teenagers are selling refreshments to raise money for the center, as well as membership cards for a dollar. It will hold the library, a snackbar, office space and recreation area....

August 6

The men (and some of us when we have time) work on the building up to 10 hours a day with a 100° sun beating down and the humidity so high one's clothing becomes soaking wet after only a few minutes work. The building is guarded at night because these people, after having had their homes shot into and having a couple of crosses burned in the middle of their community during the last few months, do not intend to have all their hard work go up in flames right away....

August 5

About 4 men or teenagers armed with rifles and pistols stand guard. Every local car that goes by has to honk a specific number of times ... If anyone *does* attempt to bomb or burn the center, they haven't got a *chance*. I live only about 50 yards away so I take over coffee, cookies, cigarettes, tobacco, etc., to the guards and talk with them....

It was finished: a 30- by 60-foot frame building open to all residents and supervised by a board of elected trustees. The roof was barely up when Harmony began moving again on the school situation.

August 10

The decision came Saturday night at a meeting in the Galilee church. The day before the Carthage newspaper came out with the shocking news: the 3 Negro schools of Leake County are opening on Monday, August 10th, three full weeks before the white schools, The reasons:

1) This was an attempt to stop the Freedom Schools two weeks early.
2) They wish to start the Negroes early so that when they pull them out of school in October to pick the white man's

cotton they can claim the Negroes can "afford" the time.

3) August 30th marks the 1st day of white registration. Due to a Federal court order the first grade is to be integrated. But if a first grader has already enrolled in a Negro school (and they'd have to do so if they went 3 weeks early), he cannot transfer. Therefore the idiocy was mainly to prevent school integration.

The parents and students of Harmony were really riled up and voted to boycott totally and use this as a "strike" for demands: equal student-teacher ratio, heat in the winter, better buses, no firing of Negro teachers for registering to vote, no hand-me-down desks, books and buses from the whites, etc.

And so today, the kids didn't go to school. It began pretty well — I'm told over half were absent....

We spent three hours in Freedom School with all the children, ages 4 through 19. It was exciting and wild — we had the older teenagers each take two or three 2nd and 3rd graders and explain to them why we are boycotting. It was a joy to hear the youngsters work with each other....

Later that month, Leake County schools were integrated after all. One Negro first-grader registered in the white school: a girl. But whether Mississippi rejected or accepted black children seemed less important at this point in history than what had happened to the children themselves.

Canton, August 30

We were sitting on the steps at dusk, watching the landscape and the sun folding into the flat country, with the backboard of the basketball net that is now netless sticking up into the sunset at a crazy angle. Cotton harvesters went by — and the sheriff — and then a 6-year-old Negro girl with a stick and a dog, kicking up as much dust as she could with her bare feet. As she went by, we could hear her humming to herself "We shall overcome" ...

Freedom School student DeLois Polk (*on left*) and Chude Pamela Allen

Sheriff Earl Hubbard photographing the Batesville project headquarters

Mississippi is really two countries —
Negro Mississippi and white Mississippi,
and the difference is startling ...

Shaw, July 19

The Other Country

THE KLAN LEDGER

An Official Publication of the White Knights of the
Ku Klux Klan of Mississippi (July, 1964)

We are now in the midst of the "long, hot summer"
of agitation which was promised to the Innocent
People of Mississippi by the savage blacks and their
community masters….

The recent events in Neshoba County and Statewide
call for a message to the general public and the
citizens of the great State of Mississippi. The arch-
traitor and long-time betrayer of patriots the world
over, Dulles, has used his lying tongue to try and
convince the American public that this organization
was involved in the so-called "disappearance". We
were *NOT* involved, and there was *NO DISAPPEARANCE*.
Anyone who is so simple that he cannot recognize

a communist hoax which is as plain as the one they pulled on Kennedy in Dallas (and which Earl Warren is working so hard to cover-up), had better do a little reading in J. Edgar Hoover's primer on communism, "MASTERS OF DECEIT" ...

There is no racial problem here in this state. Our system of strict segregation permits the two races to live in close proximity and harmony with each other and eliminates any racial problem ... Bi-racial groups are the greatest danger we face in this State today. These groups have absolutely no legal standing whatsoever ... Bi-racial groups have brought violence and bloodshed to every area in which they have been recognized. The surest way to have violence in Mississippi is for anyone to give any weight or recognize the authority of a bi-racial group....

We are not going to recognize the authority of any bi-racial group, NOR THE AUTHORITY OF ANY PUBLIC OFFICIAL WHO ENTERS INTO ANY AGREEMENT WITH ANY SUCH SOVIET ORGANIZATION. We Knights are working day and night to preserve Law and Order here in Mississippi, in the only way that it can be preserved; by strict segregation of the races, and the control of the social structure in the hands of the Christian, Anglo-Saxon White men, the only race on earth that can build and maintain just and stable governments. We are deadly serious about this business. We have taken no action as yet against the enemies of our State, our Nation and our Civilization, but we are not going to sit back and permit our rights and the rights of our posterity to be negotiated away by a group composed of atheistic priests, brain-washed black savages, and mongrelized money-worshippers, meeting with some stupid or cowardly politician. Take heed, atheists and mongrels, we will not travel your path to Leninist Hall, but we will buy *YOU* a ticket to the eternal if you insist. Take your choice, *SEGREGATION, TRANQUILITY AND JUSTICE, OR BI-RACISM, CHAOS AND DEATH....*

Moss Point, Monday, July 6

Tonight the sickness struck. At our mass meeting as we were singing "We Shall Overcome" a girl was shot in the side and in the chest. We fell to the floor in deathly fear; but soon we recovered and began moving out of the hall to see what had happened ... When I went out I saw a woman lying on the ground clutching her stomach. She was so still and looked like a statue with a tranquil smile on her face. I ran to call an ambulance and police ...

It seemed as though a signal had been given. Two days later, the Project headquarters in McComb was bombed. On Friday, a Molotov cocktail was thrown at the Freedom House in Canton; in Hattiesburg a visiting Rabbi and two volunteers were severely beaten. On Saturday night, the Shaw project workers learned of a bombing plot as whites surrounded their office. The next day in beautiful old Natchez, a Baptist and a Methodist church were destroyed by fire — two of five Negro churches burned to the ground that week.

The week of July 6 showed that while there were relatively "good" and "bad" areas, violence could explode anywhere. Natchez and McComb had always been trouble, and there was originally some debate as to whether volunteers should go there at all. Eventually a few Negro and white male volunteers went to McComb, but no white women until the summer was over. Hattiesburg and Moss Point on the other hand were considered fairly peaceable. But in the end they all added up, as the song says, to Mississippi Goddam.

Each of the incidents had something to teach the volunteers about the attitude of Mississippi police and the pattern of law enforcement. In Moss Point, on the Gulf Coast, the victim was a local Negro girl of 17, Jessie Mae Stallworth. The occasion was a voter registration rally.

Moss Point, July 9

On Monday night we had a mass meeting, and the fifth district director, Lawrence Guyot, gave a terrific speech. The gist of his speech was that people say Moss Point is an easy area, "we have nice white folks here," that everyone has what they want already. But we don't have such nice white folks here, he said, and even if we did it shouldn't make us apathetic, it should make us want to take advantage of that extra little space ... He kept saying, "What will it take to make you people move? A rape? A shooting? A murder? What will it take?"

At the very end of the meeting we were singing the last verse of "We Shall Overcome," 300 people in a huge circle. Suddenly there were gunshots, and all these people including me, hit the floor in a wave ... A few seconds later we all got up trembling. A car of whites had gone by on the road outside and fired three shots through the open door. One Negro girl was hit in the side. She is in the hospital and is going to be all right, but nobody knew that at the time. The whole thing was additionally frightening because during the confusion when everybody was taking cover under tables etc., a piece of wire or something got caught in an electric fan and made a noise like a machine gun.

All during the meeting, the deputy sheriff was sitting there and the police patrol outside. The sheriff left shortly before the meeting was over and with him the police protection. At the time of the shooting there were no police anywhere around. Instead, they came fifteen minutes later, long after the whites had gotten away....

... The boy who had been standing next to her, just outside the door of the meeting hall, said that there were four white men in the car. Kids were walking around saying, "They can't do that to us any more." It was only with much persuasion on the part of some of their friends and the COFO workers that they calmed down a little and went home. That night, the police arrested five Negro men. No white men! These five had gone home for their guns and gone out to see if they could find the car from the description given. They saw what they thought to be the car. Some men in the car apparently fired at the Negroes. The five stopped at a gas station to tell some policemen what had happened. The police searched them, arrested them on charges of carrying "concealed weapons" and never followed the suspicious car....

On the night of July 8, the pleasant-looking white frame house rented by the McComb project to serve as a "Freedom House" (living quarters and, in this case, the office too) shook to its foundations as a bomb sailed through a large picture window. The blast wrecked the wall and should have killed project director Curtis Hayes who was sleeping in that room — yet only two workers in all were injured, and only slightly at that. Like the Molotov cocktail which was served to the Freedom House in Canton two days later and failed to go off, it was one of several apparent miracles of the summer.

In the late morning of July 10, three white men and two Negro girls were returning from a morning of canvassing for voter registration in a Negro section of Hattiesburg. The men in the group were two white volunteers named Larry and Dave, and Rabbi Arthur Lelyveld, 51, a prominent Reform rabbi from Cleveland, Ohio, who was with the Ministers' Project. One of the girls, Margie, was a volunteer, the other a local resident, Janet Crosby. They were on their way to the Morningstar Baptist Church, one of six churches in Hattiesburg where Negro women of the community served the usual big noonday meal to voter registration workers and Freedom School teachers.

Hattiesburg, July 10

I was writing a letter Friday morning about 11:45 when someone ran in saying that Dave was hurt. I and several others hurried back to the house behind the church to see what had happened. There was a small crowd on the patio and two people covered with blood. Dave was half-sitting, half-leaning on the back stoop, blood running down his chest, arm and back from a wound on the back of his head which the ladies were tending. The rabbi was sitting on a wrought iron bench while the ladies tried to stem the flow of blood from a cut behind the right ear and a wicked gash over his right eye. Larry was helping, although I noticed he was favoring his arm. The two Negro girls were also there, neither was hurt. A car was commandeered to take the men to the hospital ... the kids dispersed and Margie told what she had seen and gradually began to regain control of herself.

They were walking along the railroad tracks. A white pickup truck stopped and two white men in it began shouting insults and profanities; the team walked on. Then the men got out and ran up the incline to the tracks in front of the five workers. The old man hit Dave who fell....

Dave and then Larry continue the story:

... When I saw them swing, my thought was to use the old Karate, for it wouldn't have been hard. But nobody else would have helped me, so I didn't feel I could go against the Movement. The rabbi was hit on the first blow, I on the second. I fell to the ground, dazed but conscious, pulled my knees to my stomach, my hands covering my back, as we had been taught at Oxford. The rabbi stayed standing and took a number of blows. Larry was kicked....

... The younger man with the iron rod started beating me about the head and shoulders ... he struck me, pushing me over the tracks and down the embankment on the other side into a little ravine. He followed and kicked me with his work boots and beat me with his fists. He was swearing at me, calling me such things as "nigger lover," "white nigger" and "Commie," "Jew" and different combinations of these ... At one point he grabbed up a handful of canvassing papers which had fallen down with me to the bottom of the ravine and tried to force them in my mouth. He then continued to kick me and beat me with his fists but as I had assumed the position I was able to ward off and soften the blows he gave me. When he had finished beating me he said, "Run, nigger" …

Meantime the older man had been beating the Rabbi and he fell to the ground. The Rabbi had not remembered what he had been taught in orientation or else had not had any orientation as he did not know how to protect his head and abdomen from the blows…

The two Negro girls were not attacked at all. At one point, as one of them was kneeling over Dave to protect him as we had been taught in orientation, the white man looked at her and said, "I ought to wup you nigger" and then went back to beating the rabbi.

… As I returned to the top of the bank the rabbi was kneeling and blood was streaming from his head [the men had gone back to their truck by now]. I helped him to his feet and the five of us moved on down the track trying to get to the church or into the Negro community where we would find safety and medical help. As we came to the first street which crossed the tracks, the truck —which we were no longer watching — came up behind us and attempted to run us down. We quickly stepped aside so as to put a small drainage ditch between ourselves and the truck. The truck stopped. The younger man leaped from the cab with the iron bar and said, "I'm goin' to wup 'em again" … I stepped beside the Rabbi … and said, "Haven't you hurt him enough?" The man … raised his weapon and hit the Rabbi again. I shielded the blow with my left forearm. This is where I incurred my major injury. The man then returned to the cab of the pick-up truck and they sat. We crossed the street heading toward the church as quickly as we could. I was holding the Rabbi as he was growing weak from the loss of blood. When we reached the corner, the truck sped up and came abreast with us. They glared.…

Professor Pease from Stanford University, who is working with the Freedom School teachers, and staying with me, was at a Volkswagen repair shop in Hattiesburg when the news came over the radio. He said the five white mechanics in the shop let out a cheer.

Dave had seven stitches taken in his head; Larry was treated for a fractured arm bone.

The day after the beating, Dave wrote:

We walked downtown to see the police this morning. The white people stared at us, and someone yelled from a passing truck, "what happened to your head, buddy?" All yesterday I couldn't believe that they really meant to hit us as hard as they could with those rods. Apparently they never were bothered by the thought that we were human and had feelings. I couldn't understand yesterday when the first one came swinging at us.... But somehow I understood after those stares we got downtown and the shout from the car.

Downtown we met a Negro girl in the movement. Yesterday the stares wouldn't have bothered me, but today they did. I just wanted to get away from her. I can now understand much better the feelings of those who have worked long in Mississippi. And I can see why they have ulcers. You just can never know when it's going to come.

And a week later ...

Hattiesburg, July 19

One man has been arrested on the charge of assault with intent to maim in connection with our beating. I'm not at all sure what the chances are that a Hattiesburg jury will convict him, but it could be interesting. I'm sure that the FBI did the work, not the local police. The local police have asked me for no information except my name, age and address ...

*Almost a month after the beating, a grand jury hearing took place
— supposedly to indict the man who had been positively identified
by all four in the group. Larry continues the story ...*

Hattiesburg, August 7

... Then began a four hour game of musical chairs — a
game so ironic and destructive, so tragic that a shame such
as I have never felt came over me. We watched whites come
in and out, shifting, moving chairs, and standing in order to
avoid sitting next to a Negro. Chairs were moved from their
places so that they partially obstructed the elevator door and
one stairway....

The first of our party, the Rabbi, was called into the Grand
Jury Room. He was asked to tell where he had slept in Hat-
tiesburg, whether Negroes and whites slept in the same room,
whether there were any women of any color sleeping with them
and how many beds, etc. The Rabbi asked that the relevancy of
this line of questioning be explained to him so that he could
answer the questions more completely. He was told that no one
needed to "justify" any question put to him.... The last question
put to him was whether we had been embracing the girls or in
other physical contact with them preceding the beating....

After an FBI official was interviewed, I was called, took
the oath, and sat down. It was a long room dominated by a
table and surrounded by a dozen red-faced men in open shirts
and weathered necks and hands. I was asked the address of my
family in Hattiesburg. At this time I asked if I could see counsel
before answering that question and the interrogating District
Attorney screamed, "NO!" He said, "Boy, you realize that you
may be liable for contempt of these proceedings? Do you refuse
to answer that question?" I replied politely that I would rather
see counsel before I answered. Half standing he screamed, "Get
outa this room," ... his finger trembling. I left.

... We were required to wait until 3:00 p.m. before we were told to leave the waiting room. About two minutes before we were released, two lawyers from the COFO legal office appeared, consulted with us, and we all walked downstairs together. Within that interval, one of their briefcases was stolen. Later in an interview, the District Attorney made a slip of the tongue which indicated he had read the contents of the case.

Since the hearing before the Grand Jury, we have found out that a semi-secret trial was held for Mr. Estus. He pleaded "no defense" in order to avoid having a public trial and our participation as witnesses. He was fined $500 and 90 days at hard labor — suspended. There was no newspaper coverage of the trial, the plea of no defense, or the decision.

The police in Hattiesburg had demonstrated only indifference when confronted by violence; the police in Shaw on the night of the bomb scare were — apparently — more concerned.

On Saturday, July 11, about 8:30 p.m., the Shaw project workers had gathered at the Community Center to relax a while from the 8 p.m. curfew they had been observing for security reasons. The project director, John Bradford, had gone to the nearby town of Mound Bayou and was due to return soon.

Dear Mom and Dad,

... About 8:45 a Negro boy came to the door saying, "Tell Bradford not to come by the main road — there are men waiting for him."

Our reaction was slow. It was unreal; the night's heat and mosquitoes held our attention. We called Jackson, kept the line open and tried to contact Bradford.

At 9:00 a 20-year old Negro ran to the door talking in broken sentences — he had been offered $40 to tell where we were, and $400 to dynamite us. We frantically turned out the light, moved into one small back room — 20 people and 100,000 mosquitoes — keep open line with Greenwood, call papers, local police, FBI, noises of cars passing and people outside — listening for bombs. Several people re-emphasizing their conviction that this summer is necessary and right, and glad they came down, regardless....

Love,
Heather

The road had been blockaded with police, about forty of them. But the Project workers in the back room couldn't tell what was going on.

Mississippi has put everyone in a mild state of paranoia, but this is no imaginary situation. There are four cars at one end of the block. We're on the phone right now with the legal division in Jackson. They just informed us that we are not to leave the building, we'll be here all night — sleeping on the floor if we can sleep....

... Well, we survived. The Sheriff came by this morning and told us he had put a guard around the whole Negro community last night. He was hurt that we called the FBI in. But he admitted that he should have told us about the guard. They never kept anybody away, anyway. Carloads of whites were driving by all evening until about 12:30....

The sheriff told the newspaper that the bomb scare was a hoax of ours ... But if it was a hoax, why waste forty guards on a Saturday night? And if he was really interested in protecting us, why hadn't he let us know what he was doing, instead of adding to our fear? The answer, in my mind, is that he wanted to scare us.

The volunteers' suspicion of the police was not unfounded. A lot of their activity was mere harassment: the police truck driving past a project office every 30 minutes with a German shepherd dog standing large and ominous in the back; the police cars circling at night, a spotlight turned suddenly on your face. Their favorite outdoor sport, however, was fining and arresting volunteers for traffic violations.

The volunteers expected this and took care in most cases to get a Mississippi driver's license, Mississippi tags, and the inspection sticker which is necessary for a car after 30 days in the state. They kept their eyes glued to their speedometers and you could always tell a volunteer on the road because his would be the only car to come to a full halt before the big Mississippi STOP signs at railroad crossings — when there was no train in sight.

Batesville

The police gave us a hard time. All the time trumping up traffic violations. We were riding in a Volkswagen going 35 mph with the car in *third* gear. We were ticketed for going 110 mph. By-by $17. We are hard pressed for money.

Dear Mom and Dad,   Holly Springs, July 21

Harry and I went down to Canton to Harry's trial on a charge of blocking traffic with a truck load of books. A girl who is working in Canton also went to trial on a charge of running a stop sign on a corner where there is no stop sign. She paid a fine of $21 and Harry paid $23 …

The cops waited for Harry and me to leave town. As we were going north we saw two police cars pass us heading south. They were only a few minutes apart. Then about five minutes later two cars went around me and a cop came up behind. I had been careful not to go more than 55 mph in a 65 zone. The cop stopped me and said I had been going 75. When I told him I wasn't going that fast he got mad, took my driver's license and told me to follow him.

We went north to a gas station in Pickens where he called a judge to come hold trial …The cop said "Let me warn you about this judge, he's a real hanger. See that tree outside? He's hanged 15 guys from that tree. You can still see some little pieces of rope." He made several other remarks about hanging but it didn't scare us very much; we just looked at him.

He also asked what we thought of Goldwater. Harry is from New York. The cop said "Goldwater sure ran that nigger-loving Rockefeller crying back to New York, didn't he."

When the judge came in the cop pointed at me [a white] and said "This nigger here has broken the laws of the sovereign State of Mississippi." The judge didn't ask me to plead guilty or not guilty; he just asked if I had anything to say. I told him I was only going 55 and that two cars had passed me just before I was stopped. The cop said I was "passing everything on the road and was slowing down to 75 when I caught him." The judge said one of us was a liar, and that since he had known this policeman for a long time and since I was the first person ever to doubt his word, I must be wrong. So the fine was $27 or nine days in jail.

This wasn't enough though. When I had paid the fine I asked for my driver's license. The first cop told me the second cop had it. When I asked the second cop he said I had tried to run him off the road earlier that day. He told me to follow him back to Canton. When we got there I was charged with reckless driving and sent to jail on $100 bond ...

Enough,
Larry

Occasionally an officer would come up with an original charge, like "reckless walking" (on an empty road), or provide a bit of humor by asking the volunteer to write out the ticket himself since "I don't spell too good." The police could always pick up a person for "investigation," hold him up to 72 hours — which is legal in Mississippi unless a writ of habeas corpus is obtained — and eventually confront the person with an offense.

Jackson

Three local high school students and myself were passing out hand bills about Martin Luther King's visit the next day. As we often would because of the hot sun, we stopped at a small cafe for a soda. It was about four in the afternoon. Two huge cops, noticing my car, came in. They fooled around for about five minutes and then asked my three friends for identification. Then they told the three to go with them. Up to then they hadn't said a word to me. I asked if the three were under arrest. They said "yes." I asked on what charge. I was then told to shut up or I'd be taken in also. The cops then said the three were under arrest for "investigation."

After I had called the office to report the incident, I started back. As soon as I turned into the highway, a waiting police car came in behind me. I was arrested for improper tags (I had Wash. State tags), taken to the station, charged $29, and put into jail because I didn't have it. The bail soon came and I was out. But the other three, it turned out, had been charged with being drunk. The jailer would not let the lawyer see them. The cops refused to give them a drunk test. Finally, I bailed them out at $15 apiece.

Next day we had a long trial. The three who were charged, myself, and the boy who works in the cafe testified that all four of us were drinking orange soda and had not had any alcohol that day. Our lawyer made the cops look like fools in the courtroom. When asked by the judge if they could identify the three as the ones arrested, one said, with a wave of arm, "Yeah, I think that's them three niggeresses over there." The other cop said he was sure of one, but not of the others. Finally, at the end, we were amazed at the verdict. The judge could never reflect on the good character of the officers, but dropped the charges because the cops didn't make a positive identification of the three ...

Law enforcement in Mississippi could become even more amazing if you were being attacked by local whites and called the police for help.

About a week after the Rabbi was beaten in Hattiesburg, a young volunteer in that town went to buy some poster board with two fellow workers ...

Hattiesburg, July 21

There were three of us — Bill, a Negro, Peter, white, and I [a white girl]. Realizing the risk of being in an integrated group, we first decided to split up, with Peter and me following Bill; but it was so awkward being unable to talk together, and so obvious that we were all together anyway, that we decided to abandon the arrangement.... We were walking three abreast, Peter closest to the curb, I in the middle. Bill entered the drugstore.... Suddenly a man jumped Peter from behind. I was so astonished, I hardly grasped what was happening. Peter was knocked down and curled into the non-violent protective position against the building — the man was kicking him in a fury, but almost methodically and without a word.

All I could do, in accordance with "the rules" was try to get help, and should the beating go on too long, shield Peter's body with mine. I yelled "help — police," loudly and clearly, over and over. Finally a policeman arrived and pulled the man off. (It seems he had been at the corner directing traffic and could have made it more quickly.) Another policeman quickly joined the first, who led the man away, and detained us when we started to follow — as if to let the two get out of sight so the man could quietly be released. We hurried after them anyway.

At the station house, Peter heard for the first time that *he* was under arrest, along with his assailant, for assault and battery. We all acted indignantly and vociferously, demanding how that could be. The policeman said that whenever there was "fighting" in the street, both parties were arrested. We said that there had hardly been a fight ...

Every brush with the police contained a reminder that the missing three had last been seen alive on their way to jail. There were ugly stories about what could happen to a man in the privacy of prison, in the hands of the law. But more commonly jail was just a nuisance for the volunteer.

Gulfport, July 8

We were booked and taken to a cell block on the second floor with about 8 white prisoners already in it. Standard procedure is to bribe some prisoners with cigarettes to beat up civil rights workers. However we soon made friends and in ten minutes we were removed to an empty cell block on the third floor with women, juveniles, and condemned murderers. We sang freedom songs, beat rhythm on the bars and metal table, played kazoos of tissue and combs and raised hell.

The Harrison County jail is very modern, but you sweat, for Mississippi is a hot place. Jails are so damn stupid, though. Once you're in, and the lethargy and the apathy stick, you're stuck. The theory is deterring, but who is deterred? The theory is reform, but who reforms? You just sit, or sleep, or stare, or think about something, or dwell on nothing. Jail apathy very quickly becomes life to the inmate. But this apathy permeates everything only while you are in jail. When you are set free, it explodes in one big binge of rebellion....

Kenneth Keating (R-NY) called through an aide about a half hour after our 9:00 breakfast the next day — Barry and Dave are his constituents. The sheriff came up personally to give us hell for not eating his food. We turned it down in protest against segregated jails, arrest under an unconstitutional law, and because we got better facilities outside — a dig at the sheriff. He cannot comprehend why we live with Negroes. It is so foreign and strange an idea that his mind just stops. We finally got out on $500 apiece property bond.

Unlike workers in the early days of the Movement, the volunteers usually didn't remain in jail more than overnight. But once in a while ...

Dear Family,   Batesville, Friday ca. 1:30 p.m.
                                Panola County Jail

I am writing this letter as I begin my second day in jail, but bond is set at $700 and the trial for tomorrow at 10:00 a.m., and I have read the *Sat. Eve. Post. Life, Mad,* most of a Baptist publication called *Gospel Light*, 12 pages of a pulp western, odd bits of newspaper, and parts of *Car Life*, all very thoroughly, and am now at the end of my resources. Not stir-crazy — just restless. I'm well and alone in a large bunch of cells, tolerably clean and unmolested. I just had an amiable conversation with the sheriff. But I do wish someone would get me out of here. An attorney and a law student are in town, but they don't seem to have secured bail money yet. I'm in on two charges: failure to answer questions of the D.A. and resisting arrest ...

                        Sunday, Round about Midnight

I tore these pages out of the back of a Bible. But I'm furious — and anxious to communicate the fact. Who the hell do they think they are? At my trial, the Sheriff and a State Highway Patrolman, who was in mufti when I was arrested, testified that (1) the sheriff had told me I was under arrest (2) when grabbed by the arm by the Deputy, I had raised my arm to ward him off (3) I had held back after being grabbed. All of which are untrue. The point is, they never did make a proper arrest; the others only said, "Let's go" and so on ... The D.A. also asked me what organization I belong to, and I told him COFO, Spee Club, Hasty Pudding, I hope he does some research into that.

The very same State Highway Patrolman, back in mufti after dressing up for my trial, came around to my cell. Infuriating and frightening middleaged bastard. Parts of our conversation:

"They wash that nigger smell off you?"

"I'm sorry, sir, I don't understand."

"They give you a bath to get that nigger smell off you?"

"Well, I took a shower yesterday, sir."

"That oughta help."

And when I mentioned that I had a Bible in here: "Look it up where it says about mongrelizin' of black and white degeneratin' the races."

"What chapter and verse is that, sir?"

"I don't know, but it's in there."

"The Bible is a big book, sir. I can't find it if I don't know where to look."

"You don't want to find it, that's why."

Then he launched into an analogy about mangy mongrel dogs. I never got up the courage to ask him about the "mongrelization" already accomplished, of which there is ample evidence all around. Ah, but he knows all that ... The trusty, who's a pretty likeable, apolitical, troubled alcoholic, assured me that in the past, Negroes had to be lynched, summarily "cause otherwise they'd run all over whites." It's a curious kind of reasoning, but of course it is the prevalent line of thought, world-wide.

We can't skirt the idea of Freedom and agree that first and foremost, the cops have to keep order, and *then* we can progress ... Order! I guess things are pretty well ordered on the mechanical side for most Americans. But emotionally, imaginatively, intellectually ... why can't people admit not only that they fear the chaos but that they *are* the chaos?

Later.

I can't sleep, though I've finished *Borstal Boy* and reread *Invisible Man* and *The Stranger*, attentively, and also some of yesterday's Memphis paper, and, by God, I hate this old world. To think that someone as egocentric and self-pitying and cowardly and self-righteous as myself could have some effective grasp on a simple concept of justice which evidently strikes most people as either treacherous or nonsensical or unimportant or too dangerous! Dangerous! Wow! What's dangerous is closing our eyes like we all do most of the time and hoping we'll never see the dangers. I do hope that when I'm old, and this struggle, if it *is* to be won, is won, all of us, and everyone we touch or even brush by, will live in a more gutsy, moment-to-moment, existential fashion, whether for love or for hate, for creation or for destruction. And perhaps love will come of all this. I'm not ashamed to use the word right now, for I feel very attached, very loyal to the common but infractable bits of passion and affection and desire and appreciation and enjoyment and loyalty that are what it comes down to, if one lives for any reason other than to keep from dying. Tell everyone I'm well and that if they want me to go back to Harvard in the approved style, they simply do not understand.

Monday

No action today from COFO, but the most active day yet for me inside the jail! The Deputy volunteered me the use of a razor after I asked and received permission to take a shower. Result: using a broken rearview mirror, my worst shave ever. After five days, what will you? Another result: the towels on which I wrote this. Furthermore, after the shower I had time to talk to the Negro prisoners in their cell ... They gave me a whole bunch of Superman comics. I also read the Book of Amos *aloud*. I don't know if anyone listened enough to get the point.

But most exciting of all, two young (late 20s — early 30s) respectable, white citizens were allowed back here by the deputy with the intention of engaging me in conversation, which they did. Since they were unofficial, I let myself go more than I did with the Highway Patrolman last night. Mostly the same old guff, although they seemed to believe me when I said that I wasn't a Communist. One of them owns and operates a 1500 acre plantation; I don't know what the other does. It's very hard to dig them — you know, both sides polite, furious and afraid and contemptuous of the other ... The parting shot was revelatory. "You guys are all the same. Your ideas are all shallow and philosophical, not based on practical experience with people." The weird part was that both looked my age or younger, right down to hair style. It's a depressing country, and I don't mean Mississippi. I realized, talking to them, how much money-as-status must mean to the Citizens Council types.

Oh, God, I don't know what to do about my white brothers. All the assumptions, implicit or explicit, pragmatic or theoretical, of the white-is-right-Anglo-Saxon-uber-alles variety are part of what keeps me in this jail. That's not an unfair statement, even allowing for the personal responsibility of the Sheriff and the D.A....

Just think of how I was raised! Private school, indeed. I suppose that's a bit sophomoric, but I think I'll want my children to go to some place like a city high school, where social snobbery isn't as tight, and knowledge of other social classes not so difficult to obtain ... I'm still, au fond, a moralist. There's a lot of truth about all of us — y'all too — in Eric Hoffer's *The True Believer*.

Lies — the thing about someone like Mr. Jones. His family had a plantation ... The system induced him not to *know* what the black folks thought and felt. Yet he's intelligent, he should at least have guessed sometime ... but his fine intellect was never attached to the will to be critical enough of his own environment. If moralists won't analyze and criticize environments, it's all in the hands of B.F. Skinner and BBD&O.

As you and I have found, abstract support for "Civil Rights" — the newspapers and other outsiders call it Civil Rights and we call it *Freedom* — isn't worth much to the people who are catching hell. You've got to catch some of the hell yourself ...

                                                    Tuesday

Out today at 1:00 p.m. on bond of $350 plus $100 = $450. Trial Saturday ... Don't worry 'bout me. Back to my base today, I think. I hope you can read these jottings. I write from outside jail.

> Yours in the struggle
> Morton

Harassment, arrest, jail — the volunteers quickly learned what to expect from the Mississippi police. Yet the pattern had a certain complexity. Law enforcement varied from county to county, partly because the sheriffs — elected officials whose power could be hard for a Northern city-dweller to imagine — ranged from peaceable types to notorious killers.

> Clarksdale, August 8

… Clarksdale, like so many other Southern towns, remains somewhat autonomous from state government and the local government is run by the police. Instead of a police state, Mississippi is a conglomeration of police communities …

In the courtroom, too, there was variation — at least on the surface.

> Clarksdale

Before the trial began, we had packed the courtroom. A policeman entered with a can of air deodorant, and sprayed all of us who were in the room. Since most of us were Negroes, it was a subtle reminder that all Negroes are supposed to smell bad. Most of us just chuckled.

Dear Mom and Dad,   Hattiesburg, July 21

At the hearing [for the volunteer who had been arrested after being beaten] Peter was granted continuance until Thursday, but the assailant, a Mr. Houston Hartfield, was tried and we all had to testify as witnesses for the city. The city prosecutor, oddly enough, has the same last name as mine, and a daughter named Susan. He and the judge seemed fairly reasonable; at least, though they are segregationists, they couch their sentiments in polite phrases. The attorney for the defense, on the other hand, was coarse, theatrical and stupid. The judge continually reprimanded him for his method of questioning ... But the highlight of his performance was when Bill innocently used the term "comrades" to mean friends. He recoiled, then pounced on the word, weighted it with insinuation ... Then he stepped back, inflated himself, and after an impressive pause, demanded ponderously, "Are you now, or have you ever been ..." It was quite ludicrous. Bill asked the judge if he had to answer, and the judge wearily gave an affirmative. In a completely candid and somewhat amazed fashion, Bill shrugged, "No" ...

Later:

July 24

The judge said at the outset Thursday that it was with great pain that he was forced to render the verdict — that he and the entire community were in complete sympathy with Mr. Hartfield and would very likely have reacted in the same way to "the situation" (I assume he meant ourselves as a mixed and therefore noxious group). He declared that we were destroying everything accomplished in race relations here through gradualism and education. He could say this, before a segregated courtroom in a courthouse cluttered with white and colored signs, where Negroes are addressed by their first names and must submit to derogatory appellations. It was a lengthy sermon concluding with the warning that if any of us again appeared before the court it would be extremely difficult for whoever occupied the judge's bench to remain impartial.

Mr. Hartfield was pronounced guilty and fined $40 with $20 off on good behavior. The case against Peter was dismissed. We were given by the lawyers to understand that the decision, unimpressive as it may seem, was unusual....

Love,

Susan

The one thing that no Mississippi authority wanted, from Senators Eastland and Stennis on down, was another invasion of federal officials and reporters such as had occurred in Philadelphia. That event, as much as anything, made the Summer Project less bloody than everyone had expected. And so in some areas, it seemed as though the circling police cars really were there to protect the volunteers — at least from being killed ...

Meridian

A member of the Citizens Council told me that the Meridian Citizens Council had voted in June to "ignore" the presence of COFO workers for the summer. The Meridian police are amazingly cooperative. But this decision to be patient is based on a belief that COFO would leave Mississippi with the sunflowers — and take all the radio and TV and newspaper men and the FBI with them ...

Shaw, July 7

Yesterday, the third day of our stay here, I was among four volunteers driven up by the local police chief to see the sheriff of the county. The sheriff ... told us that every Mississippian's blood boiled, that he felt a physical revulsion when he saw us; but he would protect us to the hilt in order to protect the image of his beloved state of Mississippi and of his country ...

That was the "white power structure"; what about the people of Mississippi? Probably the large majority just looked at the volunteers — but in a very special way.

Gulfport, July 29

A while before I came down I read John Griffin's *Black Like Me* and he speaks of the hate stare ... It's really the most terrifying and ugly thing imaginable. When it was first given to me I had a reaction that combined fear and shock. Fear because you realize the power that someone like that will use, and shock that the human face could be that way.

Meridian

... It's impossible to describe the type of stares one receives around here for walking or driving in an integrated group ... Yesterday there were two cars driving by the house where I'm staying and the first car slowed down ... the second driver, watching us rather than the road, nearly smashed into his colleague ...

Vicksburg, July 10

... Since so many people drive slowly past and stare at us and sometimes even bring the family and park (like a drive-in movie), we've hit upon a plan to get free meals. Put up a sign:

C.O.F.O. ZOO VISITORS WELCOME
Nonviolent Animals
PLEASE FEED

And the crank calls: sometimes a threat — "don't go to sleep tonight if you want to wake up tomorrow" — and sometimes just unflattering adjectives ...

Dear Friends,   Meridian, July 20

Once again I find myself spending the night "guarding" the COFO office, a task which consists mainly of answering a more or less constantly ringing telephone only to be greeted by the voice of some well-wisher who employs the sort of language which it would probably be illegal to send through the mails. Often these people remain merely silent and hang up the receiver, but at times they become more daring and toss off witty remarks about our mothers and our morals. Every once in a while one of them forgets his script and has to be coached by whoever is sitting next to him at the time ...

While I'm in a "lighter" mood (and you have to be in order not to get driven crazy by these callers), I'll note that the omniscient *Meridian Star* has been very instrumental in protecting us from any possible physical violence on the part of the local aristocrats. Besides calling us left-wing fanatics (which I might be ... who knows?), race-mixers, trash, and a lot of other such things, they have continually gone into full descriptions of our physical appearance. Naturally, besides being dirty, long haired ... and, in general looking like we just crawled out from under a trash can (that's their description, I'm not making it up), it seems that we all (I'm not sure if the girls are included) have beards. So far, I have yet to meet one person on the project with a beard (people were strongly urged to shave them off in Oxford).

The result is that, unless we're walking in integrated groups, it would be hard for the local citizenry to recognize us — they're all on the lookout for Christ figures or something.

Best,
Peter

Specialized harassment included the telephone company giving elaborate excuses for not installing service in a project office; the widespread tapping of project telephones; the bank's refusal to open an account; the nondelivery or delaying of mail; the inch-long tacks sprinkled across COFO driveways ... These things, like the traffic tickets, were more irritating than fearsome — yet they suggested what lay below the surface.

Hello to all friends of freedom,   Carthage, July 23

Being unsure of what I actually said to Daddy, I want to tell you all everything I can remember about the incident.

Three other girls and myself went into Carthage today to shop, do laundry, and call home. All our business was done within an hour except my call home. Having been told that our old place from which we called was frequented by "two hoodlums whom the sheriff can't control," we chose a drive-in cafe which had two outdoor phone booths in the parking lot. I went in to make my call.

I guess Daddy and I had talked about five minutes when this redneck ... came to the booth and asked me in a testing way through the half-open door if I would talk longer. I knew what he meant because of the empty booth next to me.

"I'll be through in a minute," I said.

"You'd better be through now and get out," was his response, delivered in a threatening tone.

Then Daddy asked me if that was Hank. I was momentarily puzzled as to what to do as I surveyed the situation. I was trapped in the phone booth with this character's foot in the door (my mistake to let that happen). I wasn't scared but just a little confused.

The best thing, I decided, was to frighten him away by describing him to Daddy on the phone.

"No, this is a strange man whom I've never seen before. He is about 5'6". He's wearing a cowboy hat ..."

I think I slammed down the receiver on "hat" because as I began the sentence he waved an open pocket knife at me with his right hand. When he heard my description he glared and went around to the back of the phone booth. This startled me and for some reason I thought he could electrocute me; actually he would have been hurt himself because his intention, and he almost did it, was to cut the phone wire. The girls in the car had the door open and the motor running....

At the junction with 488 we found two cars with three men in each waiting for us. Anne, luckily, was a good driver and had presence of mind. She whipped around the corner and got in front of the two cars. We had to go well over 80 mph to stay ahead of them (only one car chased us). They could have tried to run us off the road. We knew we would be safe once we got to our dirt roads....

Love,
Judy

Dear family,   Laurel, August 24

Saturday afternoon, several of us were invited out to a farm 6 miles from town for a day of picnicking, swimming, relaxation and V.R. work out in the country ... Bill Haden, a white COFO worker from Oregon, a local Negro and myself were sitting along the edge of the lake about 400 yards from the farmhouse singing some songs and playing the guitar. Just after finishing the last verse of Dylan's "Who Killed Davey Moore," we saw two whites coming towards us down the path from the farmhouse. Since we were expecting other people from the COFO office to be joining us, we didn't think anything strange about this. When they got somewhat closer and I didn't recognize them, I asked Bill if he knew who they were. He didn't know. A few seconds later, the younger man (about 5 feet 10, 200 lbs.) came up to me and asked if I knew "Dixie."

I told him, I wasn't sure, to which he responded, "Well, you'd better be sure, and quick." I told him, "Well, just sit down. Maybe we could work it out together." He told me just to play it. I've never learned a song quite so fast in all my life.

Apparently, he didn't appreciate my efforts, because the next thing I know, the guitar was out of my hands, kicked, and thrown out into the lake. Almost simultaneously, about 15 other rednecks, about 25-55 yrs. in age, emerged from the trees and brush surrounding the lake. The other man, who had first come up, began beating me with the big wooden club. I saw that it would be impossible for me to run around the edge of the lake back to the house without being further attacked and beaten. So, since I was born for the water, home I went. After I was 15 or 25 feet out, he pulled a pistol from beneath his shirt and began firing in my direction. Ten or twelve of the other men began shooting in the direction of the house and the fleeing COFO worker with pistols, rifles and shotguns.

When the bullets began hitting the water, not five feet from my head, I thought it was time to make a submarine exit. Coming up about a hundred and fifty feet further out, the bullets were spattering even beyond me, perhaps 30-40 feet. Since I didn't see any men at the other side of the lake, I was hoping to swim there, get out, and try and make it to the house. About ten minutes later, as I got out of the lake, two men came towards me out of the brush. The man in front had a forked tire iron and the man behind him had a steel chain.

Since old freedom fighters never give up, I again tried to humanize with the cat, asking him "Wouldn't you like to sit down so we can talk this thing over? Although we might have our differences…." While I was saying this, I was gradually taking a few steps back toward the lake, just in case he did not respond positively. Well, he didn't. Menacing the tire iron, he ordered me to get over to where the rest of the men were and not get wise. For a few more seconds, I tried to reason with him … Just about at that moment, one of them comes from the brush around the lake with his club. He swings it at me across the back and the man with the tire iron hits me across the knee while I think the man with the chain hit me across the ribs and back. Deciding that it was better to be a live chicken than a dead duck, I got the hell out of there. By some miracle, I was able to make it through the brush, barbed wire and all the shooting (by now from both sides) up to the farmhouse.

When I arrived, the COFO office had already been notified and I got on the phone immediately to the FBI in Laurel.

After about five minutes, an FBI agent called back and wanted to know what was going on. I told him that the Civil War was reoccurring and would he *please* come on out — with the rest of the Federal Gov't. He wanted to know if we had notified the local police and sheriff's office. I told him we had, but they refused to be of any assistance. I then asked him if he could not protect us, would he be so kind as to come out and take pictures down by the lake of the man who had been firing on us? We exchanged a few more words, and I went to lie down on the floor. I vaguely remember the sheriff arriving maybe a half hour or 40 minutes later and taking the names of everybody in the house. We asked him if he would give us protection back to Laurel or at least ride with us. He replied, "I didn't carry you trouble-makers out here and I'm sure not going to take you back." With this, he left us. About 15-20 minutes later, the ambulance arrived and we were taken to Jones County Community Hospital....

That's all for now, take care, don't worry,

Love,
Dave

The symbol of unpredictable violence was the pick-up truck with gunrack and two-way radio, and no license plate in many cases. Sometimes the driver removed the plate or covered it with a paper bag for his own sinister reasons. Sometimes he just didn't have one. You couldn't be sure.

The pick-up truck was the trademark of the redneck, the rural white — usually poor — who works all day in the open and thus gets a sunburned neck. People call them crackers in Georgia, peckerwoods elsewhere. The volunteers dreaded the redneck above all other whites, and during the summer of 1964 they generally had more to fear from him than the police. But in many areas it seemed as though there was not much difference between the antenna on a man's truck and the one on the police car.

In the small rural town of Marks, a carload of workers from Clarksdale went canvassing....

Clarksdale, August 12

I was stopped and questioned by the City Marshall, the only police officer in Marks. On finding out who I was, he cussed me out and demanded repeatedly that I hit him — if I was any kind of man. He told me to get into the car; the charge was "suspicion" because there were many "bank robberies and car thefts in the area." I was taken to the Sheriff's office and interrogated. The Marshall said he would give me and my fellow civil rights workers no protection and in fact he was looking to "get us" and if he couldn't get us some of the townspeople would and he would be elsewhere when things were happening.

On the way back to where he picked me up, he stopped at two gas stations to show the folks what a "Communist civil rights worker bastard" looked like. Then I was released ... Angry mobs of whites were gathering at street corners and it was getting late — a sure sign of possible trouble. Finally we got a group of Negroes to escort us home but at that moment "deputies" came and told all the "goddamned black bastards" to go home and told us to get out of town. We had to leave unescorted on the main highway when we had planned on a more discreet route.

We started down the highway and we saw 3 or 4 cars parked ahead and 3 or 4 cars converging on that spot from a side road. We felt sure that it was some type of road block since it was about midnight and we hadn't seen people congregated on corners and we knew that the deputies and townspeople were in close contact. I turned the car around and headed in the other direction at breakneck speed....

And in Greenwood, this is what happened to a voter registration worker who was beaten but managed to get his attacker arrested that same day:

Greenwood, July 11

... At the police station the insidious relation between the local law officials and the local law-breakers grew more obvious. A police officer was playing with a knife, rubbing his thumb over its edge. He pointed the knife at a girl, a co-worker, and said that he kept it sharp for "niggers like you." He then pushed her around. My assailant, still present, started in on one of the white workers, accusing him of being a "nigger-lover," and suggested to the officer that he castrate the boy. A bit later, he and my assailant both drove a Negro boy home who had been in jail.

We finally started to leave the station late that night, but we couldn't because all four of our car tires had been slashed. The Negro boy who had been driven home by them later told us that as they passed our car, one said, "There's the car those bastards are driving." We have good reason to suspect that the law enforcer, and the attacker, slashed the tires.

The man who beat me is now free. He paid a $25 fine. He is a friend of the judge's, of the police, and a member of the Citizens' Council. It is amazing that he was even fined, He probably would not have been one month ago. Still, it is no comfort to me. He is free, he is angry. He knows that he can get away with much worse. The FBI would not arrest him ... I have no local protection. I have no Federal protection ...

Hattiesburg, July 12

Coming from lunch the other day to the COFO office we noticed a hush unusual for that place. A boy in a bloody shirt was reporting a brutal beating via phone to the FBI ... The FBI will "investigate" and no more.

Where is the USA? It is a violation of FEDERAL LAW to harass voter registration workers. Where are the Federal Marshalls to protect these people? How do the Negroes defending "democracy" in Viet Nam feel about the defense that democracy gets in Mississippi?

On July 10, J. Edgar Hoover arrived in Jackson at President Johnson's request to open the first statewide F.B.I. center since 1946. He announced that there were now 153 agents in the state; he also announced that they weren't there to protect civil rights workers.

The F.B.I. had the power to arrest when a violation of constitutional rights was taking place. They used that power once in Mississippi on June 26, when three voter registration workers were threatened at Itta Bena. They used their arrest power once again, under the Civil Rights Act, in Greenwood.

Jackson, July 13

The FBI is acting a little more quickly — but only because of your pressure on the federal government. And they aren't much help because they're really not on our side. To investigate the bombing in Ruleville, they went around asking intimidating questions of the local Negroes....

Dear friends,   Ruleville, July 18

At around ten p.m. 14 F.B.I. agents came to interview us [a group of volunteers and staff workers jailed for "unlawful distribution of literature"]. The two staff workers were not enthused about talking with them ... In the past they have sometimes turned statements over to the local officials, thus giving away the defendant's hand. This fear was confirmed the next day. One of the guys overheard the chief of police ask the FBI for our statements and the FBI man said, "Well, we'll talk about that later." I tried to get them to promise them not to give my testimony to the police. They were evasive ...

The next morning the F.B.I. came back to interview us. They were pretty square with me, but asked some of the others irrelevant questions about their past political activities ...

Love,
Mike

A whole world had come crashing down; terms like "law and order"
or "responsible Negro leadership" became meaningless. When, on July
16, Barry Goldwater was nominated at the Republican Convention
in San Francisco and the first of the Northern city riots broke out
in Harlem three days later, the volunteers had little patience with
all the talk about white backlash. The Mississippi newspapers were
exultant about both events.

Dear everybody,   Bolivar County, July 28

... The Harlem riots have really been spread all over the
newspapers down here. After living in a Negro community for
a while it is a lot easier to see why riots occur ... Nobody has
to "agitate" Negroes to make them dissatisfied. All it takes is
something to trigger it off ...

Medgar Evers wrote that in his younger days he wanted to
start a guerrilla war in Mississippi. Some of the young people
here have come close to advocating the same thing — "Some
of the guys, they don't buy this nonviolent stuff. We want to get
out and DO something." After facing a few bombings, beatings
and jailings some of the summer volunteers felt like throwing
a few bombs back themselves ...

Yours for freedom,
Robert H.

Hattiesburg, August 12

... a brief comment on the note you scribbled across the ar-
ticle you sent me regarding the moratorium on demonstrations.
"This is what I suggested to you in June needed to be done, and
you disagreed at the time. Now the Goldwater threat is so great
that certainly rioting must cease — at least for now."

I suppose you might call riots demonstrations — but the
reverse is not true. Demonstrations are not riots. How dare you
suggest, as you do in saying "rioting must cease — at least for

now," that demonstrations and rioting alike originate from the Movement? Yes, of course the rioting must cease, and not just for now, but for always. Have you thought about what positive steps might be taken to *prevent* it?...

The volunteers had learned only too well how "violence" depends on who does it. How a society can conspire against you. With no local protection and no federal protection, fear becomes the climate of life.

Ruleville

It's night. It's hot. No lights because there aren't any curtains — meaning they can see you and you can't see them. *They*, the word *they*, takes on its full meaning here. You slap at a dozen or so mosquitoes that are buzzing in. You doze off and the phone rings again, about the fifth time, and the other end stays mum. By now you know that somebody, someone on the other side, knows where you are. They know who you're staying with ...

Violence hangs overhead like dead air — it hangs there and maybe it'll fall and maybe it won't. Sometimes it's directed at people in the movement, sometimes it's indiscriminate. Cars have been roaming around; seven or eight vigilante trucks with their gun racks and no license plates have been seen meeting at the city dump. What will they do? When? Something is in the air, something is going to happen, somewhere, sometime, to someone ... A few nights ago cars roamed the streets, empty bottles flew from their hands, striking cars and homes. They were empty that night — the next night the bottles were loaded — exploding as they hit the church and setting it afire.

Canton

When any cars come here, Karol and I do a disappearing act into the back of the house. So far we've had no trouble. Sometimes around midnight when the dogs start barking we feel rather strange. Last Saturday night they started howling about 12:30 a.m. Karol and I turned out the lights and listened. The barking came closer and got louder until we heard footsteps under our window. The chase continued around the house while everybody else slept. Karol and I sat very still and listened. "I'd like to use the pot," Karol said, "but not with the Klan watching." The barking soon stopped and we fell asleep. Next morning, a neighbor came over looking for an escaped pig. We thought our prowler would have had to have been awfully short to pass unseen under our window ...

To my brother,

Ruleville

Last night I was a long time before sleeping, although I was extremely tired. Every shadow, every noise — the bark of a dog, the sound of a car — in my fear and exhaustion was turned into a terrorist's approach. And I believed that I heard the back door open and a Klansman walk in, until he was close by the bed. Almost paralyzed by the fear, silent, I finally shone my flashlight on the spot where I thought he was standing ... I tried consciously to overcome this fear. To relax, I began to breathe deep, think the words of a song, pull the sheet up close to my neck ... still the tension. Then I rethought why I was here, rethought what could be gained in view of what could be lost. All this was in rather personal terms, and then in larger scope of the whole Project. I remembered Bob Moses saying he had felt justified in asking hundreds of students to go to Mississippi because he was not asking anyone to do something that he would not do ... I became aware of the uselessness of fear that immobilizes an individual. Then I began to relax. "We are not afraid. Oh Lord, deep in my heart, I do believe, We Shall Overcome Someday" and then I think I began to truly understand what the words meant. Anyone who comes down here and is not afraid I think must be crazy as well as dangerous to this project where security is quite important. But the type of fear that they mean when they, when we, sing "we are not afraid" is the type that immobilizes…. The songs help to dissipate the fear. Some of the words in the songs do not hold real meaning on their own, others become rather monotonous — but when they are sung in unison, or sung silently by oneself, they take on new meaning beyond words or rhythm … There is almost a religious quality about some of these songs, having little to do with the usual concept of a god. It has to do with the miracle that youth has organized to fight hatred and ignorance. It has to do with the holiness of the dignity of man. The god that makes such miracles is the god I do believe in when we sing "God is on our side." I know I am on that god's side. And I do hope he is on ours.

Jon, please be considerate to Mom and Dad. The fear I just expressed, I am sure they feel much more intensely without the relief of being here to know exactly how things are. Please don't go defending me or attacking them if they are critical of the Project …

They said over the phone "Did you know how much it takes to make a child?" and I thought of how much it took to make a Herbert Lee or many others whose names I do not know) … I thought of how much it took to be a Negro in Mississippi twelve months a year for a lifetime. How can such a thing as a life be weighed?…

With constant love,
Heather

Mike Smith in front of a church in Crenshaw

Mr. Charlie and Miss Anne

Aside from the hate stares and the traffic tickets, the conversations which weren't conversations and the beatings, the volunteers had little contact with whites as they walked from Negro homes to Negro farms or churches or Freedom School. Many of them felt that it must be possible to do more, that somewhere in Mississippi minds could be opened.

Canton

We had thought that perhaps our one chance for making contact was through the churches. Members of our group (all white), have tried to make contact with both the white Methodist and Presbyterian churches in Canton. The first time some of them went to the Methodist Church they had a chance to talk to a few people who really seemed to be interested in finding out what the project was all about....

... The next Sunday they were met at the door and told by the preacher, "You are not welcome here." The third Sunday, they were again turned away at the door and beaten up on the way home. Local Negro preachers said, "Yes, that was a white man's church. It was not God's church"....

... Then a new man joined our project, Bill Monnie, who is a Methodist and is planning to study for the ministry. He wanted to make one last attempt to get into the Methodist Church. When he and several others got to the church in his car, and stepped out, a number of men rushed down off the church steps and shoved them back into the car energetically enough so that one of the car windows got broken. Two women from our group, who had gone in another car, went into the church and signed the guest book. A few minutes later an usher called them out and asked them if they were connected with the COFO project. When they replied that they were, they were told that they were not welcome. When they returned to the car, they found the tires slashed....

... Our contacts with the Presbyterian Church have been more encouraging. Three of our group have been going there regularly....

In Clarksdale on July 5 two white volunteers went to the First Christian Church (Disciple of Christ) and were refused admittance. A six-page statement was read to them in front of the church by a member of the church's board of directors while a police car circled the area.

Clarksdale, July 6

Yesterday afternoon, Dave B. called the pastor of the First

Christian Church (Dave is a disciple and plans to become a minister) and asked him for an explanation of what happened. The pastor met with us, and we had a very friendly, understanding, and mutually informative conversation. He said that he had not known any such statement had been prepared. He appeared to be one of the few white moderates who is seriously concerned with the social situation, and he has been trying for five years to negotiate with some of his parishioners....

Another Sunday, another church ...

Clarksdale, July 14

Four of us (white) went to the Episcopal Church last Sunday, and I have never felt so much outside the Episcopalian club! I tried to look nice and smile a little at everyone, so that the returning stares were discomforting. I think two people did say good morning to us. Half a block away from the church a man came up to us and without introduction asked us, "You won't bring any niggers next week, will you?"

If they couldn't get very far with church-goers and ministers, perhaps the "intellectuals"? Hattiesburg had its University of Southern Mississippi, a number of Jewish residents, and for sixteen years a rabbi who was known to be progressive.

August 1

... I talked to a psychology prof at Mississippi Southern. This man is Jewish from New York, but southern orientation: schooled in Atlanta and Florida, wife from Atlanta, here since 1958. He too seemed very sympathetic, but not very willing to say anything; in fact I don't think he made any positive remarks, but he didn't make any negative remarks and smiled in the right places. I invited him to the Freedom Schools; he didn't say yes, but he did say maybe (I don't expect him)....

... Bob Beech got some Southern Mississippi prof to have an interracial group to his house, and what a comedy, with not turning on the porch lights when we came in so no one would see, and the general nervousness that none of his friends would unluckily drop by etc. And everybody admired his courage for having us at all, which only shows what things are like ...

Dear Mom and Dad,   July 25

Mississippi liberals are almost without exception scared stiff. Deviation from the proud old rebel flag and Our Southern Way of Life is obvious to all, and a threat or two — perhaps a few bullets fired at a house or a cross burning — is likely to leave two alternatives: silence or pulling up stakes. Boycotts are illegal in Mississippi, as is handing out boycott literature, but of course this applies only to Negroes. The Forrest County Citizens Council had no difficulty getting out a sheet calling for the boycott of several stores in Hattiesburg which had desegregated their lunch counters rather than close them down as did other merchants (after the Civil Rights Act passed) ...

I was also told that the students did not seem to get excited about much of anything; that they were for the most part apathetic. One student told about trying to get a liberal club of some sort started last fall ... It was about ready to go into action at the time of Kennedy's assassination but after that it died. The campus was stirred up; in some cases they cheered and gave parties celebrating the murder of the President....

Bill

Dear Friends: August 5

Another volunteer from the project and I sat and talked for about four hours with a dozen students; asking and answering questions. They were great kids, and most would be considered liberal in Mississippi terms — in other words, they recognize that there might be a problem, but it must be solved by the people here and the method of solution would be separate and equal. They were open and honest and we did communicate in some ways, but I could not seem to impress upon them the very basic fact of the humanity of the Negro people; their need for dignity and escape from the "great white father" relationship. As I came away from this mental beating, I cried, for it all seemed so hopeless....

In freedom and love,
Beth

To the north of Hattiesburg, at Oxford, volunteers made a special effort to establish contact with people at the University of Mississippi.

REPORT ON A VISIT TO THE UNIVERSITY OF MISSISSIPPI

On Thursday, July 22nd, I went with George McClain, the minister assigned to our project, to the University of Mississippi — in Oxford. We went first to meet the Methodist Chaplain on the campus, whom George had met on a previous visit. He had offered to take George around the campus.

We talked with the Episcopal Chaplain, who has been active in the Movement. His great concern is for the whites of Mississippi. He emphasized that, for many people, standing up and stating their position would simply mean being forced to leave the state.

The Chaplain's feeling is that people who do believe in integration are too valuable in their communities working underground with other whites to lose if they make a principled stand and are forced to leave the state. The reason why his job is not in jeopardy, as are the jobs of ministers from congregational churches, is that he is responsible only to the Bishop of Mississippi and not to a board of local people....

After eating lunch in the school cafeteria we went to visit Professor Russell Barrett of the Political Science Department.

He had been James Meredith's advisor ... He stated that he felt that there was a real lack of communication between the COFO workers and the white community. We discussed with him some of the things we were doing in Holly Springs. We then talked about getting more Negro students into Ole Miss. He said that they would all need court orders and that if we could get together some who would be interested in going to Ole Miss they could use the same lawyer and come in under the same order. He said that the Dean of Women was especially anxious to get some girls....

We then went to the home of a Professor where we met a student, Phil Patterson, and his wife ... Phil Patterson had been identified as a "nigger-lover" and was eventually forced out of first one and then another dormitory by the students. The Saturday before, an attempt at a "K" had been slashed in the front seat of his car and a threatening note left.... The professor's wife suggested that we come back another day and speak in some of the classes as a way of communicating to some of the students the purposes of our project. She said that she would contact some of the professors....

At the Journalism Building we talked with the editors of the campus newspaper "The Mississippian." We met the girl who is editor of the paper during the regular school year, Kathryn Webb, and one of the summer co-editors, plus a few more students who were around at the time. We talked for about half an hour about why we had come to Mississippi when there were problems in so many other places, etc. Kathryn Webb was one of the most vocal in the group and one of the most open-minded. She admitted honestly that she was prejudiced and that she resented Mississippi being put in the spotlight for the summer. But she was interested in talking with us and hearing what we had to say. The others lost interest before she did and we ended just talking with her.

To sum up, we learned that there were professors on the campus actively concerned about what was happening in Mississippi. One family keeps a harassment map in their living room. The students we talked with were friendly to us although dialogue could be carried on only so far before minds began to close.

A week later, the volunteers went back — this time without their minister.

July 30

Yesterday, July 29, two of us (both white) went to speak in two Sociology classes ... We spoke about our project in Holly Springs and then answered questions. While some questions were relevant, many were of the nature of: "Would you marry a Negro?" "Is your organization Communist?" and "Why are Negroes so immoral?" Both Alvin and I felt that it was fairly successful. We were able to answer most of the questions in sociological terms. The second class which we attended was an advanced class in Urban Sociology. Their questions were for the most part more sophisticated. Both classes treated us respectfully and were very attentive to what we had to say ...

A few girls came up and invited us to eat lunch in the cafeteria with them. I was told later by a professor that this move was fairly courageous on their part, as students who had eaten with two people involved with the Movement a month before had been under pressure from their fellow students.... We spoke with about seven students, though none stayed with us more than 15 minutes and none offered to renew contact. There were catcalls of "queer" and "communist"; a boy who came up and said, "I heard you were on campus and I just came up to say, 'I won't shake hands with you sons of bitches.'" Eventually we found ourselves sitting alone in a crowded cafeteria.... Our conversations at lunch depressed me but I could not really put my finger on why until after we had left.

When our car came to take us back to Holly Springs, two police cars followed our car to the outskirts of Oxford. They waited until we were at the edge of town. Then they stopped us

— three cars, four policemen. They asked for all our identifications … Before he let us go, the policeman gave us a lecture about why we should notify the police when we came to Oxford, so that they could protect us from any harassment.

Even as he was uttering these words, three burly characters were walking up and down in front of us. If we had not been stopped, we would never have been seen by these guys. When we left, a green truck pulled out *right* behind us and began to follow us. We recognized the three who had marched up and down before us as we were talking to the police. Our driver picked up speed and so did they. Soon we were driving at 90 and 100 miles per hour, with them right behind us. We finally lost them when a police car passed us coming from the opposite direction and probably stopped them.…

Later, I realized what had been bothering me about those people at lunch. It was that they were patting themselves on the back for recognizing and admitting that conditions in Mississippi were bad.…

I find it hard to care about people who say they are concerned but will not take small risks to help prevent the deaths of many other people … I am beginning to understand why people who work in the Movement come to not really care too much about the kind thoughts of some "liberal" southern and, for that matter, northern whites.

I try to fight the bitterness …

But the Summer Project did assign twenty-five volunteers to work exclusively on finding white allies. Eighteen of them, including a good number of white Southerners, went to Biloxi — a "moderate" town on the Gulf Coast. Some of the group worked on making contacts with "poor whites," the rest with middle-class residents.

In midsummer, one volunteer evaluated the job they had done thus far.

Greetings from the sovereign state of Mississippi,   July 30

It looks like the pilot phase of our White Community Project is pretty much over. We had a war council over the week-end to hash out what we had learned thus far. First of all, the group of 18 of us dropped into the community of Biloxi was too big. Eighteen people, in one place, in a community which already expects all manner of chicanery from the "invaders," and watches every move so closely that little could be done. A more subtle and selective approach needs to be taken, working with smaller groups. Second, the groups should have a more specific focus. Groups attempting to be involved in the power structure and business and religious community have to maintain a different image to be effective from a group in the poor white community. We have worked against one another in this area. Those whose interest is the poor white community enabled the rest of the white community to consider us a bunch of beatniks (which they probably would have done anyway!) and at the same time, those of us involved in the middle class were always after the others to improve their appearance for the sake of our success, causing tensions within the group.

Third, in the middle class white community, a more selective approach must be taken. With few exceptions, people in business and politics and in the churches feel they cannot speak out … This being the case, our approach must change from the attempt to involve them in action NOW, but to explain the nature of the coming changes…. This new approach would be much more quietly done. It would not consider time spent with people of commitment rigidly opposed to us as very worth while.

Soren

Fear, fear, fear: the same story over and over again. It was no white myth; the volunteers themselves saw intimidation in action.

Carthage, July 24

... Yesterday, four of us went to a radio station near here to leave off a tape of Martin Luther King pushing the Freedom Democratic Party. The owner was very business-like and agreed to run it 23 times for $37.50, which he is required to do by the FCC (since it was a paid political announcement). Today, he stopped by, gave us our money back, and signed an affidavit that his home and family had been threatened. It's easy to see why the white community wants to "move slow" on integration — they have nothing to gain and they have a tremendous fear of the lawless element. The whole thing has all the flavor of a TV western where there's a bad guy with a gun who's keeping everybody in town scared — well dammit, it's about time somebody faced up to the bad guy....

The whites were afraid of each other, afraid of the Negroes, afraid of the volunteers.

Canton, July 7

... They are scared. They are terribly afraid that the Negroes will treat them the way they have treated the Negroes if the balance of power shifts....

Dear people,   Batesville

One thing which has seemed plain to me, when reading the Jackson newspapers or talking to local officials, is that the whites are just as frightened as the Negroes. They have their own set of rumors....

One evening I drove past an auto accident; a white girl's face had been severely gashed. At the request of her date, I went to a nearby house for help. For a moment I had a cordial conversation with the white college student who came to the door. Then he figured out who I was and rushed back into his house to get his dog and shotgun. Naturally that ended that conversation — and left the girl stranded. Sometimes I think that a hot line is needed between the white and black sections of Batesville....

Geoff

Entwined with the fear was the obsession with sex; almost every conversation between the volunteers and local white people came around to that theme in the end. It seemed to run so deep that the Mississippians could not bear the sight of physical nearness between Negro and white even when the sexes were not mixed: "A newspaper editor told me that he had seen one of the white girl volunteers with her arm around a little Negro girl, playing with her hair. This, he said, almost made him vomit. The look on his face proved it was true."

Dear Mom and Dad,   Canton, Aug. 2

Karol and I went canvassing down route 43 last Friday. On the way back, close to our freedom school, a big sweaty white man who looked as if he had been drinking stopped beside us in his black Renault. We told him our names and shook hands with him. He identified himself as Mr. Green. First he asked if we wanted a ride, and we said, "No thank you," and said we were headed for the church just ahead. He turned around and followed us so we beat it into the outdoor toilet. He sat in the driveway and honked. When we came out, he stopped us.

"What are you two white girls doin' usin' that nigger toilet?" he asked.

"Using it," we replied.

"We got better places for white girls around here."

"One place is as good as another."

"But not fer white gals. How old is you?"

"Twenty-two." "Twenty-five."

"I got some kids your ages. One of 'em goes to Mississippi State."

"That's a good place to go," I said.

"You've heered of it?"

"Sure."

"What you doin' 'round here? Are you talkin' to the nig-gers?"

"We've been visiting with Negroes." His eyes got big.

"You're both purty gals — some of the purtiest I've ever seed. But you know what? I seed you the other day up at thet nigger store talkin' to the worst nigger slum in the county. Why, that nigger slum cain't even count to ten!" and he held up ten fingers.

"Yes, we've been talking to Negroes at the store," I said.

"We'd be glad to come to your home and talk to your wife and you together, but we'd rather not talk here," Karol said.

"You married?" he asked.

"No."

"No."

"You reckon you'd ever make anybody a wife?"

"We'll probably get married sometime." He shook his head and dropped the subject.

"I still can't see why purty gals like you would want to go talkin' to them nigger slums what cain't even count to ten. This place ain't fit fer white gals."

"We're here because we don't like slums, either." (I hadn't quite caught on that he called people "slums").

"But them slums is plumb mean an' ..."

"We'd still like to come to your house to talk to you one day next week, maybe," Karol said again.

"I wouldn't let the likes uv yew in mah house ..."

Love,
Kay

Columbus, July 7

... To give you some insight into the mind of the white southerner, dig this. I'm the communications and security officer in the project here and this entails answering the telephone whenever I'm here. Following are some of the things I've been greeted with by southern white women: "Is this the place where poor white trash and black bastard niggers live together?" "Nigger, would you mind singing for me?" One day I invited a young lady to come over and we would explain in detail our purpose for being here. She said "and get raped?"

Dear Betty, Carthage, July 15

... I was in Jackson overnight Tuesday and had my first brush with the Mississippi lawmen. No beatings or anything but they weren't what you'd call polite.... When I told them I was a medical student, they accused me of being down here to do abortions on all of the white girls who are pregnant by Negroes. But this seems to be an obsession all across the country. One of the girls gets a letter from her father almost daily asking her "to come back home and start associating with decent people again." ...

Sincerely,
Clarke

Dear friends, Ruleville, July 18

Time and again they talk about how we are just spoiling a beautiful relationship. They take great pride in their solicitude for Negroes. When I ask Negroes about whether whites are just lying or really think they are good to the colored, Negroes always answer that they are lying. They can cite cases where the very man I was talking with had beat up a Negro. What's more, the lopsided power relationship in this system makes the Negro lie to whites in order to stay alive. This lying reinforces the whites' illusion and destroys the Negro's self-respect ...

In the ideology of non-violence we talk about being against the system, not the man. However, this is damn hard to practice, for the man is so implicated in the system that any attack on it is a real threat to him. At the same time, I don't think you'll be able to really communicate the wrongs of the system to the man on top without attacking it. The system has numerous mechanisms for dealing with challenges from within. One must find a very direct and compelling, even coercive means of cutting through these mechanisms and reaching the man ...

Best,
Mike

In Vicksburg, a volunteer from Harvard wrote of how his ideas about white Mississippi had changed — and not changed — during the summer.

Dear people,

At Oxford, my mental picture of Mississippi contained nothing but an unending series of swamps, bayous, and dark, lonely roads. Of course the real Mississippi is nothing like that — but there was a certain logic behind my misconception. It had, quite simply, been impossible for me to believe that the skein of uncivilized atrocities that one knew had covered this state, could have spread through an area that looked as modern and developed as the places we came from.

A white lady with whom I dined one night in Vicksburg uncovered this attitude of mine. "You Northerners all think that every Mississippian is a bare-footed redneck," she complained. She and her husband had invited another summer volunteer and myself to their large, modern ranch-style home. We were eating steak, which had been cooked over a barbeque pit, and drinking wine. "Some of us are different."

All night she had been calm and charming but now, as

she talked, her eyes became teary and her voice wavered. Her feelings were not hard to understand. Our characters and backgrounds had been subjected to similar distortions here in Mississippi. My hostess was no closer to the Erskine Caldwell characters I had expected to find dominating this state than I was to the immoral, unwashed Communist dupe who, rumour here once had it, would persuade all Negro cooks to poison their employers' food.

I wanted to tell her all this in a tone that would leave her believing that I, a reasonable man, had come to this state and quickly seen the error of my prejudgments. But I couldn't: this state is actually worse than anything I had anticipated. I could more easily accept atrocities that took place in the swamps and woods — in pre-civilized surroundings — than I can accept the daily harassments and threats at factories, gas stations, and hotels: places which, for me, fall into the familiar context of American life.

I was eager to establish a friendship with her. But as she talked of her Mississippi, I kept thinking of the state familiar to the young Negroes I teach at our freedom school: a world light years removed from her carefully decorated ranchhouse and her excellent steak dinner.

She had told me that not every Mississippian was a barefoot redneck, and I knew she was right. Wearing shoes and a comfortable collar, a gas station owner several blocks away had fired one of the young Negroes who attend our school, and had apparently been privy to nightly threats on the student's life. I tried to mention this incident to my hostess. "I know the man you're talking about," she said. "He's one of the lower class people around here, and they're always harsh with Negroes." But was there really so great a distance between the fellow townsmen?... Both husband and wife undoubtedly ate, without much discomfort, at restaurants which had refused to serve Negroes weeks after the Civil Rights Act passed. If we developed this point, the distance between our attitudes would become too great, so we went on to another subject. By Mississippi standards it had been a good conversation: each of us had learned something. Yet too much stood between us. She called herself American and so did I ... But, in her state, whenever I pause for a moment to reflect on the history of a particular person or acre, I cannot help but feel like a depressed and confused alien, and wonder whose land I am really in.

Paul

At worship

Take this hammer, Carry it to the captain.
Take this hammer, Carry it to the captain.
Take this hammer, Carry it to the captain.
Tell him I'm gone, boys,
Tell him I'm gone.

If he asks you, Was I runnin'
If he asks you, Was I runnin'
If he asks you, Was I runnin'
Tell him I was flyin', boys,
Tell him I was flyin'.

If he asks you, Was I laughin'
If he asks you, Was I laughin'
If he asks you, Was I laughin'
Tell him I was cryin', boys,
Tell him I was cryin'.

Captain called me, Nappy-headed nigger.
Captain called me, Nappy-headed nigger.
Captain called me, Nappy-headed nigger.
Ain't my name, boys,
Ain't my name.

The Greenwood Story

How to convey the magic of place names unknown to the rest of America; how to explain that the map of Mississippi could become in a single summer more rich in associations, even nostalgia, than the whole geography of childhood and school — more fabulous than the cities of Europe which one might have known in another kind of summer? The young volunteers said Neshoba, McComb, Tallahatchie in a way that other generations say Barcelona, Iwo Jima, Stalingrad. Not because the Project was like a war, although it sometimes seemed that way, but because both sets of words transmit echoes of pain and courage, and images of a particular sky or earth color or human being. The words became possessions:

Batesville, July 30

Last night we gathered together from all quarters and corners of the county for a four-hour staff meeting. We talked about things in general, but chauvinism kept creeping in. Somehow the Crenshaw people always got the talk around to Crenshaw; the Sardis people, to Sardis; the Crowder person, to Crowder, the Como person, to Como....

The names could even sound like the places they stood for: Natchez, off-limits to white volunteers, exotically evil; Pascagoula, with its slippery Uncle Toms; Yazoo City, lawless like the Wild West. Indian names, Anglo-Saxon names, a town named Midnight and a river named Big Black. The irony of names, which produced a sign in COFO offices everywhere:

> *There is a street in Itta Bena called Freedom*
> *There is a town in Mississippi called Liberty*
> *There is a department in Washington called Justice*

Each name and the place that went with it had its uniqueness, its history, and none more than the Delta town of Greenwood. At first glance it might seem typical ...

Greenwood

"He jes' grew up on the wrong side of the tracks." The proverbial phrase is loaded with meaning for the Negro child here. The railroad tracks divide the Negro community from the white. The houses in the Negro neighborhood are perched precariously on several stacks of bricks. They are old and often unpainted, with cardboard instead of glass at many of the windows. Most often the property of whites, the houses received little attention from the owners. They are never vacant: there is no other housing for Negroes.

Yard space is at a premium — 60 sq. ft. in front is almost a luxury with little more in back and none on either side. Some people fill the space with every variety of flower — the temptation to stop and smell the freshness is overwhelming. More frequently yards are bare or non-existent. A sign hanging on a porch advertises "Cockroaches for Sale" (for fish bait). Who would have to *buy* cockroaches?

In the poorer section, the yards and even the porches are gone. No series of "Good mornings" greets the white civil rights worker here, only closed doors and the frightened looks of undernourished children sitting on the steps. Many of them seem not even to have the energy to brush away the flies. Untreated cuts and vicious-looking scars already identify them as inmates of the ghetto.

West McLaurin Street. Skid Row of the Negro district. The five block section is broken only by one of the grade schools. The street is lined with taverns and joints. Brave talk about what "Ah's goin' a do next time Ah meet Mr. Charlie (the white man)." For all the defiant speeches and camaraderie, this area is most resistant to active participation in the movement. Fear and disillusionment brought them here and it will keep them here until tangible signs of hope appear....

The statistics were familiar too: Greenwood is about half Negro, half white. It is the seat of Leflore County, whose entire Negro population (30,500) far outnumbers the white. Some 258 Negroes were registered to vote in that county, as of 1963.

But Greenwood had a history of exceptional violence. Ten years earlier, the body of 14 year-old Emmett Till had been found in the Tallahatchie River which runs by the town; he had been killed just north of there in a place called Money. Greenwood was now the home of Byron de la Beckwith, twice tried for the murder of NAACP leader Medgar Evers and twice freed by a hung jury.

In June of 1962, Sam Block of SNCC had come to town. He was joined by Willie Peacock and the two went out together to talk to the people about voting. Somehow they weren't killed. But once Sam Block had to live for a week in a car parked in a junkyard because nobody dared take him in.

That fall, so many Negroes went to register that the county Board of Supervisors stopped distributing the surplus food which 22,000 people depended on. By mid-winter their situation was desperate. Friends of SNCC groups across the country sent shipments of food and supplies. People kept on going down to the courthouse.

In February, 1963, white men fired thirteen bullets into a car carrying James Travis and Robert Moses of SNCC, and Randolph Blackwell of the Voters Education Project, a new coordinating agency. VEP asked all voter registration workers in Mississippi to move into Greenwood immediately. In March their office was destroyed by fire. The white world didn't give an inch, but black Mississippi began to move.

This was the Greenwood to which a large group of volunteers came in 1964. A 20-year-old white Harvard student from New York tells the story of the summer in a series of letters.

Dear Family: Greenwood, June 22

Things are very quiet as of now — so quiet that the old-timers are worried. We were out this morning passing out a notice for a mass meeting tonight. All of us were followed by the police, but none were even questioned or stopped. A guy who went out to get some cartons for packing the books that are downstairs where the national office of SNCC is going to be was followed all over town, but not stopped. The theory here is that the cops are trying to convince the reporters who are still thick here that nothing is going to happen, and then lower the boom as soon as they leave for more troubled waters....

By the way there is a large Chinese community here, of all things. [They are descendants of laborers brought in to build and work the railroads which connected inland Mississippi with the River when it was a major artery of commerce and travel.] They all run food stores, and about half of the stores are Chinese-run. The kids speak with a real Southern accent, but also speak Chinese to themselves ...

The meeting tonight was really something. Over two hun-

dred people were there and they were very hip. We all introduced
ourselves. Stokely [SNCC project director for the Second Con-
gressional District, Stokely Carmichael] gave a good speech, very
sound politics. He didn't give them any of this better-street-lights
crap, but talked the question of power. Power is not abstract if
you know how Eastland controls the appointment of every single
judge in the whole damn county ...

July 2

Canvassing is dirty work. It is very tiring, and frankly
boring after the first hour or so. (Three hours is about all most
people, including myself, can stand). It is almost impossible to
overcome the fears ... And the courthouse people make sure
that you have to wait a long time, and make sure that there are
no chairs around. They only let three take the test at one time,
in an office large enough for ten ...

We have mass meeting two or three times a week. The
trouble is that one gets the feeling that it is the same people all
the time. There is a wonderful preacher around here who yells
and haw-haws during the speeches. When he speaks himself
he comes up with things like, "If you can't go ten blocks to the
courthouse, how are you going to go nine million miles up to
heaven?" and "If they don't believe in integration, how come
they's so many half-white Negroes around? — somebody's been
integrating for a long time."

We are planning a Freedom Day for July 16, hopefully over
the whole area, but at least for Greenwood ... This consists of
large numbers of people going down to register. It will mean
trouble of some sort, but we have to use it to stir the community
into united action. Taking a few down a day is not going to
break Martha Lamb [the registrar].

July 3

Had a great time canvassing today, in spite of sour report about the boredom of canvassing in my last letter ... Finally I have met a guy who works at the only large factory around here — Baldwin piano. Segregation works in funny ways here. Some Negro men, no Negro women. Each operation is done completely by one race or another, and the only contact is when parts are being passed from one department to another. The restrooms and smoking rooms are segregated ...

Getting ready to canvass in Greenwood

Where else but in Miss. can you have a dry state and a tax on liquor? The cops come into a place, pick up their $100 a month apiece and a fifth of whiskey (used to be a pint) and walk out. The guys who run the cafes display their tax stickers prominently. They are called 'privilege taxes,' or something ...

July 9

The NAACP flying wedge of integrators is not well liked around here — and I am not just talking about the white folks ... the places they integrate are not places that the ordinary non-middle class Negro is likely to visit. Also, they must be blind not to see that places which are open to them will be closed to the ordinary Negro. No violence when the group is there with its press entourage — but just wait until tomorrow afternoon when they are hundreds of miles away. These guys also give people the idea that they have their freedom now, and can run all over the place integrating everything. Some kid tried it last night at the white movies and got beaten up by six guys. The police came and rescued him, (by taking him to the station), but did nothing to the guys who were still standing around. The same thing happened to the kid's brother, last week.

Keep your eyes open for news on July 16th — that's Freedom Day in Greenwood. One wonderful story about what happened last Freedom Day. Some whites brought a monkey down with a little sign around its neck saying: "I want to vote too." They took him into the registrar's office, but soon came out gleefully proclaiming the fact that he was refused because he couldn't read either. Then they took him across the street to where the whites were because he was insulted at being on the same side of the street with the niggers. But the final laugh was on our side. Some old lady couldn't see too well, and had never seen a monkey before anyway. Nobody could convince her that it wasn't a 65 year old white woman!

We had a meeting of all Delta area people. It was really wonderful, seeing the people who seemed like old friends, even though I had only known them for a few days at Oxford. Now I understand why snick [SNCC] people hug each other when they meet. We are so glad to see each other alive and well!

July 11

It seems as if things are about to break now. The NAACP leader's tires were slashed right in front of his home last night. The night before, his windshield had been stoned for the second time. Three of the stores that carried posters announcing Freedom Day had their windows smashed. More people have been going to the white movie. Last night a group of about 5 saw most of the picture, and then it stopped right in the middle, and the manager asked them to leave and come back Sunday night. He gave them a full refund, and receipts. They left the theatre in the face of a small mob that didn't do anything except call a few names. The local NAACP guy was with them, which is very good ...

The white swimming pool has been full of water but temporarily closed for the last week. Just yesterday, however, the city voted to give the pool to the Kiwanis Club for its members. It's gonna have a lot of white members, methinks ...

July 13

Two snicks just got married a few minutes ago — guess we have to call it a Freedom Wedding.

The brief service was held in a little chapel on the ground floor of the office. Flowers were scotch-taped to the wall. Strings were hung from wall to wall: sprigs of spruce alternating with Mississippi Freedom Summer leaflets hung along the way. Some of the kids had spent the afternoon using glue and sprinkle-glitter things to make a cross and a Jewish star. All, including the bride, wore jeans. The service was not the usual religious one, but a personal appeal to God to guide these two children to do what is right, and so on. When it was all over, Jim Forman stood up and yelled in that wonderful booming voice of his: "ONE MAN — ONE WOMAN — TWO VOTES!"

We are going out canvassing at 4 in the morning tomorrow

to catch the people as they load up on buses which will take them out to the fields to chop cotton. (Chopping is hoeing weeds that grow after a day or so of rain, so that chopping is seasonal within a season. Picking comes later. Typical wage from 5 a.m. to sunset is about 2 to 3 dollars. And soon picking will be almost all done by machine around here.)

Some ministers arrived to take part in Freedom Day. I drove some of them to their houses just now. Driving back alone (along the road where Jimmy Travis got his) was rather scary. You imagine all sorts of cars following you. Beckwith lives in a motel down the highway, incidentally.

On Freedom Day a large number of people were taken down to register; with them went about 100 volunteers, staff and local people carrying "One Man — One Vote" and similar signs. They were testing the antipicketing law recently passed by the Mississippi legislature.

July 17

Here is the Freedom Day special issue....

Wednesday nite Stokely spoke at a very large mass meeting. He had been stopped by a well-known highway patrol goon some miles north of here, and told the folks about his interview. The cop asked him how come some niggers always laugh and smile so much, hoping to make Stokely mad. How come some niggers sit on the porch, how come they drink so much and cut each other up. Stokely said "that's right — niggers drink too much — but they learned it from the white man. Niggers are lazy, and they learned that from the white man, — haven't you seen white folks sitting up on their porches?" With Stokely talking about niggers all the time, the cop couldn't get him by using the word. And Stokely said, "Now we're learning from the white man about how to vote, baby, so they'd better watch out."

In the morning I helped coordinate the transportation to the courthouse, and went around the neighborhood trying to get people to go down to register. Went down with one car, arrived just in time to see the first group of about 30 pickets going off to jail. They were banging on the windows and screaming FREEDOM at the top of their lungs. Later in the morning, I got word that a cattle prod had been used, and that a 7-months pregnant woman had been dragged down the sidewalk with a billy stick under her nose.

Down at the courthouse, in the afternoon, the third wave of pickets was about to be launched. People waiting to register were lined up all the way down the steps. Martha Lamb was still only letting 3 people in at a time. They did allow us to bring a water cooler down for the people outside.

We tried to take a blind guy up, to test what they would do in his case. (Before, they had just refused to give him the test on the grounds that he couldn't read or write!) As I walked up the steps of the courthouse with him, one of the county sheriffs called over and asked me why I was bringing up a stupid old nigger who couldn't read or write or even walk up the steps alone. "What's the matter, don't blind people vote around here?" I asked. "Don't get smart with me, boy — I'll hand you over to my bouncer here and we're gonna whup your ass down these steps."

Towards the end of the afternoon it started to rain, not too hard at first. We decided to see what would happen if we went up on the porch of the courthouse to get out of the rain. We were thrown off, of course, back into the rain — which was getting worse. The whole gang of cops and sheriffs, up on the steps, really got a kick out of seeing people try to huddle under the few umbrellas that we had.

That night we had the largest mass meeting ever, back at the Elks Hall again. Jim Forman was the main speaker ... I remember him talking about how it wasn't the poor white man who was doing so much against us. The guys who shot

Jimmy Travis are well-known, and as Jim says, anyone who has fifteen huge tanks of Standard Oil gas is not poor. People reported having been fired that very day. And all the people there agreed that they would not work for those families. The guy who dragged the woman off in the morning has a store in the Negro neighborhood, but that won't last long now, I can assure you. Jim said that soon we have to form a community welfare fund to support people who lose their jobs for freedom.

After the meeting we had a long staff meeting that lasted until 2 a.m. We first thought that we must picket, to keep up morale, and because the people would expect it. Some feared violence, because the Negroes were certainly mad about what happened, and would fight back. Jim Bevel [of the SCLC], the wonderful reverend who wears a skull cap, was there … He didn't think violence was a problem. The people will believe you, he said, we used to take a bushel basket around to the gathering place for a large march and explain to the people that if a cop was cut, the whole thing was finished. They would then fill the basket with the knives the people had brought. Bevel says you shouldn't keep on going to jail unless you have so many people ready to go that the whole country will take note, and you get immediate action. (We had orders from Jackson that no more staff should be arrested.) Halfway measures just run your bail up a few thousand dollars …

The lawyers came up with the idea that was finally adopted. We would take picket signs into the voter registration line and stand there with them. People waiting to register would carry signs saying: "I WANT TO VOTE," snicks would carry signs saying: "REGISTER TO VOTE," and so on. The people who showed up for picketing the next day agreed to this. The police drove their bus up that afternoon but didn't arrest anyone at all. They really couldn't call it a picket line, and we were definitely covered by the Bills of '60 and '64.

July 22

Much water has passed under the old dam since I last wrote. Been too busy, since we who were out of jail had to do all the work. I ended up more tired than my bed-mate, who spent the week-end in the jug. I slept at the office most of the time — on the floor — and he at least had a hard bed. Some cat came in from Jackson and they assigned him to the other half of my bed. He ended up with the whole thing, as I was at the office all night.

You probably know the story of how the city tried, convicted and sentenced all of the kids. [Over 100 had been arrested.] All got 30 days and $100 fine. We finally got them out, just before they were about to be sent onto the roads to work ...

I went to the county farm to pick up some of the people who had been kept out there (all Negro). Aside from a one-minute visit to Stokely by one of the lawyers on the first afternoon, the whole bunch of about 50 were kept entirely cut off from all relatives, lawyers, doctors, or anyone. When I drove up, they were all yelling FREEDOM NOW and really kicking up a storm. I yelled back that we had come to get them out, and they started singing and cheering ... As they came out, 6 at a time, they embraced us, and asked when we wanted them to go back to jail ... "We had a ball in there," was the general consensus. The jailers had really had a hard time with these kids, (some of the "kids" were over 60 years old, by the way) — they had stopped up the drains and flooded one floor. They had started 3 fires, and had torn boards off the walls and thrown them out the windows....

De la Beckwith is now on the auxiliary police force, by the way. He rides a cop car with a gun and a club.

What I have been feeling for over a week now was just confirmed by a long memo from Jackson. I don't think we should spend any more time taking people down to the courthouse to get spiritually beaten down. Now we should put all our efforts into Freedom Democratic Party work. At the same time, more Mrs.

Hamers and Mrs. Grays [Mrs. Victoria Gray of Hattiesburg] will be emerging as local leaders — people really capable of running the Movement and making the decisions.

Too bad I didn't go to jail and lose some weight. They had a hunger strike going for five full days.

July 26-27

A real hum-dinger of an evening. More about Jake and Silas McGhee, the two brothers who have been integrating the movie theatre. You know that the FBI made the first arrest under the Civil Rights Act in connection with the beating of Silas.

Well, they went down again tonight. After the film was over, they called and asked if we could come pick them up. Nothing doing as yet, but they didn't like to try it alone. By the time we sent an all-Negro car down there, a mob of over 300 people had gathered, and the situation was really bad. We were on the phone all the time with one of the brothers. He described the movements of the crowd, and told us that the theatre manager was demanding that they get out, since the theatre was about to close for the night. The police were there, but refused to give them any protection. He couldn't see too well whether our car had pulled up yet. Then, with 3 of us listening on our different extensions, he told us that he was going to shoot his way out. It was really tense for a few minutes, as we pleaded with him. He promised to hold out until our car arrived.

Bob Zellner and Phil M. and I jumped into another car to see if we could find out anything. We rode with windows up and doors locked tight. We got to the theatre and found it deserted. Whatever had happened — had already happened. Bob leaned out the window and asked in his deep Southern accent where were the goddamn niggers at. Nobody knew....

We found out that they had been picked up by our car after finally getting a police escort from the theatre. As they got in the car, the police stepped back, and as if on signal, the mob rushed the car, and a coke bottle was thrown through a window — the glass from the window and the bottle cutting both brothers over the eye. They went straight to the Leflore County Hospital and were treated promptly.

Another car went down to the hospital to see if everybody was all right. That car was shot at on the way, but finally managed to get safely to the hospital.

The situation was at this time fairly bad. Cars full of whites were riding up and down in front of the hospital. Five guns were seen, .22s and .38 pistols. Later, the mother of the brothers came with their older brother, Clarence, an army man with 12 years of army experience behind him (Korean War paratrooper) in full uniform. All were holed up at the hospital.

We were very afraid the hospital would demand that they leave the place [since the two younger brothers had been discharged after treatment]. We gave our people instructions not to leave unless they got a full escort and guarantees of safety. The local police refused outright, and the Highway Patrol said it would look in on the case.

We were on the phones like mad, talking to FBI, congressmen, trying to get the Pentagon to rescue the soldier in uniform, and so on. On the phone from the hospital, the soldier told us that if we didn't get him out in 30 minutes, he was taking his family out any way he could.

By this time, the FBI had finally decided to do something. Not on their own, of course, but after many, many phone calls, and many protestations on their part that they did not protect people. Two agents came over here to see the broken car window, and to see if they could get any fingerprints from the bits of coke bottle. At least 6 agents later showed up at the hospital, very hostile but taking statements like mad.

Meanwhile, we were getting a steady stream of information from the hospital. It seems that one of the kids was beaten on his way from the theatre to the car. With a policeman standing right beside him. The cops told them that they got themselves into it, and they had to get themselves out. This while in the middle of a mob, and while one of the kids was being beaten right and left.

The Hiway patrol and the sheriff both sent people down to the hospital and Chief Larry also went down. The soldier had been convinced to stick it out, and not try to get out the bad way. The sheriff finally agreed to escort them, but said that they would have to come over to the other side of the hospital and come out that way. To get to the other side, you have to cross the driveway where the white cars were moving around. No dice. Our people said they wouldn't move until they had a car in front and one in back and were escorted to their cars out *their* door. Finally they got an escort — and are home safe. They were headed off by a white car on the way back, but the police went over and cleared them out — the first positive action by the police during the whole incident....

July 30

Two nights ago we had some real trouble over an integration attempt. Whites rode through the Negro section of town firing shots into stores, and so forth. Some Negro kids threw bottles through white car windows, and it is just lucky that enough whites were scared off before they started using the guns they all had with them. We decided that the time had come for us to organize the kids into a militant but hopefully non-violent group that would do things during the daytime — when the danger of shootings is greatly reduced. If the night riders come at night in retribution, people will shoot back in defense of their homes, Robert Williams style.

Last night we had a great meeting of local, "violent" kids, here at the office. The McGhee brothers were there, but they were not the war-hawks. I think the McGhees were somewhat sobered — but God knows not scared — by their experiences. Silas had it right: when coming out of the movie theatre, just taking the coke bottle by the neck and not shooting back saved his life. When he was pulled into the car with the white men who had lead pipes, he lived by fighting hard enough to get away.

Zellner made a key speech: "I have lived in Alabama all my childhood days, and moved around a lot because my daddy was a preacher. I had to fight every day the first couple of months, when we moved into a new town. Had to take on all the kids my size and bigger. If some joker comes up to me outside here, he may beat me up, but brother he's going to know he's been in a fight. When I'm on a picket line or in a demonstration, it's a different matter. The Man is just waiting for you to hit him so that he can put you away. You pull a knife and he'll shoot you so dead so fast, and nobody in the county will say he was wrong to do it. You go on a man's property, and he shoots you down, and no jury will touch him. I've been in 15 jails in 5 southern states, and I've been beaten to that you wouldn't recognize me, so many times…. One time there were 500 people waiting to beat me up, and I was hanging onto a railing. 18 people were trying to pull me off, and I was non-violent as Hell holding on to that railing. All 18 of um couldn't pull me off, and I'm alive here today."

Our law student, who is about 10 times as good and hard working as most lawyers, explained the legal situation: what your rights should be, and what they are. Not everyone, by any means, was convinced. But the back of the war-hawk group was broken … We decided to put on a concerted effort to get Slim Henderson out of business. Slim is the cop who dragged the 7-months pregnant woman down the sidewalk. He owns a grocery store in the middle of a Negro neighborhood. We decided to go around the neighborhood with pictures of Henderson dragging the pregnant woman away. We also gave the kids Freedom Democratic Party information to hand out at the same time. After we had worked the neighborhood, we organized the kids to march around shouting: *Slim Henderson's Store Must Go!* This was very good for them, releasing some of the tension …

We just received another shipment from FASC. FASC is a little-known national organization: Friends and Admirers of Stokely Carmichael. We keep on getting these wild Care packages with all sorts of soap and toothpaste and candy, and those towelettes, and baby powder, and prickly heat powder and shampoo and insect repellent and shoe polish and more soap and so on. There is great merriment amongst the people who happen to be in the office when they arrive. Stokely sits in the middle of the pile and hands the stuff around and makes little comments:

"Young man, tell FASC what you want and FASC will see to it — FASC is generous and fair."

"Oh, my people saw me on TV and got a look at my shoes, and here is shoe polish: 'Yours from the FASC.'"

We have a good time here when we are not getting beat up or shot at or threatened ...

August 2

So much has been happening that my arrest seems like a small bit of information that I should pass on.

Three different cars tried to run me down when I was in a parking lot of a large supermarket registering people. A whole bunch of the not so non-violent youth started taunting a white man in one of those cars. He got out of the car and started threatening them with a knife. At this point Clarence McGhee stepped onto the scene, the big brother of the two kids who have been down to the theatre. He stands well over six feet. He understands the need for non-violence, and has helped us calm some of the kids down a couple of times. But if some-body touches him — look out! Well, with thirty screaming kids standing around, daring the white man on, Clarence just stood there with a little smile on his lips, his head cocked slightly to one side, and waited for the guy. He didn't shout or taunt or anything, he just stood there and stated the facts: "You've got the knife, come and get me." The yellow peckerwood turned away, of course. The sight of Clarence standing there certainly was the prettiest sight I have seen so far in the state.

Well, then we all walked down the street, the kids still going strong, and me trying to calm them down somewhat. A cop came along and five helmeted police jumped out and told us to stop and started warning us that they would arrest the whole bunch of us if we gave them any more trouble. Just at that point a white man ran out from a store, and fingered me: "He's the one, he's the agitator, he's been causing trouble all day." They put me under arrest, frisked me, and started strong-arming me toward the car on the other side of the street. I tried to ask what the charge was, but they were shouting back at the man, asking him if he would testify, and telling what time the hearing would be. Half way across the street one of the cops hit me hard in the right rib. I thought it was a fist, but people on the street said that it was a club. I slumped down in the street, and the cop who had my arm twisted behind my back dragged me along the rest of the way and threw me sideways into the car. As we went down to the station, one of the cops turned around in his seat and suddenly reached over and pulled a fistful of hair out of my arm. Later he yanked my snick pin off and jabbed me in the leg with it. Real kid stuff — absolutely senseless.

Two FBI men came around to the jail later and asked if I had been brutally beaten. The first bit of humor so far. I told them no, not brutally ... Finally Chief Larry came into the cell, and said I could go.

Great trick we could have pulled on the FBI, but forgot to do. Our office was shot into [just after I got out of jail]. The FBI came and got up on a ladder to check the bullet marks. He was sort of nervous up there, and the people down below kept on making comments about cars on the street and so on. The ladder apparently began to shake visibly, and the FBI asked whether people were watching the street all right. Dottie says she should have said at this point: "Sorry, we are not in the protection business, we will, however, investigate the matter to see if any Federal Law has been violated." That, brother, is a perfect analogy of how we feel all the time: up a ladder with your pants down, and the FBI's running saying that they really can't do anything until we are messed up and something has been violated....

Looking forward to seeing you all soon. Write more.

Yours in the struggle,

Bill

Another volunteer continues the Greenwood story.

Dear Folks,   Greenwood, August 17

... Last night at the mass meeting, Greenwood was fed a double-barrel blast of fame in the persons of Harry Belafonte and Sidney Poitier. It was a deeply exciting experience, and a strange and enlightening one. It was exciting when James Forman entered from the back of the packed auditorium after we had waited two hours and cried, "Freedom! Freedom!" and the two tall straight men moved in thru the people and their screams like gods, their faces holding the same dramatic intensity, by association, that they hold in the most effectively contrived photographs. And it was strange and enlightening when these two seemed fumbling and amateurish and, most of all, awed on stage, lacking the showman's composure and command. Belafonte gave a shamed, beseeching little talk about how his heart and his body as well as his money have been with the Movement since it has begun, and this is probably true. And then Poitier stepped forward and in an almost matter-of-fact but decided tone made this embarrassingly frank and dramatic statement: "I am 37 years old. I have been a lonely man all my life.... until I came to Greenwood, Mississippi.... I have been lonely because I have not found love, but this room is *overflowing* with it."

There is the danger that I am being unjust and inaccurate with this description. But in general this is what happened;

they moved from the grandiose, the sublime, towards the pathetic. We saw public figures become private ones, and we saw human beings informed more fully before us. But when I allow myself to recall this experience as I felt it, it is saddening and then almost embittering. I think it was sad because I don't feel the room was overflowing with love and their perception of it describes their need, most of all, and reveals perhaps an expectation of a spiritual experience that they haven't found in the North. Also, as I said, it was embittering, because of the vision of the North that they brought with them, the "Canaan" where everybody can vote. You wonder: is freeing the Negroes to that end desirable? Is it freeing them at all? And the problem becomes insupportably large because you realize that the character of an entire nation must be changed. And it is also embittering not just to see they mistook the crowd as including ideal qualities of soul, but because my own vision of that perfect emotion has also been "tarnished" in that the crowd was people that I knew, and not "Southern Negroes" ...

A special news bulletin has just come over the air reporting the shooting of Silas McGhee. He was sitting in his car in the Negro section and someone in a passing car shot him through his left temple. The report claims that he's in satisfactory condition, that he needs surgery, that he will recover ... His older brother, the Korean war veteran, is now in the Greenwood jail on an old assault charge which is supposedly trumped-up.

This is the next morning. Silas had driven a bunch of Snick people to a cafe after a staff meeting and was sitting across the street in one of the radio cars sleeping over the wheel. Witnesses say that a new white station wagon slowed down beside his car and shot thru the closed window and into Silas. People in the restaurant, hearing the shot, rushed out and opened the car door, and Silas fell out bleeding onto the street. They called for ambulances but supposedly none was available. The latest news is that either they could not or else would not perform the operation on him needed to dislodge the bullet. So he was driven to Jackson a hundred miles away. It is our feeling that

Silas was refused treatment. A similar incident occurred about three years ago when a civil rights worker [James Travis] was struck by bullets meant probably for Bob Moses right outside of Greenwood. The delay involved in arguing with the hospital and in taking him to Jackson nearly killed him. We are waiting to hear now whether Silas survived the operation. Whether he dies or not, the important point in terms of the civil rights movement in Greenwood is that they meant to kill him....

The battleground between blacks and whites in this community recently has been the several stores owned and run by white men but patronized primarily by Negroes. The first of these to be boycotted was Slim Henderson's. Several arrests have been made during demonstrations near there and at least twice the police have stood guard all day with rifles, preventing cars from passing the store and in general attempting to frustrate the boycott. This man has nearly been run out of business.

A boycott had also been started on a man who tore down a civil rights sign that was posted across the street, who has supposedly been "fresh" with his girl customers, and who has cheated those customers of his who are on credit. Another woman, who has claimed that she would shoot dead anyone who tries to boycott her store, has successfully boycotted herself by threatening everybody with a shotgun. That has been a scene out of Faulkner, this lean woman with straggly hair brandishing that huge gun, leveling it now and then at the crowd and watching them run. She has fired it several times, so far always high in the air. Now she threatens to drive the streets shooting at every civil rights worker she sees....

The Student Nonviolent Coordinating Committee places a large order when it asks people to meet this kind of violence with non-violence. So far in Greenwood, they have been able to make their point — that non-violence is tactically necessary in demonstrations and wherever the ends of "the movement" are concerned. But SNCC has also, I think, encouraged self protection, and it has proven difficult to discern where self-defense and "defense of the community" are distinct from each other.

To these young people, as to most, violence is not at all a last, and regrettable, resort. To be violent has usually been, in the minds of Southerners, to be courageous. The boycott, powerful economic blow or not, does not satisfy the repressed urge of these young people to strike back. Silas' shooting last night came close to touching off unspeakable things ...

I am enclosing a statement that one of these boycotted store-owners made over the radio ... it is very frightening to know that anything *they* do they justify on bases of principle, and to realize that much of what they do is inspired by moral fervor. Playing on their sense of guilt is a dubious, even negligible weapon, it would seem. I saw this perverted moralism translated into violent action the other day when I was chased out of the white neighborhood with stones and curses, a car finally ran me off the road and forced me to dive into a Negro's chicken-coop for safety. That little gimp-legged man with the wild blue eyes who was not a good enough shot to hit me with the rocks, who ran after me down the street with his cronies, who roared after me in his car and came up onto the dirt after me with it, who swung at me with his left hand as he went by but missed again, believed that he was striking blows for freedom, among other things — for all that is good and right. I suppose all you can do for a man like that is pray for him. Is he wicked? If he isn't, then maybe no one is and maybe that's the proper conclusion: There are no evil men in the world, only scared ones and indignant ones and hateful ones. But if there are no evil men, there *is* evil; you feel it come into yourself when you view these men....

Love,
Bret

Silas McGhee lived.

THE STUDENT VOICE

VOL. 5 NO. 21   STUDENT VOICE, INC.   6 Raymond Street, N. W.   Atlanta, Georgia 30314   AUGUST 19, 1964

THE THREE MOTHERS OF THE THREE SLAIN RIGHTS WORKERS leave service for Andrew Goodman. Mrs. Chaney, Mrs. Goodman and Mrs. Schwerner (l to r) leave the Ethical Society auditorium after services for the slain worker.

DEMO CONVENTION FACES SHOWDOWN

MORE THAN 800 DELEGATES OF the Freedom Democratic Party from over 40 counties met in Jackson to choose 68 delegates and alternates to the National Democratic Convention.

NATION MOURNS SLAIN WORKERS

PHILADELPHIA, MISS. -Neshoba County Sheriff Lawrence Rainey refused to speak to FBI agents investigating the death of three civil rights workers.

Approached by two agents, Rainey asked if they had a warrant. When they replied "no," Rainey told the agents, "Come and see me when you got one and I'll be glad to talk to you."

Meanwhile, services were held for the three slain workers.

Memorial services were held in Meridian, Miss. for James Chaney and in New York City for Andrew Goodman and Michael Schwerner.

Concurrent memorial services have been held throughout the country to commemorate the workers' deaths.

In Mississippi, the FBI was reported to be keeping several persons under surveillance while it searched for a weapon to match the bullets taken from the bodies.

Dr. David Spain, a New York physician, who examined the body of Chaney, reported that he found evidence of a severe beating, probably with a blunt instrument.

Pathologists in Jackson found five bullets, three in Chaney, one each in Goodman and Schwerner.

OMNIBUS RIGHTS SUIT FILED AGAINST MISS.

JACKSON, MISS. - A suit asking that 16 laws which hinder civil rights activities be struck down has been filed by Mississippi rights leaders.

The suit, filed in U.S. District Court here, contends that the laws abridge freedom of speech, press, right to assemble peacefully, petition for redress of grievances and have deprived Negroes of "life, liberty, and property without due process of law."

It was brought by SNCC Mississippi Project director Robert Moses, Aaron Henry, Dave Dennis and Hunter Morey.

They contend that the people they represent "have been and will continue to be arrested, incarcerated, tried and convicted without due process of

CONTINUED ON PAGE 4

BOYCOTT THREATENED

ATLANTIC CITY, N. J. - "A proven lawless element is attempting to blackmail the President into preventing the seating of the Mississippi Freedom Democratic Party (FDP) delegation," an FDP spokesman said.

The spokesman was referring to a meeting of the governors of Mississippi, Alabama, Arkansas, Louisiana and Florida in New Orleans. They announced that if the Freedom delegation is seated their states would boycott the convention.

"It is horrible to think that the President would submit to political blackmail, especially by men who have defied the Federal government and one who is under indictment for criminal contempt," the spokesman continued.

STATE BANS FDP

Meanwhile Mississippi State Chancery Judge Stokes Robertson, Jr. issued an injunction banning the operation of the Mississippi Freedom Democratic Party.

The suit, filed by State Attorney General J. T. Patterson, banned the FDP from acting as representatives of a "pretended political party" in Mississippi.

Patterson's suit charged that last week's state convention of the Freedom Democrats was designed to "intimidate and embarrass the lawfully existing Democratic Party and to create confusion in the minds of the electorate and bitterness, hatred and discord among the citizens."

Named as defendants were Aaron Henry, Rev. R.T. Smith, Mrs. Victoria Gray, Mrs. Fannie Lou Hamer, Lawrence Guyot, Leslie McLemore, Miss Peggy Connor, Rev. Ed King and Dr. A. D. Biettel.

Robertson's injunction barred the Freedom Party from using the name "Democratic."

FDP CONVENTION HELD

Over 800 delegates attended the state convention of the Freedom Democratic party in Jackson Aug. 6. The participants elected 68 delegates and alternates to the national convention in Atlantic City. Aaron Henry heads the delegation while Mrs. Fannie Lou Hamer is vice-chairman. Rev. Ed King and Mrs. Victoria Gray were elected National Committeeman and Committeewoman. Lawrence Guyot will head the state executive committee.

The first four mentioned have been unsuccessful candidates in

CONTINUED ON PAGE 4

August 1964 edition of *The Student Voice*

We are soldiers
in the army
we have to fight
although we have to die

We have to hold up
the freedom banner
we have to hold it up
until we die

Freedom Song

Philadelphia, August Third

Greenwood, June 29

We have heard rumors twice to the effect that the three men were found weighted down in that river. Both stories, though the same, were later completely dropped in an hour or so. How do you like that guy Gov. Johnson saying that they might be hiding in the North or maybe in Cuba for all he knew ...

Tchula, July 16

Yesterday while the Mississippi River was being dragged looking for the three missing civil rights workers, two bodies of Negroes were found — one cut in half and one without a head.

Mississippi is the only state where you can drag a river any time and find bodies you were not expecting. Things are really much better for rabbits — there's a closed season on rabbits.

Como, August 3

About three weeks ago there was a flying rumor that they had been found in a rural jail. Tonight it was said that three graves had been found near Philadelphia. How the ghosts of those three shadow all our work! "Did you know them?" I am constantly asked. Did I need to?

The bodies were found on August 3 and identified the next day.

Meridian, August 4

Last night Pete Seeger was giving a concert in Meridian. We sang a lot of freedom songs, and every time a verse like 'No more lynchings' was sung, or 'before I'd be a slave I'd be buried in my grave,' I had the flash of understanding that sometimes comes when you suddenly think about the meaning of a familiar song ... I wanted to stand up and shout to them, "think about what you are singing — people really have died to keep us all from being slaves." Most of the people there still did not know that the bodies had been found. Finally just before the singing of "We Shall Overcome," Pete Seeger made the announcement. "We must sing 'We Shall Overcome' now," said Seeger. "The three boys would not have wanted us to weep now, but to sing and understand this song." That seems to me the best way to explain the greatness of this project — that death can have this meaning. Dying is not an ever-present possibility in Meridian, the way some reports may suggest. Nor do any of us want to die. Yet in a moment like last night, we can feel that anyone who did die for the Project would wish to be remembered not by tributes or grief but by understanding and continuation of what he was doing …

As we left the church, we heard on the radio the end of President Johnson's speech announcing the air attacks on Vietnam … I could only think "This must not be the beginning of a war. There is still a freedom fight, and we are winning. We must have time to live and help Mississippi to be alive." Half an hour before, I had understood death in a new way. Now I realized that Mississippi, in spite of itself, has given real meaning to life. In Mississippi you never ask, "What is the meaning of life?" or "Is there any point to it all?" but only that we may have enough life to do all that there is to be done.…

Meridian, August 5

At the Freedom school and at the community center, many of the kids had known Mickey and almost all knew Jimmy Chaney. Today we asked the kids to describe Mickey and Jimmy because we had never known them.

"Mickey was a big guy. He wore blue jeans all the time" … I asked the kids, "What did his eyes look like?" and they told me they were "friendly eyes" "nice eyes" ("nice" is a lovely word in a Mississippi accent). "Mickey was a man who was at home everywhere and with anybody," said the 17-year-old girl I stay with. The littlest kids, the 6, 7, 8 year olds, tell about how he played "Frankenstein" with them or took them for drives or talked with them about Freedom. Many of the teen-age boys were delinquents until Mickey went down to the bars and jails and showed them that one person at least would respect them if they began to fight for something important … And the grown-ups, too, trusted him. The lady I stay with tells with pride of how Mickey and Rita came to supper at their house, and police cars circled around the house all during the meal. But Mickey could make them feel glad to take the risk.

People talk less about James Chaney here, but feel more. The kids describe a boy who played with them — whom everyone respected but who never had to join in fights to maintain his respect — a quiet boy but very sharp and very understanding when he did speak. Mostly we know James through his sisters and especially his 12-year-old brother, Ben. Today Ben was in the Freedom School. At lunchtime the kids have a jazz band (piano, washtub bass, cardboard boxes and bongos as drums) and tiny Ben was there leading it all even with his broken arm, with so much energy and rhythm that even Senator Eastland would have had to stop and listen if he'd been walking by....

And Andrew Goodman: he had been in Mississippi little more than twenty-four hours.

On August 7, James Chaney's funeral and memorial service took place in Meridian.

Meridian, August 8

... The service was preceded by several silent marches beginning at churches throughout Meridian and converging on the First Union Baptist Church. I have been on a large number of walks, marches, vigils, pickets, etc., in my life, but I can't remember anything which was quite like this one. In the first place, it was completely silent (at least, the march I was on), even though it lasted over 50 minutes, and even though there were a fair number of children involved....

Meridian, August 11

... In the line I was in, there were about 150 people — white and Negro — walking solemnly, quietly, and without incident for about a mile and a half through white and Negro neighborhoods (segregation is like a checkerboard here). The police held up traffic at the stoplights, and of all the white people watching only one girl heckled. I dislike remembering the service — the photographers with their television cameras were omnipresent, it was really bad. And cameras when people are crying … and bright lights. Someone said it was on television later. I suppose it was.

Dave Dennis spoke — it was as if he was realizing his anger and feeling only as he spoke. As if the deepest emotion — the bitterness, then hatred — came as he expressed it, and could not have been planned or forethought …

Dear Folks,   Laurel, August 11

… The memorial service began around 7:30 with over 120 people filling the small, wooden-pew lined church. David Dennis of CORE, the Assistant Director for the Mississippi Summer Project, spoke for COFO. He talked to the Negro people of Meridian — it was a speech to move people, to end the lethargy, to make people stand up. It went something like this:

"I am not here to memorialize James Chaney, I am not here to pay tribute — I am too sick and tired. Do YOU hear me, I am S-I-C-K and T-I-R-E-D. I have attended too many memorials, too many funerals. This has got to stop. Mack Parker, Medgar Evers, Herbert Lee, Lewis Allen, Emmett Till, four little girls in Birmingham, a 13-year old boy in Birmingham, and the list goes on and on. I have attended these funerals and memorials and I am SICK and TIRED. But the trouble is that YOU are NOT sick and tired and for that reason YOU, yes YOU, are to blame. Everyone of your damn souls. And if you are going to let this continue now then you are to blame, yes YOU. Just as much as the monsters of hate who pulled the trigger or brought down the club; just as much to blame as the sheriff and the chief of police, as the governor in Jackson who said that he 'did not have time' for Mrs. Schwerner when she went to see him, and just as much to blame as the President and Attorney General in Washington who wouldn't provide protection for Chaney,

Goodman and Schwerner when we told them that protection was necessary in Neshoba County ... Yes, I am angry, I AM. And it's high time that you got angry too, angry enough to go up to the courthouse Monday and register — everyone of you. Angry enough to take five and ten other people with you. Then and only then can these brutal killings be stopped. Remember it is your sons and your daughters who have been killed all these years and you have done nothing about it, and if you don't do nothing NOW baby, I say God Damn Your Souls....

Dear Blake,   Mileston, August 9

... Dave finally broke down and couldn't finish and the Chaney family was moaning and much of the audience and I was also crying. It's such an impossible thing to describe but suddenly again, as I'd first realized when I heard the three men were missing when we were still training up at Oxford, I felt the sacrifice the Negroes have been making for so long. How the Negro people are able to accept all the abuses of the whites — and the insults and injustices which make me ashamed to be white — and then turn around and say they want to love us, is beyond me. There are Negroes who want to kill whites and many Negroes have much bitterness but still the majority seem to have the quality of being able to look for a future in which whites will love the Negroes. Our kids talk very critically of all the whites around here and still they have a dream of freedom in which both races understand and accept each other. There is such an overpowering task ahead of these kids that sometimes I can't do anything but cry for them. I hope they are up to the task, I'm not sure I would be if I were a Mississippi Negro. As a white northerner I can get involved whenever I feel like it and run home whenever I get bored or frustrated or scared. I hate the attitude and position of the Northern whites and despise myself when I think that way.

Lately I've been feeling homesick and longing for pleasant old Westport and sailing and swimming and my friends. I don't quite know what to do because I can't ignore my desire to go home and yet I feel I am a much weaker person than I like to think I am because I do have these emotions. I've always tried to avoid situations which aren't so nice, like arguments and dirty houses and now maybe Mississippi. I asked my father if I could stay down here for a whole year and I was almost glad when he said "no" that we couldn't afford it because it would mean supporting me this year in addition to three more years of college. I have a desire to go home and to read a lot and go to Quaker meetings and be by myself so I can think about all this rather than being in the middle of it all the time. But I know if my emotions run like they have in the past, that I can only take that pacific sort of life for a little while and then I get the desire to be active again and get involved with knowing other people.

I guess this all sounds crazy and I seem to always think out my problems as I write to you. I am angry because I have a choice as to whether or not to work in the Movement and I am playing upon that choice and leaving here. I wish I could talk with you 'cause I'd like to know if you ever felt this way about anything. I mean have you ever despised yourself for your weak conviction or something. And what is making it worse is that all those damn northerners are thinking of me as a brave hero....

Martha

Laurel, August 11

... As I was riding on the bus back to Laurel from Meridian after the service, all this kept running through my brain, along with the fact of knowing that nobody has ever been brought to justice in Mississippi for all those murders, that the

Federal Government just bought some property with Beckwith for $27,000.00 (almost like Barnett's handshake after the first mistrial). No, the FBI is only an investigative body ... The Justice Department can do nothing ... Welcome to Mississippi, the Magnolia State ... Help Save Your Country, IMPEACH EARL WARREN ... Six months sentence, suspended to take care of tobacco crop ... It isn't nice to have a stall-in ... two more churches bombed ... it isn't nice to picket the President ... wouldn't have happened if they stayed in their part of the country ... it isn't nice to block a door ... white grand jury refused to indict ... It isn't nice ... kill 'em, burn 'em, kill the bastards ... it isn't ... Not Guilty ...

On the road between Laurel and Meridian

Claude Weaver (*far right*), Panola County project director and Harvard student, and Geoff Cowan in the center

Canton, July 20

I gave Kay a laugh the other night. She came into the kitchen about midnight and I was sitting there eating cold lima beans and humming "We Shall Overcome"....

The Nitty Gritty

Dear Ruth and Carl,   Holly Springs, August 9

It is Sunday, and I have driven over 2,000 miles in the last three days. I am tired. I want to go very much to a movie, or to watch TV even. I want to be in Berkeley and do stupid things and don't look behind me in the rearview mirror. I want to look at a white man and not hate his guts, and know he doesn't hate me either. I want to talk about the White Sox and be admired by somebody who isn't going through worse than I am. I want to get out of the 90 degree weather and go swimming ...

Love to you,

Bob

Getting down to the nitty gritty: the facts, the realities, the how-where-when-who of carrying out a big idea. The important problems have been described by the volunteers in other chapters; the smaller ones could seem just as bad.

Dear Mom & Dad,   Holly Springs

It is a little easier working within the Freedom Schools but you still have … the pressure of a group of almost forty living fairly closely and the tempers and moods of your leaders and the guys in the field who sometimes find release for their tension by attacking others … One of the hardest things is that you almost never have a chance to take a break. Sundays can be one of our hardest working days as everybody goes to church and some don't get back until late afternoon….

Wayne's death exhausted all of us [Wayne Yancey, a Negro volunteer killed in an automobile accident]. Very few were actually close to him but his death was so useless and wore down our nerves. I think that all of us have felt in the back of our minds a little nagging thought that sooner or later someone would have a serious accident. Our project is responsible for about seven counties in northern Mississippi and we have had a number of minor accidents. The constant worry about policemen and hostile cars plus fatigue makes the chances for accidents much greater….

                                    Love,
                                    Pam

                                    Carthage, August 9

I cannot wait to discuss something besides civil rights. Sometimes we make conscious efforts to discuss Plato or what's the best color for toilet paper — but it's useless. In thirty seconds we're back to C.R.…

Meridian, July 25

I'm a Northern white intellectual snob. I can't do anything at all about the Northern or the white part; I try (believe it or not) to subdue the snobbery; but I'm a college intellectual phoney by choice ... And in my short range of rather sheltered experiences, I suppose I have never spent this much time in such a culturally sterile place ... I got a letter from Dave today describing the most outrageous and absurd Mahler Cycle with which he was torturing our neighbors once again, and I must admit, the thought of listening to 7 of those symphonies, more or less one after another, has never been more appealing to me ...

Dear All,   Carthage, July 14

Transportation is still our main problem. Farms are far apart — sometimes miles; roads are terrible, etc. One day Hank and I rode mule bareback. It was all I could do at first to hold on with my legs around his belly ... Soon I got the hang of it and did all right — didn't hold on or anything. Then a farmer gave Hank a horse and saddle, which he has been riding for two days all over the place. Talk about saddle sore, Hank the cowboy has to even sleep on his stomach....

Love,
Judy

Hattiesburg 3:30 a.m.

Boy, love life around here is really something. My experiences wouldn't make even *Junior Catholic Messenger* ...

Dear Gretchen,   Clarksdale, July 7

I'm sitting in a junkyard. It used to be a cotton stamping

and processing plant. Some of the plant is still in operation, but most of it has collected dust, debris and rust ... next to the yard is a clearing and a group of Negro kids are playing softball — without gloves, without shoes and without bases.

I went walking to try to get away, but I can't. Wherever I go, I see kids without shoes; wherever I go, the air is heavy. The tension has subsided a great deal in Clarksdale, but there is no escape from the psychological and physical poverty ...

In many ways this reminds me of camp. In the first weeks, kids and problems will be of special interest and they will be a constant topic of conversation. Later, people get sick of talking about the same problems and topics and start making jokes about it to get away from it. Conversations seem superfluous unless you find a person with whom you may be comfortable. There is no one I can relax with plus there is no place to relax and forget about problems that you no longer want to think about or waste words on ...

Hope to hear from you soon.

Lew

Gulfport

The roads are clay and dusty. Red dust that kicks up when the breeze passes. It gets into your clothes and your hair. The red mud on the side of the road left over from yesterday's rain storm clogs your shoes and somehow leaves stains on your pants. But somehow none of this matters when you are welcomed into a person's home and talk to him about registering for the vote ... and so clothes cease to be a real concern. "Image" ceases to be a real concern. If it ever was. In spite of the national Council of Churches' advice, we crap on the clean, antiseptic, acceptable, decent middle-class "image." It is that decency that we want to change, to "overcome." It is that decency which shuts these "niggers" in their board shacks with their middle-class television antennas rising above tarpaper roofs. So crap on your middle class, on your decency, mister Churches man. Get out of your god-damned new rented car. Get out of your pressed, proper clothes. Get out of your unoffensive, shit-eating smile and crew-cut. Come join us who are sleeping on the floor ... Come with us and walk, not ride, the dusty streets of north Gulfport ...

Life in a Project "office" had its own special quality.

Gulfport, June 24

The SNCC shack is across the road, a two room wooden shack, plastered with pictures of Freedom candidates and CORE and SNCC posters. One room is just beginning to be an office, with five typewriters and a mimeograph machine and newly installed windows. The other room is devoted to sleeping — with mattresses on the floor....

Leland, August 10

The present office is upstairs in a place called the "Athletic Club," a place that is neither athletic, nor a club, but does sport a small "snack" bar, where beer and wine are served, and in the back of the place is a long room where card playing takes place, a juke box is ensconced, and some dancing is done among the small clientele. Upstairs is our office-bedroom combination ... we are not plagued with any of the normal problems, such as rats, mice, and cockroaches, or even mosquitoes — the reason is very simple — we have minuscule ants that literally infest the damn place, eat all refuse that happens to be left around ...

Perhaps the hardest part of being an office worker was the sense of being removed from the action, behind the front. Yet nothing could have been more important than the work of the communications people, particularly at the COFO headquarters in Jackson.

Dear parents,   Jackson, July 3-6

This office is almost beyond description. Hot — the air-conditioner is still broken [the only one in a Project office], very full of people doing very important things apparently without any order. The office is one long room partitioned by plaster board. No windows! Perspiration runs down the back of my legs at 4:00 a.m.! Plywood desks are nailed to the walls around the room. Dogs, paper, pop bottles, glasses, newspapers and people are strewn everywhere. A visitor would see no order in the madness, but it *is* there. With the difficulties of the first

COFO Office (Peter Rabinowitz at desk)

week and the very busy job of dealing with the press and trying to perform as security agents for the entire project, we had little time to think of organization. Things are looking better, however. I am generally impressed by the ability of the leadership though I find it necessary to exercise my own judgment.

The Negro SNCC workers know how to be 'cool'; some of the whites think they do, and don't. But that is a small matter.

I am very happy tonight, though I have had no sleep in 2 days, hardly, and only one meal today. We in communications have the responsibility of running the telephone system and handling the press, knowing where everyone in the state is. We are the security system. The FBI, local police, Justice Dept, press from around the nation, are our constant "phone companions."

Since I am now chief WATS operator, I will describe to you how it works. The WATS is a "Wide Area Telephone Service." It costs about $500 a month to have a state WATS line but you can make an unlimited number of calls around the state per month. By means of the WATS line we are able to keep in close contact with the projects across the state. Almost all information that comes into the office comes over that phone. It is absolutely essential to security and transfer of all information. The WATS operator types up all vital data received in the conversations she has with the field concerning a million different things. The WATS line digest is compiled from these typed reports. There is another WATS line used for program calls which involve long discussions of detailed plans. There is also both a state and nation-wide WATS line in Greenwood, where the SNCC headquarters is located ...

This evening I happened to be the one who answered the phone to hear "emergency" from Moss Point. One more incident you will see in the morning paper about the 'battle for civil rights in Mississippi.' The strange thing is that even here in the heart of the organization and of the state, I have a hard time believing what really goes on....

Love,
Margaret

Jackson and Greenwood were headquarters for the security system, but "security" was a mystical word which haunted Project workers all across the state. Some workers considered the do's and don'ts very important; staff members often had less patience, especially with the sign-out, sign-in system, which applied equally to a hop down to the corner for a pack of cigarettes or a 20-mile trip into dangerous rural territory.

In mid-July, an important new safeguard was added....

Valley View, Aug. 26

Our security precautions are as good as they could be. The house is set back about a hundred yards from the road, and there are three searchlights which are kept on all night. We also have two dogs, appropriately named Freedom and Now respectively. The most effective precaution, though, is the new 2-way radio. I've learned to use the code numbers and names. We use it whenever anyone goes any distance from the house or at night, checking in at each destination and giving estimated times of arrival, etc. One girl walked home tonight as it was getting dark — with the radio. I wasn't too happy about it, but she seemed to know what she was doing. She called once or twice, because a car was following her for a while, but it turned out all right....

The two-way radios were installed in cars as well as offices, using the "Citizens' Band" which operates on 23 frequencies. Whites did some jamming, but destroyed only one installation, in Natchez; they seemed to prefer to fight back by increasing their own supply of two-way radios.

Sometimes the volunteers slipped away from all the tensions for a while — to New Orleans for friendly white faces and legal bourbon or to Hodding Carter's swimming pool in Greenville. But then the old problems might come along too ...

Clarksdale, July 12

I went to Mound Bayou with four Negroes — it is an all-Negro community about 28 miles south of Clarksdale. We just talked, drank, ate fried chicken and danced. It was a night of relaxation except for the fact that we kept discussing the Negro problem and the Jews — since they asked me if I was Jewish. As we talked and drank, tongues grew looser and out came Negro resentment towards whites — misconceptions like all whites have money — but Negroes are still better, etc. They think they're all hip — which is true — and that whites want to be hip like them — which is sometimes true.

The tension at Oxford between volunteers and staff members, whites and Negroes, did not vanish in Mississippi. The Northern white volunteers were less awed now than at orientation; they had fresher energy than the veterans, less patience with a casual approach to the job, and often a strong leadership drive. Usually they were better educated and better "adjusted" than Negroes in the Movement: local people as well as staff.

Dear John & Cleo,   Canton, August 12

… Several times I've had to completely re-do press statements or letters written by one of them. It's one thing to tell people who have come willingly to Freedom School that they needn't feel ashamed of weakness in these areas, but it's quite another to even acknowledge such weaknesses in one's fellow workers. Furthermore, I'm a northerner; I'm white; I'm a woman; I'm a college graduate; I've not "proven" myself yet in jail or in physical danger. Every one of these things is a strike against me as far as they are concerned. I've refused to be ashamed of what I cannot change; I either overlook or purposely and pointedly misinterpret their occasional thrusts of antagonism; I think twice or more before asserting myself or pronouncing my opinion on any affair in which they have more experience, and so far have had no really unpleasant moments at all …

"No bad moments at all" does have one exception — a run-in with a 17-year-old fellow who's been with the Movement in the south since '60, has served countless jail sentences, was a participant in the bloodiest of freedom rides and considers himself, rightly so, a true veteran. He's quite loud and swaggering and hypersensitive to criticism or insult (imagined or real). One afternoon he was knocking away (literally) at a guitar with neither knowledge nor talent. The guitar's owner (a white boy) appeared and requested the instrument. Request ignored. Owner took it away. Injured feelings flamed immediately into an anti-white tirade that was carried on for 15 minutes straight. I had been trying for the last hour to write a report and was getting very tired of the racket. So I foolishly asked the ranter why he didn't join the Muslims if he so badly hated the white man's guts. No rational response, just further venom directed at us. I'd given him a new target — a white woman. My temper ran away with me at a certain remark from him and I childishly commented on his super-friendly behavior toward certain other white gals.…

Love,
Jo

Biloxi, August 16

Another problem has to do with a local volunteer, an ex-drunkard who is finding something in life in the movement. He has a great need for being in the center of attention, and is usually arrogant and spiteful to all he meets. In one of our staff meetings he came in drunk and started attempting to take over the meeting. George put to us an ultimatum: either agree with him or else he would leave the group. After he walked out, many of us felt that he would be harmful to the movement if he stayed, but the NCC minister with us, a very gifted and articulate worker, brought up the question of just what our purpose

Kathie Sarachild in the Batesville office

was down here and just how we had failed if we could not help George rather than lose him, if we could not have some respect for his problems. The rest of us soon fell to attacking ourselves for our attitude, and we talked about what we had done wrong and what we could do. It was a beautiful act of what we are here for — to build a society where the problems of the individual can never be forgotten, a world where understanding and love are the keys to success....

Ruleville, July 27

... The question is how much energy and resources can we exert in helping people like this, who have personality problems, and still meet the tasks that have to be met. So far we haven't been able to give them much constructive attention. It is frustrating to know that you can't be an effective case-worker with our resources and thus must continually avoid getting really involved in people's personal problems ... However, I find the broad attack on the system much more satisfying than the case work approach....

Yet amidst all the tensions, the moods of irritation and despair, perspective remained.

Hattiesburg, July 27

(Written on an opened-out paper bag)

I got a letter from a boy in Altadena who wants to come here for the rest of the summer. It was sort of a strange letter: He wakes up in the night with just one word pounding in his heart and his head. The word is *Mississippi*. He wants more than anything to come here. I wrote asking him to question his motives, and if he thought he had reasons instead of just feelings for going to Mississippi, he should come ... The boy wrote that he called you. Encourage him to come if you see fit; my letter may have been discouraging ...

Chris Williams cooling off in Panola County

Go tell it on the mountain
over the hills and everywhere
go tell it on the mountain
to let my people go

Democrats for Freedom

Clarksdale, July 22

… The heat the last two days has been so unbearable that work has been virtually impossible … Harassment continues at a low level but steady … Voter registration has been stalled for over a week —the registrar has closed the courthouse …

The one bright spot is the Freedom Democratic party.…

Dear friends, Greenwood, August

To my way of thinking, the most exciting aspect of this summer is the politics of it, especially the grass roots elements of politics down here.

The Freedom Democratic Party, which accepts the political

processes of America, including party politics, is something even newer than other forms of political action such as demonstrations, sit-ins, freedom rides, etc. A freedom ride or demonstration has short-term, usually symbolic goals. When a person sits in at a hamburger joint, he is protesting discrimination in all white public accommodations. But it is time now to go after the long-range goals of political power through direct participation — through the right to vote. This must be done by the FDP, because the Negro is denied these rights in the regular Mississippi Democratic Party.

Until court orders finally demand it, the registering of Negroes on the official books of the state seems a hopeless task: 94% of the eligible Negroes in Mississippi aren't registered. Old Martha Lamb, the official registrar of Leflore County, just won't give in to the waves of black faces which confront her every day. Earlier this month, three Congressmen came by to observe voter registration practices in Miss. A young Negro girl, age 24, had tried to register nine times in the past three years. Each time she failed. When we asked her to try again, she broke down in tears, saying she just couldn't take any more degradation. However, Bill Ryan, one of the Congressmen, demanded to see her back tests. (We were never allowed to see them ourselves.) He felt strongly that her answers were better than some of the whites who had passed. So Ryan convinced her to try again. (We learned later that she *did* pass, with Congressman Ryan breathing down Martha Lamb's neck. She was the only Negro to be registered in Leflore County all summer.)

Because official registration is hopeless for the moment, we are concentrating our efforts on FDP registration. But this is tough too. The Negro community in the South, particularly Mississippi, has had absolutely no political education. And whenever he has tried to take the bold step into politics, he has been beaten back into submission and kept in ignorance. The closest thing to politics around here is church elections when they elect Deacons ... As for the expression of interests and needs through the political process, the Negroes are totally inexperienced. If nothing else is accomplished this summer, at least a good education in politics and political expression will have been achieved by the Negroes, paving the way for more effective action in the future....

I still feel, and always will, that political power is the most powerful instrument of peaceful, legitimate change. And as the Negro gets the vote, he gets representation. With representation, the powers of the state must begin to look more to his interests, and as the whites adjust to this power change, then progress is made on all fronts. They don't have to love each other, but they do have to accept the realities of change.

The FDP meets the standards of a regular party. Its meetings are open, its meetings are documented. Legal proof, showing not only voter intimidation by the whites of the regular party, but also the qualifications of the FDP meetings and elected delegates, is being gathered and sent to the Credentials Committee of the Democratic Convention which starts at Atlantic City on August 24. But besides meeting basic requirements and being open, we have a larger claim to acceptance by the National Democratic Party. We support the national party and its platform and candidates. The regular Democratic Party does not. Senator Eastland of Mississippi has voted against most of the major bills proposed by this administration. This time, the regular Mississippi Democratic Party will probably not support Johnson ... When the FDP presents its legal and political credentials to the National Credentials Committee, these credentials should be accepted. If not, the Negro in the South is left with few other avenues of expression.

The FDP is a product of imaginative and responsible thinking. Hopefully, the American people are still imaginative enough to accept this move ...

> Best regards,
> Phil

Although both regular voter registration and organization of the Freedom Democratic Party had been carried on simultaneously from the start, by late July the emphasis of the Summer Project had almost totally shifted from regular registration to getting people "Freedom registered." A simplified form was used, modeled on that of a northern state, and the purpose was to show how many people would register if they could in Mississippi. Their numbers would support the convention challenge at Atlantic City.

The underlying idea of the FDP was as real as grits, but it didn't always seem that way to a volunteer standing on somebody's porch trying to explain the national Democratic Party and Mississippi Democratic Party and Mississippi Freedom Democratic Party and how they were related thus and so. On the other hand, Freedom registration had the advantage of being secret — unless the police arrested a worker and seized his forms, which happened once in a while. But still....

Greenville, August 19

One of the difficulties is that most Negroes in Mississippi are instinctively apprehensive of the word "registration." They connect it with going to the courthouse and answering a lengthy trickily worded form. Also, some ask if they have to pay any money, associating it with the poll tax which is still required in state elections in Mississippi (the 24th amendment to the constitution of the U.S. applies only to federal elections.)

Dear Mom, Dad and Vickie, Rural Madison County, July 28

Yesterday we canvassed ... One lady couldn't work because she had cut her leg badly with the hoe while chopping cotton, and her leg was full of stitches. She lived in a two-room unpainted shack (kindly provided by the management). You climbed on the porch by stepping on a bucket — there were huge holes in the porch for the unwary. The woman was sitting dejectedly on the bed as she couldn't walk very well. She was surrounded by shy children, some of them naked … We tried to explain what Freedom Registration meant — it seemed like a rather abstract approach to her problems.…

Another time, we were walking behind the church where we have our Freedom School and saw the gleam of a rooftop between the trees and heard children's voices. I went back and asked the Negro girl who had come with us if it would be all right to visit the house and she said "Yes." So Karol, Minnie Pearl and I undid the latch and walked down the lane. Tall pines lined the road with blackeyed susans and great elm trees in between. The house, if you could call it that, was made of unpainted boards … Three planks served as porch steps. Two little girls on the porch disappeared into the house as we reached the gate. A woman in a ragged dress looked out of the door and told us to come on in … Several children who looked about the same age came out to see us, their little stomachs sticking out with the bloated look of starvation and their eyes dazed and listless. Inside a baby cried. I asked the mother how old the baby was and she said two months and added that her oldest was seven. She had six children. I started explaining about the Freedom Democratic Party and she listened, saying "yes mam" to everything I said.…

The construction of the place was very shabby and would have been unbearably cold in the wintertime. The house belongs to a white man whom the couple works for. They work in the cotton fields from 5 a.m. to 5 p.m. and when I asked what they do with the kids while they are in the fields, the lady said "We have to take them with us." The seven-year old, she said, takes care of the baby.… She signed a Freedom Democratic party registration form, but I'm not sure she understood it. I found out her age when I filled out the form for her — she is only 22 …

Love,
Kay

Dear Folks,   Columbus, August 1

The state quota for Freedom registration is 100,000, but with only about three weeks to go there are scarcely 50,000 forms in our Jackson (main) office…. In Columbus, where for some reason the people are more apathetic and afraid (for their jobs, not physically, I think), a good day's work was twelve forms. In West Point, where I am now, I have gotten 29. Most of the time you harp on education and jobs, and, if it's an old person, on relief ($50 per month). The hope for a better future ("I'm too old, I'm going to die soon") or a better future for children ("But I don't *have* any kids" or "They're all up North.") … I stop at one house and find someone who not only nods, but says "That's true" or interrupts with complaints of his own and who signs and maybe takes one for his wife, and a few for his mother and father. The more prosperous houses probably mean good luck, with one major exception. Any teacher in the schools is absolutely unsignable …

Love,
Joel

The first test of the FDP undertaking came with the precinct meetings, which would elect delegates to county meetings; then the counties would choose people to send to caucuses in each of the five Congressional districts; and finally the FDP state convention would be held — in other words, a parallel structure to existing party organization.

Vicksburg

Fear reigned at first — but soon people were excited about the prospects of a new party and neighbors were talking to neighbors about the "New Thing." Block Parties and mass meetings were being held many times a week in various parts of town. Spirit grew. Hundreds of people risked their lives and jobs to come. Representatives were elected after the election of a permanent chairman and secretary. Resolutions were introduced, minutes were kept ... The precinct meeting was one of the most exciting events of my life ...

Dear family,   Greenwood, July 22

Last night we had the FDP precinct meeting for Leflore County. we got some of the community leaders together and had a workshop with them on how to run the meetings. The meetings were run by the local people, with snicks as 'parliamentarians.' We gave advice and assistance when needed.

We had to go through a lot of red tape getting people seated in the right areas in the hall, and making sure they were freedom-registered. This was very much worth it, though, as it gave the people some feeling of being in a real organization. The meeting hall was done up like a convention hall. There were placards for the different precincts, and banners proclaiming LBJ FOR PRESIDENT, and ONE MAN — ONE VOTE, and so on. The place was jammed, and bits and pieces of the audience were lit by powerful TV lights, giving a wonderful appearance of activity as you went in. The delegates all wore different colored tags to identify them as precinct members.

Martin Luther King spoke before the meetings. He said lots of fancy things, many of which — I think — were over people's heads. Fantastic use of metaphor. "The cancer on the body politic," etc. And he had some specific things to say ... "Mississippi doesn't worry about states rights when they receive more than twice as much aid from the Feds as they send up in taxes. It's only when it gets down to the Negro that the Federal Government is overstepping."

Freedom now,
Bill

Greenwood

What a meeting it was — a totally unorganized group of people had come together for the first of many steps in organizing a local political party. And it was truly democratic. Hundreds of people came from each precinct, compared to the five or ten Mississippi whites who show up for their precinct meetings ...

Dear folks,   Columbus

The precinct meeting was the first political experience for those who attended, and we were sure that the job of explaining to them nominations, delegations, resolutions, would be impossibly complicated. It was tremendously interesting to watch and indicative, I think, of the innate political nature of all men. Within ten minutes they were completely at ease and had elected a chairman, secretary, and ten delegates to the district convention in Tippah. The delegates were teachers, housewives, packinghouse workers, a toy factory worker, in short, a genuine cross-section of the community ...

Love,
Joel

Greenwood, August

Of even more significance than the precinct meetings was the County meeting. Here all the delegates from Leflore County met, and a real convention was held with candidates vying for election — with serious discussions of issues and of problems facing the community, the county. You should have seen me after the meeting. I was so excited that I kept running around outside. I was overwhelmed by the history of the meeting!...

Moss Point, July

… The County convention was held here last Saturday. It was just amazing seeing these people, many, or rather most, of whom have never had any experience at all in politics running the meeting, electing the people and passing resolutions for a state platform. These people, housewives, unskilled workers, many, but not all, uneducated, are fantastic. People who have never spoken publicly before get up and make the greatest speeches …

Vicksburg, August 3

After those great precinct meetings which I told you about on the phone, the county convention was a disappointment. The Old Guard — the Warren County Improvement League — the comfortable middle-aged "We Don't Want Any Trouble" Uncle Toms — monopolized the meeting and the votes. Most of the Great New Blood which pulsed through the precinct meeting was slyly siphoned out. It was a sad night for all of us. We had forgotten that machinery is quickly formed even in something as new as the FDP and our defenses were down …

Carthage, August 3

I went to Meridian Sunday for the District Caucus — 4th District … there is an aware, sophisticated group creating the Party, so the extreme lack of sophistication on the part of the delegates was, for now, unimportant. It would be very easy for a small group of people to control the party, but there is no such group and the leaders really want this to be a learning event for the people … One man from Neshoba was elected a delegate to Atlantic City — there were three at the Caucus from Neshoba, and they got a great round of applause. It was a vision of things to come, the whole day.…

Meanwhile, the regular Mississippi Democrats held their state convention in Jackson on July 28. Not a single Negro delegate attended. To support the FDP challenge of discrimination, Negroes had attempted to participate in the regular Democratic precinct meetings around the state on June 16, and a week later in the county meetings. The results were as one would expect: exclusion by intimidation or trickery.

Goldwater support was so rampant at the state convention that it adjourned until after the national convention, thus avoiding commitment to the Democratic candidates and platform. This came as no surprise: in 1948, the Mississippi Democrats had bolted the national party convention. In August 1960, they had rejected the Kennedy-Johnson ticket and platform, and successfully campaigned for unpledged electors who then voted against that ticket. And in 1963 they had issued campaign literature for Governor Paul Johnson that stated: "Our ... party is entirely independent ... of any national party ... long ago separated itself from the National Democratic Party ... both the National Democratic Party and the National Republican Party are the dedicated enemies of the people of Mississippi ..."

About a week later, the FDP held a very different kind of state convention.

August 6, 1964

From the floor of the State Convention of the Mississippi Freedom Democratic Party:

This is the most exciting, moving and impressive thing I have ever had the pleasure of witnessing — let alone be a part of.

Miss Ella Baker presented a very stirring keynote address. She hit very hard on the necessity for all the delegates to work and study very hard so they can prepare themselves for the new type of fight — a political fight. She also put great stress upon the fact that these people here today have braved extreme danger and now must redouble their efforts to get all their neighbors to join them in this struggle for Freedom.

Right after Miss Baker's speech, there was a march of all the delegates around the convention hall — singing Freedom Songs, waving American flags, banners and county signs. This was probably the most soul-felt march ever to occur in a political convention, I felt, as we marched with a mixture of sadness and joy — of humility and pride — of fear and courage, singing "Go Tell It in the Mountain," "Ain't Gonna Let Nobody Turn Me Round," and "This Little Light of Mine." You would just about have to be here to really feel and see what this means to the people who are here.

Attorney Joseph Rauh, a member of the Credentials Committee of the National Democratic Convention, then addressed the group. Mr. Rauh is also Walter Reuther's attorney and his appearance indicated the support of Mr. Reuther who is, of course, one of the powers of the Democratic Party.

Mr. Rauh presented quite an optimistic picture concerning the chances of getting the FDP seated in Atlantic City, explaining that if the Credentials Committee does not want to seat us it will only take the support of eleven members of the 108-member Credentials Committee and the support of eight states to get the matter onto the floor of the convention where we will almost certainly win the fight ... Bob Moses didn't seem so confident. President Johnson is afraid he will lose the whole South if he seats the FDP. My own opinion is that we will not be seated, but will have won partial victory by exposing the terrible situation in Mississippi, and by forming some groundwork for progress in later years....

The delegates then elected and ratified the district choices of delegates to the National Convention. There will be 44 delegates and 22 alternates going ...

Moss Point, August 6

Thursday I was in Jackson at the state convention of the Freedom Democratic Party. Man, this is the stuff democracy is made of. All of us here are pretty emotional about the names of the counties of Mississippi. Amite and Sunflower and Tallahatchie have always meant where this one was shot, where this one was beaten, where civil rights workers feared for their lives the minute they arrived. But on Thursday Amite, and Tallahatchie, and Sunflower, and Neshoba didn't mean another man's gone. They meant people are voting from there, it meant people who work 14 hours a day from sun-up to sun-down picking cotton and live in homes with no plumbing and no paint, were casting ballots to send a delegation to Atlantic City. As the keynote speaker said, it was not a political convention, it was a demonstration that the people of Mississippi want to be let into America ...

Love,
Rita

No Negroes had attended the regular state Democratic convention, while at the FDP state convention a white man — Rev. Edwin King — was chosen National Committeeman (Dr. Aaron Henry became Chairman). However, the total number of white FDP delegates remained small.

Dear friends,   Greenwood, August

The FDP is not for the Negro alone. It is for everybody. Every person over the age of 21 has the right to join the FDP. But it is difficult to get whites to register. We can't canvas the area, because that means that we will have to go up to their door steps and on their property, where there is a good chance that we'll get shot ...

At the moment, three whites in Greenwood are registered. What we are left with, then, is that legally we are in fact an open party, despite the small number of whites who will register with the FDP. We have attempted to publish every day, starting two weeks in advance, the date, time and place of our precinct meetings. When we wrote to the *Greenwood Commonwealth*, the local newspaper, requesting them to print our notice in their announcement column, accompanied by a very good letter to the editor, we were answered by the editor in go-to-hell terms, and our notices weren't published. All correspondence relating to FDP is being notarized and will be presented to the Credentials Committee as proof of our being open. Whites don't come to FDP meetings, but this is their choice (not the other way around), and we have done our best to encourage them to join us ...

Phil

There were some volunteers who tried to do more.

Dear folks,   Greenwood, July 9

It is not enough to say that we do not discriminate against whites, we must have absolute proof that will stand up in the credentials committee, which is run just like a court of law. Stating that we *would* have, if we *could* have, is a statement of INTENT, and intent does not hold much weight ...

I have written a leaflet which I want to take into the white community. It explains the FDP, and invites people to join. Leafletting a place doesn't involve any incriminating contact on the part of the white man who is leafletted, for most of the leaflets will be left in his mailbox. The National Office is in favor of it — but the staff here is dubious of risking it. I will read the draft to a full staff meeting tonight and see what the final decision is. My plan is to take four white kids and a car into white neighborhoods in a precinct which includes parts of the Negro community. Two people to a house, four people to a street, the car following them. If we are careful, no one should get beaten up. At the end of the summer we will be able to call the leaflet exhibit x, and say that so many hundred were distributed in the white Greenwood community. Incidentally, we will never be able, nor want to be able, to tell the National Convention just how many whites we have. We do not believe in keeping separate records, as you might guess ...

Love from the struggle,
Bill

De Soto County, July 21

Usually when we canvas, we ask where the white folks are on the road — and avoid them. This morning, there were two white families on the road and I was considering talking with them. Reports from Negro neighbors made it clear they weren't rabid, so after consultation with the group I decided to try to sign them up for the FDP.

At the first house were Mr.___ and his wife. I asked if I could come in and talk. The folks were poor white and cordial ... I told them right off who I was ... that I was in Mississippi because there was injustice and too many lies. I told them some of the lies about the happy Negro, about the civil rights workers, the poor white — that the poor white was stupid and violent. We both laughed at the idea that he would jump in his pick-up and look for someone to shoot if he heard of civil rights activity (heh heh). He murmured concern about the violence that actually took place. His wife wandered off to let her husband do the talking. I then talked about how the rich white played the poor white and Negro against each other. They were receptive and friendly but the man couldn't read or write and was somewhat embarrassed about being illiterate; he was still in the same economic state as the Mississippi Negro. He finally said he wouldn't sign because he wasn't too sure of what he was doing, and told me to talk to his neighbors ...

Next door was a woman, several baby-doll type southern girls, one of them 21. There was a visitor from Arkansas who looked very unfriendly — about 30, complete with red neck. This family was even poorer than the first. By this time I was close to shaking visibly. Mrs.____ was friendly. The man from Arkansas was not unfriendly. The girls were giggly. I talked much as I had at the first house about their economic plight. Mrs. ____ showed strong racist attitudes, but of ignorance not hate. I hit each one of the myths she raised with common sense and she was forced to laugh with me. She signed after I made great pledges of secrecy and security — she didn't want any of those white idiots shooting up her house. She seemed to be most convinced by my arguments about roads and the rich power structure.

The volunteer returned. At the second house...

August 6

Mr. ____ was home; he was working on a car and talking to some friends. I went in to tell Mrs. ____ of the meetings of the FDP. We were soon joined by an eighteen-year old Mississippi racist, who told me in no uncertain terms what he thought of niggers and what I was doing. His entire performance throughout the visit was fascinating; he made all sorts of threats in a vague hypothetical way; he spoke of what would happen to someone who did such and such — while continually offering me the potato chips and popcorn he was eating. After listening to this cat for a little while I went out to talk to Mr. ____. From this point on it was a constant battle to get across to the receptive Mr. ____ over the little punk ... eventually the punk turned out to be an asset: Mrs. ____ and the eighteen year old niece started to take my side, at first out of friendliness. Then, as he got more ridiculous, they themselves became responsible southern moderates ... They were even clear-headed enough to back me up on the miscegenation hangup, insisting that it wasn't the issue ... Mr. ____ finally was won over to the party; he said he would sign because he didn't see any harm in it. As I left he told me to be sure to come back....

But these were rare exceptions.
The total number of people registered in the FDP—60,000—

was not as high by the time of the national convention as Project workers had hoped. A number of volunteers made quick trips home to press for support of the FDP by their local Democratic leaders. The challenge began to look serious: by mid-August the Democratic committees of ten important states had adopted pro-FDP resolutions of varying strength. There seemed to be enough support at least to get a minority report urging recognition from the Credentials Committee — and a floor fight.

Laurel, August 18

I'm looking forward to the convention. I'm not sure what our chances for success are, but we seem to have the Mississippi delegation worried. They have a court injunction against the Mississippi Freedom Democratic Party and have been serving injunctions on all the local leaders to keep them from participating. It seems they've found an old law which would prohibit our using the word "Democratic" …

But neither the injunction nor the jailing of the chairman of the FDP's Executive Committee, Lawrence Guyot, stopped them. They came: sixty-eight determined Mississippians plus many volunteers and staff people. The modest, almost shabby Gem Hotel was their headquarters; many of the staff slept on the floor of a church.

What happened then, between August 23 and 26, went beyond the greatest expectations of all those young people who had trudged the backroads with their registration forms, worrying about quotas. It justified all the dreams of developing indigenous leadership in black Mississippi. There, by the sea, across from a huge billboard with a picture of Barry Goldwater and the inscription "In your heart you know he's right" (later someone wrote in underneath, "Yes — extreme right"), a band of people from nowhere brought the machinery of a powerful national party to a halt for four days. They told their stories of oppression and terror — Mrs. Hamer, fired the day she registered, later beaten unconscious for voter registration work — while the Credentials Committee listened and the Mississippi regulars made

*feeble replies. The nation watched it all on television: the FDP had
become the only issue at the convention.*
  They watched in Mississippi too.

Dear people,   Batesville, August 25

  Black Batesville is perhaps the most politically conscious
community in the country today ... Every house glows with
its little, blue-gray television light. Not just to see Mr. Miles or
C. J. Williams or Mrs. Lloyd or Reverend Middleton on the
convention floor, but to watch the entire fight. Bull Connor is
hissed when he talks Birmingham-tough and the Michigan
delegation is cheered when it announces that it will support
the Green compromise — unless something better is offered.
People who still pronounce "registration" as "restoration" use
with understanding terms like "credentials committee" and
"eight states needed for a floor fight ..."
                                                    Jim

*The complex story of what happened behind the scenes at Atlantic
City belongs to another book. For this record, the Credentials Com-
mittee adopted a "compromise" which provided for the seating of
the regulars; the recognition of Dr. Aaron Henry and Rev. King as
delegates at large from the FDP and all others as honored guests; a
promise that the Democratic National Committee would obligate
states to select delegates for 1968 in a non-discriminatory way and
that it would establish a special committee to aid states in meeting
this standard.*

  *The Mississippians rejected the compromise, in the face of argu-
ments voiced by such national figures as Bayard Rustin and Martin
Luther King (who were present) that it should be seen as "a great
victory." There was a sit-in by the FDP delegates. The volunteers
who had been busy lobbying for support and taking part in a round-
the-clock vigil on the boardwalk, helped in this too.*

August 30

At 7 p.m. we met ... and arranged a system of runners to bring badges from regular delegates inside the hall to FDP delegates outside. I was appointed to receive badges inside and carry them outside to a person who passed them on to delegates waiting in small groups on street corners near the hall. I made about four or five trips in and out — it was really exciting. I felt like Mata Hari and the French Resistance and the Underground Railroad all rolled into one. I had very little trouble getting back into the hall, because I wore a press badge which was honored. Just to disguise myself further I wore a red, white, and blue striped vest of the kind worn by the Young Citizens for Johnson who were roaming around ...

All in all, I think we came off rather well at the Convention. We got lots of sympathy and we didn't compromise ourselves by accepting a phony compromise ...

Why was the compromise "phony"? The FDP had several reasons for rejecting it. The two seats were considered token recognition — and the Negro people of Mississippi had seen too much tokenism in their time. They had come there as true representatives, not as "delegates at large." The compromise still recognized the regulars, despite the mass of evidence to prove they had no business there. The promises for 1968 offered no genuine relief because they referred only to Negroes already registered; even if a few Negroes could attend party meetings four years later, the people were no more likely than before to have a voice in decision making. The compromise contained no precedent for eventual recognition or patronage. To the FDP, it was a one-shot affair — their anguish, their demands, their cause, were not.

Ruleville, August 30

This morning, Sunday morn, I was just in the middle of doing some washing when in marched Mrs. Hamer, sweat beading her face, dressed in old flat shoes and a short cotton dress gathered from the bodice so that it just flowed round her huge form, her hair plaited in half a dozen tiny braids standing out from her head. She embraced me the warm southern way, and launched into a high-powered, oft-times bellowing account of the Convention in Atlantic City.

She told how she had finished her speech by asking the question that was being asked all over the country: "Is this America?" She spoke of the effect of the exhibit of the car and the photographs of the three young men, of the way in which the vigil on the boardwalk grew from 18 people to 3,000 and of how Negroes and whites alike came to say how much it meant to them. She insisted, and I'm sure she's right, that next year the FDP will be the regular party. She said how disillusioned she was to find hypocrisy all over America. She felt Johnson had really showed his hand against the FDP by preventing a floor fight. She declared that King, Roy Wilkins, Bayard Rustin, James Farmer, and Aaron Henry had been willing to sell out the FDP by their willingness to accept the compromise. However, when I urged the wisdom of not splitting ranks, she said that at the end all of these people had congratulated them on their sit-in ... She insisted that the FDP would have been prepared to split the votes with the regular Democrats, but that two votes at large was no deal.

On Friday night here at the mass meeting I realized that for southern Negroes, Mississippi Negroes especially, to see that crowd sitting down meant something that would have been completely lost if a compromise had been accepted that simply hushed everything up. One woman at the mass meeting said, "I looked at that Convention from the time it started. All the time til now I never seen no nigger in a convention, but they was there! Lots of them! Big ones and little ones, they was there!"

This may be the last time
This may be the last time
This may be the last time
May be the last time, I don't know....

The Road Back

Dear Ruth and Carl,   Holly Springs, August 9

Our director, a Negro, has been assigned to Yazoo City, and only the two of us are left. My mind is getting all on edge over leaving. I am abandoning the best people I ever met. It is a genuine hangup to face this responsibility. How much can I cater to my own desires, how long can I wait, how much disengagement — even to become a lawyer — is justified? Depending on what should be irrelevant considerations, my answer changes momentarily.

We had a slew of people depending on us in DeSoto County and we got pulled out to go to Tippah to start the FDP there. The same dependence developed, and we had to leave there. I let down new friends, people who risked their lives and families to let us have a floor to sleep on, and suddenly we disappear. We might be dead, and there is no communication to tell them we are sorry. But the work had to be done in two places and we had to leave. We returned to both places and people were hurt. They were worried. We had let them down. It was the right thing to do, but it hurt. What shall I do? You just keep wondering, and then an important decision comes and you make it. Then you start wondering all over again.

Show this letter to Mom and Dad, and tell them I love them more than ever in all my life (I'm learning).

Love to you,
Bob

Dear Family,   Batesville, August 13

I must tell you that I am reconsidering my decision to return to school this fall. As I told you before, the question of continuing my work in Mississippi has been on my mind for quite a while … My involvement here is quite deep. I find that I have some talent for this kind of work.… I can organize, explain, and I have found that I'm able to keep my head when I need to. When the project director went to Jackson last week, I was left in charge.

There is the question of my not being Negro. Ideally, us white folks could go home this fall, and Negroes could run things. But there are not enough who can. I can see a job that needs to be done and I can do it.

Occasionally one gets very lonely down here. I go downtown and see the Illinois Central train which could take me all the way to Chicago. The idea of riding from here to Chicago is sort of strange. I could just get on a train, ride, and be back in a free country … I really don't know what to do. I'm going to meetings in Jackson next week for those interested in staying, but then I'm coming home for a while to decide.

Love,
Gene

As early as mid-July, many volunteers were already debating whether to stay on at the end of the summer or go home — which usually meant going back to school. They dreaded an outburst of retaliation against the local people after their departure in the fall. And in fact by mid-August violence had already accelerated. On August 8, the Jackson Clarion-Ledger *issued an open invitation with its banner headline: "COFO WORKERS TO ABANDON STATE ON AUGUST 24." The story was false, but the weekend which followed its appearance seemed an evil dream come true — bombings, shootings, cross burnings across the state.*

The volunteers wrote home pleading with family and neighbors....

People of Winchester: Mound Bayou, August 16

... Violence in Mississippi this summer has been avoided because of terrific pressure brought upon the political and economic power structure of Mississippi. This has been done through the President, through Congressmen from various Northern states, through the words of Northern industrial powers. This pressure must be continued, must be made even stronger ...

You should realize, I think, that the President did not send more FBI agents into Mississippi, send the Justice Department into Mississippi, exert pressure on Governor Johnson, just because of a great humanitarian surge in his breast. If that had been the case, the federal government would have been in Mississippi three years ago, seventy years ago ... The President acted this summer because he knew that there were a lot of parents, relatives and friends who had power and influence ... He realized also that he could not afford to be forced to send troops into Mississippi. He will react to your letters ...

Larry

Some of them decided to go home on vacation briefly and then back — to Mississippi. Others returned to school as planned, thinking it the longer but better road back to this Mississippi or another. And some made no bones about being glad to get out of the state and back home.

Dear Friends,   En route back to Meridian, September

Many people, including those who supported my going to Mississippi as part of the Summer Project, and those who believe that the Summer Project has been an important thing, have expressed shock and disapproval at my decision to go back to Mississippi, and have attempted to dissuade me from returning. I have been amazed at this response.

There is a certainty, when you are working in Mississippi, that it is important for you to be alive and to be alive doing just what you are doing. And whatever small bit we did for Mississippi this summer, Mississippi did ten times as much for us. Working there has given me clarity about what I want to be learning in college that three years in Widener Library could not give. Now that I have taught, I know what I want to learn about teaching. Now that I have helped people understand what it means to be a citizen in a democracy, I know things that I still have to understand. Now that I have worked with people to change the society in which they live, I know what I want to learn about societies and how other people have changed theirs....

I guess the thing that pulls me back most are the people who made us a part of their community. People I knew in Mississippi could honestly and unselfconsciously express affection in a way that few people I know in the North are able to do. They did not have to be "cool" or "one up" or "careful" ... In Mississippi I have felt more love, more sympathy and warmth, more community than I have known in my life. And especially the children pull me back....

I should tell you that it is not as easy to go back to Mississippi as it may sound from this letter. I am frightened by the probability of much greater violence ... I will be working a lot more on my own, and it will probably be much lonelier....

Gail

Greenville

For awhile it seemed that nothing I could do would be more important than staying directly active in the Movement. What I have decided is, I must learn much more about political theory, philosophy, etc. I am not sure I can stay in art. What I would like to do is finish at BU in art — then go on to some kind of profession. Maybe medicine if that's not too preposterous. Think what a doctor who was dedicated to the movement could do. At least I want to be in some position — a valuable one — where I would come in contact with many people all the time.

Dear Mom and Dad — Ruleville, August 3

I know you are very concerned that I finish college, and you fear I may not if I stay out a year. I am very concerned that I finish college too, but I want to take a year off to stay in Mississippi ... I want to take it now so the year I have left in college will be more meaningful, so I won't be in college just to be graduated ...

I found that Swarthmore is a dried-up hell unless one knows what one wants to do with what one gets from school. I'll go back next year even if I don't get a better idea from a year here, because I know the diploma means security and I'm no good to these people if I'm starving too ... A year at Swarthmore now will make me hate education and get me a diploma. A year of directed learning will make me more able to pursue whatever field I choose in the long run. I'd be miserable and waste a great deal of your money at Swarthmore. I must stay now. I will go back in September 1965.

Much love,
Gretchen

In Canton, there was a 21-year-old volunteer from Galesburg, Illinois and Knox College. Johns Hopkins had granted her an impressive fellowship for graduate work in history, to begin in the fall. When she first came to Mississippi ...

Dear John and Cleo,   Canton, July 13

    ... Leaving Galesburg was terribly hard; I feel wrenched irreparably away from all that was helping me grow and be strong and seek faith. Probably it was good to plunge immediately into this; no chance for drowning in self-pity ... maybe when this is over and the urge to introspection can be honored again, I won't hurt so much as I did when the bus pulled away with me one Thursday night not too long ago....

Jo

Dear John and Cleo,   Canton, August 24

    Some of them are beginning to realize, now that we're talking about the end of school and our departures, that we're not saviours and we're not staying forever and we're not leaving any miracles behind. We've awakened great expectations and now will vanish leaving folks with only a deepened sense of their destitute state and a deepened longing ... When we talk now with our pupils about college and scholarships they respond as if we are telling fairy stories....

Jo

Dear John and Cleo,   Canton, August 24

    I now realize (after a couple of sleepless nights and a couple of solitary walks — despite security) and various attempts to ignore or rationalize away my strongest impulses — that nothing short of staying on here, becoming permanent staff with $10 per month which others are and have been living on — nothing short of this will satisfy me....

I made the decision the night before I was scheduled to leave. I sat down to answer your letter and found myself writing that of course the end of the Summer Project is not an end of progress in Mississippi. But it's no thanks to the departing volunteers that it's not an end, it's thanks only to those who are staying on. At that point I threw away that letter and wrote to Barker and the dean of the graduate school at Johns Hopkins ...

Maybe the immediacy of the sufferings and dangers here *is* overwhelming me and blurring out the essential "larger view," but I can simply no longer justify the pursuit of a Ph.D. When the folks in Flora have to struggle to comprehend the most elementary of materials on history and society and man's larger life, I feel ashamed to be greedily going after "higher learning." And when I feel the despair of youngsters who can't even get through high school because cotton planting prevents them, I almost feel ashamed of my college diploma. And when I reflect on the terrors and deprivations in daily lives here, I cannot return to the relative comforts and security of student life.

My love for the people, the hurt I felt when 50, 60, 70 year old men and women would plead with me to keep on with the school.... I knew that it would be living a kind of lie to leave here now, lamenting about how terrible leaving was and yet leaving anyway....

I've been trying quite seriously to dredge up all possible motives and pass judgment on them. I think often of a little story told by Bayard Rustin — he was participating in a vigil for peace and was fasting, when he saw a huge woman walk by and suddenly realized that one reason he was fasting was his desire to lose weight. I suspect that some of my motives in this situation may be no more worthy....

Love,
Jo

Dear John & Cleo,   September

The man who was to have been my advisor at Hopkins has written that neither is he overwhelmingly surprised at my present action nor will he be overwhelmingly surprised if I begin looking toward Academe again in a year or two. There are some moments even now when I'm almost sure he's right, but other moments when I'm equally sure that I'll never feel like settling down into the isolation and discipline of student life again. I suspect, tho', that some sort of synthesis is possible eventually and that maybe I can become a sort of rabble-rousing scholar....

Love,
Jo

Those who did not stay had several kinds of feelings.

Dear Mother and Father: Gulfport, August 12

I have learned more about politics here from running my own precinct meetings than I could have from any Government professor ... For the first time in my life, I am seeing what it is like to be poor, oppressed, and hated. And what I see here does not apply only to Gulfport or to Mississippi or even to the South.... The people we're killing in Viet Nam are the same people whom we've been killing for years in Mississippi. True, we didn't tie the knot in Mississippi and we didn't pull the trigger in Viet Nam — that is, we personally — but we've been standing behind the knot-tiers and the trigger-pullers too long.

This summer is only the briefest beginning of this experience, both for myself and for the Negroes of Mississippi.

Your daughter,
Ellen

Hattiesburg, August 18

Somehow, as I prepare to leave tomorrow, knowing that I will be easily integrated again into society, I wonder if I will have the perseverance to keep on trying hard to change society. Maybe I'll just fall back into line …

Columbus

You write that big parties are being arranged for the returning volunteers. This is a mistake. Everyone should be staying down here … to give the movement strength…. People might have decent reasons for not staying, but the people who really need support or deserve "glory" (if anyone deserves glory) are those who are staying … A hell of a lot of the volunteers who never planned to stay, are staying. The rest (me included) know they ought to be. Reasons for not staying are easy to amass, but everyone, including the rationalizer himself, suspects these reasons. We can't feel as though things are solid enough to keep going without us. It's impossible to justify quitting now, because this is really only the start. Nothing is conquered; no project is completed; some summer volunteers have to leave, and that's nothing to celebrate.

The first days back in the North were strange.

Late night, August 25-26, Memphis, Tenn

We drove up to Memphis this noon, and I sat in the Greyhound bus terminal for a few hours. At a barber shop I suddenly realized that the barber was the first strange white man to come so close to me in months. He worked swiftly — how different it was from the leisurely hour haircut Mr. Whiting gave me in Como. I felt uncomfortable with white folks; I was seeking out the Negroes to talk with in the waiting room …

August 31

My first day back, I found a group from Downtown CORE raising funds for Mississippi on the corner of 8th Street. I stopped to talk with one of the fellows and after a few minutes I began to feel odd…. Suddenly I realized what it was: he was Negro, and we were on a corner crowded with white people. If we'd been in the white section of Hattiesburg, there would have been real danger.

A few days later, I was headed for the "downtown" train — in Hattiesburg that meant the white business district.

I've felt depressed since I've returned. I don't know how much is personal, and how much it is reaction to that place and the people I've left behind, and a heightened awareness of so much that is wrong up here….

Chicago

As we got into our car a lean Negro squatted down by the window next to me and warned us not to leave. This was his territory, he boasted. "We may be bums, but if you want some wild excitement we can find it for you." When we told him that we were just looking for some friends, he changed his pitch. "See those guys down there," he pointed to a gang at the end of the block, "there's Eskimo, and that's Shorty and Johnny. I'm Blackboy. I'm the boss." In a moment of innocence I stuck out my hand. Blackboy ignored it.

"As long as you're with us," he continued, "You're safe anytime you come down here. We'll even watch your car for you. Ask anybody for Blackboy. But mostly just look for this" — he held his wrist up to the window, baring a silver-studded leather strap…. "You won't see another one like it around here. Just give us seventy cents for a drink." Blackboy was in his middle thirties. He wore a blue windbreaker and blue jeans. I gave him a quarter and a half dollar, and we were allowed to leave.

Blackboy rules the four blocks south of Ohio Street on Clark Avenue in Chicago. In Mississippi we might at least have communicated. One friend of mine remarked that he was upset every time he passed a Negro — they don't come to embrace you for what you've done, and up here you can't even wave without being counted queer. But Blackboy is real too....

Harrison, New York, August 30

I find that whenever I meet someone around home who hears I've been to Mississippi, he says "Oh, what was it like?" People want a nice handy three-word phrase to be able to repeat to neighbors ... They ask me a question, then start talking before I can answer. And I grope to find words to explain what it was like — but can't.

Back in the Southland, the Summer Project had become the Mississippi Freedom Project. Some 200 volunteers — "old ones" from the summer plus new people — carried on the programs. The FDP was already preparing for a Freedom Vote in November and the congressional challenge of 1965. The bombings and jailings continued; everything seemed different, yet the same. Philadelphia, the town of death, had changed in one notable way: workers were living at a new project base there.

Dear Mom and Dad,   Philadelphia, October 4

As I write this letter I am on the roof of our headquarters observing a sunset I cannot even begin to describe. The hills of red dirt, the pine woods, the mountains and shacks silhouetted against the blood-red sun and clouds, all this and the rest of it takes my breath away. Now and at all such times I find myself possessed by a deep melancholy, a heart-rending feeling for the black and white toilers of this state; both the victims of a system that they neither created nor flourish under.

There have been incidents of violence and intimidation but they hardly seem worth noting at a time like this. I only know that I must carry on this struggle that other people have died in, and that some day the system will be changed....

                    Love,
                    Tommy

Freedom School Poetry

Freedom School Poetry

PUBLISHER'S NOTE: *Freedom School Poetry* was first compiled by Nancy Cooper, a volunteer in the Canton project, and published by the Student Nonviolent Coordinating Committee in 1965. The booklet is reprinted here just as it was originally, with the addition of an introductory note by one of the freedom school co-ordinators, Wally Roberts, who is also an original contributor to *Letters from Mississippi*. Every effort has been made — and continues to be made — to re-establish contact with the freedom school poets.

"Teaching" Freedom

Wallace Roberts

There were two main components to the Mississippi Summer Project, the establishment of Freedom Schools in about 20 communities throughout the state and voter registration and traditional political organizing. The Freedom Schools had two explicit goals. One was to provide students with remedial education, based on the known fact that the quality of their education in the segregated local public schools was grossly inadequate — by design, in order to keep Black people disenfranchised and impoverished. The other goal was to teach the kids Black history, which was an almost unknown subject, not only in the South but in the whole nation. A third goal of the Freedom Schools, related to the second, was not explicit that I remember, but was clearly important, and that was to use the Freedom Schools as a way to inspire the students, especially those in high school, and to recruit them to the Freedom Movement.

The Freedom Schools used a variety of strategies to achieve these goals. In some places like Hattiesburg, the schools were quite formal and did a lot of work in remedial education and Black history and had great success. Many students were starved for a good education, which they knew they were being denied, and they embraced the opportunity. For the work in reading, writing and math, the Freedom Schools had to rely on donated books and on the amateur tutoring and teaching supplied by the Northern volunteers. COFO assigned experienced teachers to be the coordinators of the Freedom School, so we had some minimum competencies.

For Black history, COFO put together a reader with photocopied selections from other publications on prominent African-Americans, the real story of slavery and Reconstruction, Jim Crow, the Ku Klux Klan, and so on. This introduction to Black history opened up a whole new world to them, as it did for us Northern white volunteers.

I was assigned to be the Freedom School Coordinator in Shaw, a town of about one thousand people in the Delta. There were about fifteen of us, half teachers and half voter registration workers. Once we found families in the community who agreed to take us in, and a building to rent for the school, we began to recruit students. We soon discovered, however, what seemed like an insurmountable barrier. In this part of Mississippi, the students had no summer vacation because they were given a month "vacation" in the spring to chop cotton (weed the new plants with hoes) and then another month of "vacation" in the fall when they were needed to pick the cotton.

What this meant for us was that after a full day of regular school in July and August in a building with no air-conditioning, the students were not about to attend another school, even a Freedom School. At first, we were at a loss what to do, but the students themselves solved that problem by coming to us and saying, "What we want you to do is to help us become Freedom Fighters. We want to go on picket lines and do protests. Teach us how to do that."

We were in something of a quandary: The COFO staff had instructed us not to let the kids get involved in this kind of activity because it was dangerous, especially in the Delta, and because there were not enough experienced COFO staff members to help out. We discussed this with Staughton Lynd, a white college professor who was the director of the Freedom Schools for the state, and with Stokeley Carmichael, who was the SNCC staff person in charge of the Delta. They both agreed we should go ahead, train the students in non-violent protest tactics, work out a protest strategy with them, and go from there. We did. It was exhilarating for all of us.

Not all Freedom Schools that summer experienced the kind of transformation ours did, and some had to contend with more violence; but, as the poems in this book show, just the existence of the Freedom Schools — the fact that a safe place had been created where children could express their hopes and fears about their lives — was immensely liberating.

And in that safe place, many students for the first time encountered literature that was liberating, the poetry of Langston Hughes, the stories of Zora Neale Hurston, the essays and books of W.E.B. Du Bois and James Baldwin. It was clear to me at the time that the kids were excited and grateful to have the opportunity to discover the ideas found in literature written by authors like these, but it was not until a few years later, when I read the *Narrative of the Life of Frederick Douglass, An American Slave*, that I really understood how important literature like this can be to someone who's been deprived of it.

It's comforting to think that we did a good job that summer, but we did not bring Freedom to Mississippi nor did we teach Freedom. It was already there in the hearts and minds of our students, their parents and every other African-American resident of the state. All that was needed for it to begin to flourish openly was the feeling that it could be expressed safely, and just our presence gave them that. They took it from there, and have begun to make a better world.

To the memory of Emmett Till

In the summer of the year 1955, Emmett Till, 14 years old, was murdered in the state of Mississippi for allegedly "whistling at a white woman."

Nine years later — out of the same society that allowed the killings of Emmett Till, Herbert Lee, Lewis Allen, Medgar Evers, Andrew Goodman, Michael Schwerner, James Chaney, and many more whose names we will never know — these poems and paintings have come. These are the expressions of the young freedom school students of Mississippi.

Foreword

Goodmorning, Poetry!
Poetry, how-do-you-do?
I'm worrying along —
So I come to worry you.

To modify a line from an old blues, this means that poetry possess the power of worriation. Poetry can both delight and disturb. It can interest folks. Poetry can convey both pleasure and pain. And poetry can make people think. If poetry makes people think, it might make them think constructive thoughts, even thoughts about how to change themselves, their town and their state for the better. Some poems, like many of the great verses in the Bible, can make people think about changing all mankind, even the whole world. Poems, like prayers, possess power.

So goodmorning, Poetry!
Poetry, how-do-you-do?
I'm writing a poem
To see if it takes on you.

Langston Hughes —
to those who write
these poems in
this book.
Spring,
1965.

by Ida Ruth Griffin, age 12, Harmony, Carthage

I am Mississippi fed,
I am Mississippi bred,
Nothing but a poor, black boy.

I am a Mississippi slave,
I shall be buried in a Mississippi grave,
Nothing but a poor, dead boy.

THE HOUSE OF LIBERTY

by Joyce Brown, age 16, McComb

I came not for fortune, nor for fame,
I seek not to add glory to an unknown name,
I did not come under the shadow of night,
I came by day to fight for what's right.
I shan't let fear, my monstrous foe,
Conquer my soul with threat and woe.
Here I have come and here I shall stay,
And no amount of fear my determination can sway.

I asked for your churches, and you turned me down,
But I'll do my work if I have to do it on the ground,
You will not speak for fear of being heard,
So crawl in your shell and say, "Do not disturb."
You think because you've turned me away
You've protected yourself for another day.

But tomorrow surely must come,
And your enemy will still be there with the rising sun;
He'll be there tomorrow as all tomorrows in the past,
And he'll follow you into the future if you let him pass.
You've turned me down to humor him,
Ah! Your fate is sad and grim.
For even tho' your help I ask,
Even without it, I'll finish my task.

In a bombed house I have to teach my school,
Because I believe all men should live by the Golden Rule,
To a bombed house your children must come,

Because of your fear of a bomb,
And because you've let your fear conquer your soul,
In this bombed house these minds I must try to mold;
I must try to teach them to stand tall and be a man
When you, their parents, have cowered down and refused to
take a stand.

(*Written for the opening of the McComb Freedom School on the
grass before the bombed-out private home at which the school had
to be held*)

LONELY

by Wilma Byas, Clarksdale

Outside it's raining
And here alone am I.
The wind is blowing, blowing
As I gaze into my fire.

My heart is slowly dying,
Inside me it is paining,
And here I sit so lonely, lonely
While outside it's raining,
                    raining,
                        raining.

FIGHT ON LITTLE CHILDREN

by Edith Moore, age 15, McComb

Fight on little children, fight on
You know what you're doing is right.
Don't stop, keep straight ahead
You're just bound to win the fight.

Many hardships there will be;
Many trials you'll have to face.
But go on children, keep fighting
Soon freedom will take hardship's place.

Sometimes it's going to be hard;
Sometimes the light will look dim.
But keep it up, don't get discouraged
Keep fighting, though chances seem slim.

In the end you and I know
That one day the facts they'll face.
And realize we're human too
That freedom's taken slavery's place.

OUR LARGEST AND SMALLEST CITIES

by Nettie Rhodes, age 14, Jackson

Large towns, small towns,
Vacant cities, busy cities,
sports coats, nightgowns,
laughs, cries, sighs, pities.

All these build our largest and smallest cities.
Candy bars, grocery stores
hold the hearts of our gay kiddies
and the gossip of our neighborhood biddies.

Loud cries, mumbled noises,
Teen-agers, small kids' voices,
Freedom-riders, Jackson Advocate subscribers,
neighborhood people, political bribers.

Large towns, small towns,
Vacant cities, busy cities,
sports coats, nightgowns,
laughs, cries, sighs, pities,
All these build our largest and smallest cities.

WHO AM I?

by Sandra Jo-Ann O., Hattiesburg

Who am I, let me see,
Am I a dog or am I a bee?
Am I a maniac who's out of her mind?
I think I know and I'll tell you
I'm not the girl I used to be.

Who am I? I have to know
So I may tell it wherever I go.
I'll tell it to men of all the land,
I'll tell it to kids who shake my hand,
That I am free and it shows
To everyone over all the land.

Who am I? I'll tell you now,
I'll have to find words, but I'll tell it somehow.
I am a Negro who fought her best
To earn her freedom and deserves to rest.
So do as I did, and you'll be free,
Just don't hit back, and you'll win
Your rest.

A LEADER

by Roosevelt Redmond, age 16, Indianola

A leader is a white mouth
        — I agree with him —

A leader will not take a stand
he sits down, and says yes SIR
        — I agree with him —

A leader will not take a risk
When everybody else is taking a
big and great risk, he is a yes SIR.
        — I agree with him —

A leader will stand up and be
heard, speak of the rights of others
        — I boo him —

A leader will take a risk even
if it is against him, or hurt him
        I boo him

A leader will take many beatings
or even give his life
        I boo him he is a Fool.

ISN'T IT AWFUL?

by Edith Moore, age 15, McComb

Isn't it awful not to be able to eat in a public place
Without being arrested or snarled at right in your face?

Isn't it awful not to be able to go to a public library and get an
                     interesting book
Without being put out and given a hateful look?

Isn't it awful not to be able to sleep peacefully nights
For fear you may get bombed because you want your rights?

Isn't it awful not to be able to get your schooling where you please?
Just because of our race, color and creed we cannot feel at ease.

A NEGRO CONDITION

by Lillie Mae Powell, Pilgrim's Rest

On day while I was visiting a certain
City this is what I saw. A Negro
Soldier with a broken arm who
Was wounded in the war.

The wind was blowing from the
North; there was a drizzle of
Rain. He was looking from the
Last place; his arm was in a sling.

The Negro soldier didn't go
Home. He was looking to the east
And to the west. His broken arm
Was in a sling.

WHY DO THEY HATE US? WHAT HAS THE NEGRO DONE?

by Florence Seymour, Gulfport

It's enough to make you wonder, its enough to make you cry,
That every race hates the Negro, good Lord, I wonder why?

You can travel, and travel, you can travel this country through,
You'll find every race hates the Negro, no matter what they do.
You can scrub and mop their kitchens, and work from morning
        'til night,
But every race hates the Negro, and just won't treat them right.
You can wash and shine their cars and have their meals ready when
        they come,
Now tell me why do they hate us, what has the Negro done?

They say that monkeys are our ancestors, the beginning of our race,
But we have never killed a President, kidnapping children is out of
        our place.

We are Jim Crowed on every corner and everywhere we go,
Not only in the South, but clear to the White House door.
We are Jim Crowed on the trains and in restaurants when we want
        a meal.
But they never Jim Crowed the Negro when he was on the battlefield.
They won't allow us to have our business, no where in the heart of town.
And if we own too fine a home, they will come and burn it down.
We have to live in rat dens, and huts on the edge of town.
It doesn't matter where we live, they mean to keep us down.
They pay us the lowest salaries, and work us almost for fun.
Now tell me why they hate us, Lord? What has the Negro done?

WHAT DOES FREEDOM MEAN?

by Madeline McHugh, age 24, Hattiesburg

Whenever I think about sunlight and fresh air, or peace and springtime, I think about men wanting to be free.

There are men who want freedom all their lives and never get it: there are men who have freedom all their lives and never know it.

… but I think men who know they are free and try to help other men get it show how precious freedom really is.

BECAUSE I'M BLACK

by Ruth Phillips, age 16, Meridian

Sometimes I ask myself why did I have to be born black?
And there are times when I feel as if I want to turn back!
But then I ask myself again didn't God put me here for a
       purpose? Then I know that's why I'm not going to
       be satisfied within the Negro circle.

Just because God saw fit to paint me black; I'm the one
       that always sits in the back.
I'm a man and I want to be treated as a man and
       not as a left hand.

One day God's gonna lift his hand over this great land,
       I don't want to be a left or a right but a man.
I hope we all be around when God brings the high
       and mighty to the ground.

I AM A NEGRO

by Rosalyn Waterhouse, age 11, Meridian

I am a Negro and proud of its color too,
If you were a Negro wouldn't you?
I am glad of just what I am now
To be and to do things I know how.
I'm glad to be a Negro so happy and gay
To grow stronger day by day.
I am a Negro and I want to be free as any other child,
To wander about the house and the woods and be wild.
I want to be Free, Free, Free.

THREE STRIKES TO FREEDOM

by Mary Zanders, Gulfport

Freedom is like a baseball game,
You have to be set and have an aim,
When that's done, now you're ready
To bat the ball with an arm that's steady.

Strike one, selfish is the ball,
Missing this one is like missing them all,
But you can strike it if you try,
Kindness won't let anything pass you by.

Strike two, the ball is hate,
If this ball could be struck before it's too late,
The world would be better than just,
Having everybody together because they must.

Strike three, equality is last,
Miss this one and your back in the past;
Remember you can't sit still and wait
For everything to stop and suddenly be straight.

FREEDOM IN MISSISSIPPI

by David Marsh, age 16, Indianola

In the middle of the night,
a stressive bell of Hope is ringing
Everyone is on the eve of fear and success
is not yet come

Until Everyone Wake up and Speak out
in an overcoming voice, the slums will still Remain.

Let Not the pulling out of a few
go down the whole crowd.

If this remains we will forever be
under bowed.

WHY DID I MY DON'TS

by Sandra Ann Harris, age 17, Jackson

why did I my don'ts
why did I my dids
what's my didn'ts purpose
is it to fulfill my dids

what isn'ts have I proclaimed
what ises have I pronounced
why can't I do my doings
my couldn'ts do renounce

my wouldn'ts are excuses
my couldn'ts couldn't be helped
my weren'ts were all willful
my were of little help

the haven'ts were just there
my didn'ts did believe
that all my won'ts are daring
my wills to receive

SEGREGATION WILL NOT BE HERE LONG

by Allan Goodner, Clarksdale

Segregation will not be here long
I will do my best to see it gone

And when it is gone the world be
So very full of equality.

The people will sing and begin to shout;
And everyone will know what it's all about.

They will leap for joy with a sigh;
Praise the Lord ... Some will cry.

Glory Hallelujah ... blessed be;
God is a just God ... for all eternity.

Forv we've been buked for such a long time;
Being Black ... was such a crime.

And when it's over ... the world will see;
God made us all brothers ... Even you and me.

On every corner ... you will hear us say,
We're FREE ... Free and Free to stay.

Even on the street ... from every side;
We're free ....We're free ... and God was our guide.

They've killed us … and hung us from trees so high;
But we knew some of us would have to die.

Dying was not really oh so bad;
We've got equality … and we're really glad.

So how it's obvious and plain to see;
God made us all equal … You and Me.

DON'T GIVE A SUBJECT

by Shirley Ballard, age 17, Jackson

Don't give a subject
because I don't give a dang
some people do care
but me, to you, go hang

many people get up and
talk on a subject, topic
spend time and energy
when they could spend time in the tropic

Oh! hang you. Oh! hang me
what in damnu, I, you, they,
they them, him, her, care about
that subject see

give something me, to, that's
right off the brain. Well,
let's have a little nonsense now
and then. But! don't give it
a subject.
           subject.
           subject.
           subject.

ONCE I WANTED TO FILL THE EARTH WITH LAUGHTER

by Lynda

Once I wanted to fill the earth with laughter
and ease the world of all its grief and pain
To make the world a marvelous place to live in
As in the woods after a summer's rain.

when I had finished; nothing would it lack
I had not learned, as yet, my skin was black.
The world will heed neither my help or desires
It doesn't care what comes from within.
It silently sits and turns to me deaf ears.
For it has seen the color of my skin.

TIME

by Shirley Ballard, age 17, Jackson

Time goes by so slowly

my mind reaxcts so lowly
        how faint

how moody
        I feel,
                I love not
        I care not.

Don't love me.

Let me live.
        Die
        Cry
        Sigh

All alone
        Maybe someday I'll go home.

MR. TURNBOW

by Lorenzo Wesley, Milestone

I know a man who has no foe
His name is Mr. Turnbow
He is about five feet six
Every time you see him he has a gun or a brick.

If you want to keep your head
Then you'd better not come tripping around his bed.
When he talks to you
His fingers talk too.
Some people will never understand
But Mr. Turnbow is a good old man.

NOV. 22, 1963

by Arelya J. Mitchell, Holly Springs

The day was still and sad.
And in my little town it was
        windy, dark, and wet.

The day went on and on so slow.
Oh, how I wished it would end!
Then it came on the radio,
        that the President had been shot.
"Shot," said I.
        "Shot," said I, "Oh no, that can't be true!"
But in the emergency room they tried their
        might to ssave him, but the hope was slowly
        dying away as the afternoon began to fade
        promptly away.
Everyone just stopped and prayed. Their
        hearts skipped thump after thump as their
        throats began to lump (with tears).
Then the radio began to speak,
        "He's dead. The President of the United States is dead."

All was still.
All was sad.
A thunderbolt had hit our path.

Eyes fell down.
Tears fell down.
No one made joyful sound.

A knot curled in my throat —
          a knot that seems to have not been broken.
That phrase had hit us as if in answer to our prayers.
Why an answer so deep and sad?
Why an answer that has not a care?

All these questions and not any answers to me
          or no one else but Thee.
The next day was different —
          as different can be for the flag
          was lowered at half staff, you see.
All that had happened the other day seemed to have been
but a dream.
Some believing.
Some unbelieving.
Some just staring and looking.
This was the date the world cried.
This was the date the world stood still.
This is the date we'll never forget!

OTHER CHILDREN

by Airvester Bowman, Milestone

Some children live in palaces
behind an iron gate
and go to sleep in beds of gold
whenever it gets late.

Someday I'll travel 'round
and visit every land
and learn to speak the language
that each child can understand

They wll want to ask me questions then
and I will ask them others
and until we understand
like sisters and like brothers.

ROADS

by Airvester Bowman, Milestone

A road may lead to anywhere
To Texas or to Maine
To take you where you want to go,
Having no one else to blame.

It might lead past the Tailor's door
Where she sews with needle and thread
With three children sitting by her side
With hats on every head.

Oh, a road may lead you anywhere
To New York or to a bad man,
Then it might just fool you,
And lead you back home again.

LIFE, PEOPLE, THE MYSTERIES OF TIME

by Charlie Brown, 16, Indianola

Life, people, the mysteries of time,
Commencing, ending, but not ending,
Understandable but often misunderstood
This is the mystery.

At times they are both terminated
Not by nature but by people
This is what mystifies us
The mystery is ours, let's keep its objectives.

THE WIND

by Cora Saunders, age 14, Greenwood

The wind is a very strange thing.
The winter it will always bring.
Sometimes it brings a full breeze,
That sends away the dried leaves.
It twirls and it whirls the leaves around,
Then all at once
It settles them down.

SPRING

by William Smith, Clarksdale

It was a hot spring day
And the flowers were gay and sweet.
The Call of Spring was whispering through
The air like a drum with a soft beat.
The grass stood tall and its color
Was as bold as the sky.
Everyone was welcoming spring
And waving winter goodbye.
The sun was glowing like a ball of fire;
The heat was hot as steam.
But the trees were as green and gay
As a cool breeze in the month of May.

POEM

by M. C. Perry, age 18, Indianola

I was walking through the Woods of Green
When at that moment of the hour
I seem to have seen the figure of a flower

There amongst the Weeds
Where the wind had blown
Grew some stray weeds
That had taken root and Grown.

WHO WHAT DROPPED WHEN
?

From the Freedom School at Moss Point

Jesse Harris was dropped soft
into a deep hole, only
not too deep because when Wade
dug (and I watched) Wade hit it
(the coffin of Jesse Harris' grave)
and that disturbed the joy
of a good shiny possum only
not only that hitting of the coffin
did that, but this jumping light
too, that slid out of that not too deep
not too open hole, disturbed that joy
I had with Wade. So the dogs ran
and we were just as fast. Now
who dropped Jesse in his hole?
And who, oh who, dropped that light
around this place and all through
the trees after us? Well, he inclined
to believe it was Thomas Jefferson,
who was well known to hate Harrises,
and whose grandson loved
to bury fat possums. But the light,
we never knew what dropped that around the place.

MINE

by Alice Jackson, age 17, Jackson

I want to walk the streets of a town,
Turn into any restaurant and sit down,
And be served the food of my choice,
And not be met by a hostile voice.
I want to live in the best hotel for a week,
Or go for a swim at a public beach.
I want to go to the best University
and not be met with violence or uncertainty.
I want the things my ancestors
thought we'd never have.
They are mine as a Negro, an American;
I shall have them or be dead.

CHANGING THE AMERICAN STAGE

by Elnora Fondren, Clarksdale

America is a stage life land,
All people have parts to learn in hand.
If I were to walk down the street and say,
"I want my freedom this very day,"
I'd raise my fingers and lift my face,
But my people would look at me in disgrace.
"Why should I try to be free?
I already have my liberty."
The people are walking as statues do;
I have no right to look at you.
My face is different, my face is black,
But why should you want to hold me back?

We are a nation, and it is said,
"A Nation when parted is a stage that's dead."
I was once a patriot true.
Now you try to take me with you:
Not to be brothers and to let me be free,
But only to take care of thee.
I still have to play my part;
I am still a slave in my heart.
To look at our flag, and say to thee,
"I am here, but am I free?"
The Nation of America is never to be
Until we have our liberty.

If Khrushchev walked to my hometown,
I'd try my best to show him around,
Even though he is a man in wrong,
I still would try to help him along.
A man is a man, and life is life;
I am a man, and he is in life.

The trail of freedom is all around,
I wish it would come through this sorrowed town.
In this nation, I want you to know,
I am a citizen, and I want to be treated so.
This nation has to get together
And leave it to God to decide who is better.
I am here to testify,
I want my freedom, and that ain't no lie.

So Mr. Charlie, you are the best,
But I am as equal as you and the rest.
I am telling you the earnest truth,
We are people just like you.
So get ready for the fright of your life.
These people are going to get their freedom in height.
Try to be ready, try to be strong,
But you won't hold the black man down for long.

THE VOICE OF FREEDOM

by Robert Lee, age 18, Greenville

I am the voice that is heard everywhere;
Each day I struggle to get segregation away from here.
I am the voice that men call upon
   for Unity
     for Brotherhood
      for Now
        for Eternity
I am trhe voice of Freedom.

Gaining me is America's task;
Through striving and sacrifice
Segregation will be unmasked.
I am the voice that speaks with great pride:
Segregation and discrimination will be cast aside.

I am the voice that proclaims,
   "I will bring justice,"
     "I will bring equality."
I am the voice that shouts, "Segregation is dead."
I am the voice of freedom.
I will be — America!

SAY FREEDOM!

by Mitchell M., Hattiesburg

There shall come a day
When every man will say
FREEDOM!

When your heart desires,
When your soul's on fire,
Say FREEDOM!

How my voice sings out
Above the loudest shout,
Say FREEDOM!

Notes

p. 3

"**And that freedom train's a comin**'"The lines come from a song usually called "Freedom Train," based on the hymn "Old Ship of Zion." It was also sung in a union version as "Union Train" in the 1930s and 40s.

Mayor Allen Thompson of Jackson: Not only did Mayor Allen Cavett Thompson (1906-1980) get the infamous "Thompson Tank" named after him, but the Jackson airport, built during his five terms as mayor (1948-1969) also carries his name.

p. 4

Western College for Women: Organized as the "Mt. Holyoke of the Midwest" in 1855, Western College for Women became known for its international studies. It merged with Miami University in 1974. In April 2002, a plaque and memorial to Freedom Summer were dedicated near Peabody Hall on the campus.

Citizens Councils: The first White Citizens Council had been organized in Indianola, Mississippi (following the Supreme Court decision in *Brown v. Board of Education*) in 1954, as a middle-class, ostensibly nonviolent opposition to integration. Citizens Councils spread rapidly throughout the state, throughout the South, and as far north as Maryland. Officially, they employed legal and economic tactics against activists, but these occasionally included physical intimidation. They liked to be distinguished from the Ku Klux Klan organizations, which were seen as more lower class and directly violent.

p. 6

Baldwin: James Baldwin (1924-1987) had most recently published *The Fire Next Time* (1963) a pair of essays that eloquently expressed not only the intellectual and physical oppression of black Americans, but also wrestled prophetically with the themes of anger, revenge, love and forgiveness.

Frank Smith, from Atlanta, Georgia was a student at Morehouse College and a SNCC field secretary. He later moved to Washington, D.C., became active in local politics along with other SNCC veterans, and served there on the City Council.

p. 7

fat ugly registrar: Theron C. Lynd was the county registrar of Forrest County. His discriminatory policies and delaying tactics when he was asked for his records by the Justice Department in 1965 resulted in the Fifth Circuit Court issuing an injunction against him.

p. 8

Jimmy Travis: James Travis (b. 1942) now lives in Jackson, Mississippi, where he was born. After joining and then leaving the Nation of Islam in 1967 he began working with Headstart programs, emphasizing local control and a community voice in the program, an occupation he stayed with for fourteen years. In the mid-1980s, Travis went to work at Levi Strauss, also helping to gain union recognition there. When his oldest daughter was diagnosed with HIV in 1987, he became active in HIV-AIDS education, which he now sees as the main focus of his life.

Jesse: see note on p. 343.

p. 10

Jim Forman: James Forman (1928-2005) grew up in Chicago, spending much of his childhod with family in Mississippi, and graduated from Roosevelt University after military service. He was active in the black civil rights movement in North Carolina, Tennessee and other areas before becoming Executive Secretary of SNCC (1961-66) as well as its Director of International Affairs. Later he moved to Detroit, to work with the Black Workers Congress there, and then on to Washington, D.C. In 1974 he began to direct the Unemployment and Poverty Action Committee in that city, focusing on voter activism, the fight for D.C. statehood and other struggles. He published five books, including *The Making of Black Revolutionaries*.

p. 12

Medgar Wiley Evers (1925-1963) was an active leader of the NAACP in Jackson, Mississippi, whose assassination in his own driveway focused national attention on Mississippi in June 1963. His killer, Byron de la Beckwith, had been tried and acquitted twice by the summer of 1964. He was finally convicted of the crime in 1997, and died in 2001. Medgar Evers' widow, Myrlie Evers Williams, (b. 1933) served as chair of the NAACP from 1995 to 1998.

Ed King: R. Edwin King (b. 1936) was a white Mississippian who served as chaplain at predominately black Tougaloo College. He became the Mississippi Freedom Democratic Party's candidate for lieutenant governor on the 1963 Freedom

Vote ticket headed by Aaron Henry. In 1964, he was an MFDP delegate to the National Democratic convention. He continued to be active in MFDP politics, running for Congress in 1966.

Bob Moses (b. 1935) was raised in Harlem, attended Hamilton College and Harvard University, and was teaching math at Horace Mann High School when he went to work first for SCLC and then SNCC. He was one of the pioneering staff-workers in Mississippi organizing voter registration in 1961, and became the architect and key director of the 1964 Mississippi Summer Project. He left SNCC in 1966, moved to Tanzania in 1968, and returned to the United States in 1976. He now directs the innovative and successful Algebra Project to empower otherwise disadvantaged students.

p. 13

Charles McLaurin (b. 1941) a citizen of Jackson, Mississippi, was a pioneer in SNCC's early voter registration work and became one of its leading field secretaries. After the summer of 1964, he stayed on organizing in Sunflower County, remaining close to Fannie Lou Hamer until her death in 1977.

p. 14

Charles Morgan (b. 1930) practiced law in Birmingham, Alabama, from 1955 to 1963. Following the Birmingham church bombings, he took a strong public stand against them, and left Birmingham shortly afterwards. From 1964 to 1972 he headed the southern regional office of the American Civil Liberties Union, and then moved on to head the Washington, D.C., office from 1972 to 1976.

p. 15

Rev. James Lawson (b. 1928), an exponent of Gandhian nonviolence, became one of the leaders of the Nashville, Tennessee student sit-in movement in 1959. As a result, he was expelled from Vanderbilt University where he had been a student at the divinity school. The Nashville activists, especially Lawson, were leaders in the founding of SNCC in April 1960, to co-ordinate the black student movement that had erupted all over the south. He later became a pastor in Nashville and was one of the leaders who made the Memphis garbage workers strike national news in 1968.

John Doar, Burke Marshall: John Doar (b. 1921) was assistant attorney general during the Kennedy and Johnson administrations, known for his sympathies to the civil rights movement in general and the Mississippi Summer Project in particular. After leaving government, he was active in New York school desegregation controversies in 1967, and became Chief Counsel for the House Judiciary Committee during the Watergate hearings.

Burke Marshall (1922-1976) was the assistant attorney general for civil rights in 1964, left government in 1965, and became dean of the Yale Law School in 1970.

p. 17

"We Shall Overcome": Originally a church song, "I'll Overcome Someday," "We Shall Overcome" apparently began its political life among an integrated group of unionized mine workers in Alabama in 1908. (See *Sing Out!* volume 45, #3, p. 66.) Folk singer Guy Carawan, who attended workshops for grassroots southern activists, is widely credited for helping to transform the song into the "anthem" of the civil rights struggle. Movement workers also learned it at the Highlander Folk Center in Tennessee. Since then, people engaged in struggles for freedom and justice around the world have adopted and sung "We Shall Overcome."

Traditionally in the movement, the song was sung ritually, as can be seen in numerous photographs. The singers stood, hands crossed in front of their bodies (usually right over left) clasping hands with their neighbors, and swaying with the rhythm of the music.

"We'll Never Turn Back": words written by Bertha Gober, became the signature song of the Mississippi Summer Project.

This song, as well as many others quoted in *Letters from Mississippi*, is printed in full in *Everybody Says Freedom*, by Pete Seeger and Bob Reiser (Norton: New York, 1989).

Lee: Herbert Lee (d. 1961), a farmer in Amite County, Mississippi, was shot and killed in cold blood and broad daylight on September 25, 1961, by state representative E. H. Hurst. Lee had been active in the struggle for voting rights. The incident had a powerful effect on the sense of responsibility SNCC staff workers, especially Bob Moses, felt for the lives of the people they were working with.

Vincent Harding: Vincent G. Harding (b. 1931), historian and professor, was head of the Institute of the Black World in the late 1960s, and, since 1981, has been Professor of Religion and Social Transformation at the Iliff School of Theology in Denver, Colorado.

p. 18

The Student Voice: This was the newsletter of the Student Nonviolent Co-ordinating Committee, widely distributed on campuses throughout the North as well as among SNCC workers and supporters.

Mrs. Hamer's face: Fannie Lou Hamer (1917-1977) was driven out of her home on a Mississippi plantation for applying to register to vote. She went on to become a SNCC field secretary, and a powerful spokeswoman and activist in the freedom movement. After the Atlantic City challenge, she continued with a challenge to the seating of the white Mississippi Congressional delegation in 1965. She stayed politically active, opposing the Vietnam War and organizing against poverty, and for housing and medical care until her death from cancer.

Eastland: Senator James Eastland (1904-1986) was the United States senior senator from Mississippi in 1964. Elected as a Democrat in 1941, he served until 1976, chairing several powerful committees.

Gov. Johnson: Governor Paul B. Johnson. Jr. (1916-1985) succeeded Ross Barnett as governor of Mississippi in 1964. In

1966, he was elected chairman of the Tennessee-Tombigbee Waterway Authority.

p. 22

Look Magazine: *Look* settled on Donna Howell, a pre-med student from the University of New Mexico who worked in the Ruleville project.

p. 31

Mrs. Rita Schwerner: Now Rita Levant Bender (b. 1942) has been practicing law in Seattle since 1975.

p. 34

Stokely Carmichael: Kwame Ture (1941-1998) was born in Trinidad and raised in Harlem. He attended the Bronx High School of Science and attended Howard University, from which he joined the SNCC campaigns. He became Chairman of SNCC in 1966, popularizing the call for "Black Power," advocating increasing militancy and renouncing nonviolence. He left SNCC in 1967 and joined the Black Panthers. In 1969 he moved to Guinea and changed his name to Kwame Ture in honor of Kwame Nkrumah and Sekou Touré, and dedicated the rest of his life to promoting socialist pan-African unity.

p. 35

Bayard Rustin (1910-1987) was a civil rights activist and militant advocate of nonviolence. He was the chief organizer of the Washington, D.C., March for Jobs and Freedom in August 1963. As an adviser to Martin Luther King, he was targeted by the FBI for his sexual orientation.

p. 37

"They say that freedom is a constant sorrow ..." The song is more generally known as, "They say that freedom is a constant struggle," words and music originally written by Roberta Slavitt.

p. 38

Mario: Mario Savio (1943-1996) returned after the summer of 1964 to the University of California at Berkeley, where he was a graduate student in philosophy. In October of that year, he seized control of the microphone during a speech by University President Clark Kerr on the steps of Sproul Hall, an act which has been pinpointed as the beginning of the Free Speech Movement and a critical moment in student radical politics of the 1960s. He later went on to teach mathematics, philosophy and liberal studies at Sonoma State, without ever abandoning his political commitments.

p. 42

Dave Dennis (b. 1940) became active in CORE in Louisiana, where he practiced law. As CORE's leader in the Summer Project, he was well respected by SNCC and other co-workers in Mississippi. Later, he moved to Jackson and helped Bob Moses found the Southern Initiative of the Algebra Project in 1992, which he continues to direct.

p. 43

Dr. Aaron Henry (1922-1997) was the son of a sharecropper who became the head of the Mississippi state NAACP in 1959. He ran for governor on the MFDP ticket in the shadow Freedom Vote of 1963, and was a delegate to the 1964 Democratic Convention. When he tried to run for Congress as an independent, he was kept off the ballot by the authorities, who claimed he lacked the number of signatures necessary to qualify. He won another Freedom Vote when he ran for the Senate, but came to reject the MFDP as too radical. He led the loyalist Democrats who stayed with the national party in 1968 and 1972. A certified pharmacist and owner of the Fourth Street Drug Store in Clarksdale, he considered himself a down-home businessman who should not leave Mississippi. He became a key figure in bringing Head Start, housing, employment, and health services to Mississippi.

p. 44

"Caesar" Byrd: Actually Cecil Byrd, sheriff of Jackson County.

p. 47

Rosa Lee Williams: *"Miss Rose — as everyone called her: When I was in Mississippi in 1994, I asked . . . where she was or if she had died and when . . . but no one knew. I do remember that on the wall in her living room she had a newspaper clipping about her husband, I believe his name was Fred. It had a photo of him next to a bale of cotton. He had set some sort of cotton-growing record in that year."* (Roy Torkington note)

p. 59

"This Little Light of Mine": (traditional) This song became particularly associated with Fannie Lou Hamer.

Go Tell It on the Mountain: A 1954 autobiographical novel by James Baldwin, focusing on his coming of age as a teenage preacher in Harlem.

p. 61

Mallette, Clemens, and Sheehan: Of these three, Sheehan is most likely Archbishop Fulton John Sheen (1895-1979) an outspoken opponent of segregation.

p. 63

the other America: *The Other America*, a seminal analysis of poverty by Michael Harrington, was one of the books on a reading list provided to volunteers before their training at Western College for Women. The other books on that list were W. J. Cash's *Mind of the South*, W. E. B. Dubois' *Souls of Black Folk*, V. O. Key's *Southern Politics*, Martin Luther King, Jr.'s *Stride Toward Freedom*, and Lillian Smith's *Killers of the Dream*.

p. 64

Louis Allen: Louis Allen (d. 1964) was a witness to the shooting of Herbert Lee. At first he supported the killer's declaration that the killing was in self-defense, but a month later he told Bob Moses he had lied under coercion from local white men, and Moses informed the Justice Department. A local deputy sheriff later told Allen that he had been tipped off by the FBI to Allen's change of testimony. Allen was found shot to death on January 31, 1964.

p. 66

Snopes: an unattractive family of poor white characters whose rise in fortune is depicted in William Faulkner's trilogy *The Hamlet*, *The Town*, and *The Mansion*.

The Reverend John: John Maurer (b. 1925) a Presbyterian minister from Delanco, New Jersey, returned from Mississippi to New Jersey, later moved to a congregation in Connecticut, and still later left the ministry. Over the years, he worked as a taxi driver and an interstate truck driver, then became a drug counselor and a counselor in prisons. He now lives in Waterbury, Connecticut.

p. 75

They say in Mississippi: "Which side are you on?": composed by Florence Reese in Harlan County, Kentucky for a coal miners' strike in 1932, was adapted by James Farmer of CORE for the freedom movement while he was in jail in Mississippi's Hinds County as a freedom rider. The song is printed in full in *Everybody Says Freedom*.

Ross Barnett (d. 1987) was elected governor of Mississippi in 1960 as a champion of white supremacy, and helped provide state funds for the Citizens Councils. Barnett, who had pledged himself to stand forever against integration, protested the admission of James Meredith to the University of Mississippi in 1962. The 5th U.S. Circuit Court of Appeals in New Orleans, which had ordered Meredith's admission, cited

Governor Barnett for contempt of court for his role. He never served time or paid a fine, and charges were dropped in 1965.

Howard Zinn (b. 1922) was the chairman of the history department at Spelman College when he became involved in the civil rights movement. In 1964 he published his first book, *SNCC: The New Abolitionists*, but he is best known since for his *People's History of the United States*. He is now professor emeritus at Boston University and a popular speaker about current social issues.

closed society: James Wesley Silver (1907-1988) a professor of history at the University of Mississippi had recently published his study of Mississippi racial politics and their consequences, *Mississippi: The Closed Society*. The book was banned in the state, and Silver was subsequently forced out of his position and out of Mississippi.

p. 76

TVA: The Tennessee Valley Authority, established under the Roosevelt administration in 1933, officially managed the development and control of natural resources in the watershed of the Tennessee River, an area of more than 40,000 square miles.

p. 80

Albert Darner: *"Darner is a misprint. It should be Garner. Albert was a local activist. He participated in the training in Ohio, and I believe he and his wife were on the bus when we left Ohio for Mississippi. The quotation from him is in dialect because, when he said it, he said it in dialect. Ordinarily he did not speak in dialect or with a heavy accent."* (Roy Torkington note)

p. 86

Sheriff Hubbard: Earl G. Hubbard (1902-1998) served as sheriff of Panola County from 1964 to 1968.

p. 89

Hodding Carter's *The Delta-Democratic Times*: In 1959, Hodding Carter III (b. 1935) had taken over the *Delta Democrat Times* in Greenville, Mississippi, a prize-winning liberal newspaper under the direction of his father, Hodding Carter, Jr. (1907-1972). In 1961, Hodding Carter III won the Society of Professional Journalists' national award for editorial writing. He worked on two presidential campaigns — Lyndon Johnson's in 1964 and Jimmy Carter's in 1976. In January 1977, he became a spokesman for the Department of State and served as assistant secretary of state for public affairs in the Carter administration, most notably during the Iran hostage crisis. He is also known as a television commentator.

p. 90

Hollis Watkins was the first Mississippi student to become involved as a field secretary (in 1961) in the Mississippi Voting Rights Project, and has been active in empowerment activities in the state ever since. He became a core participant in successful community-based redistricting efforts in Mississippi in the early 1990s, and was the lead plaintiff in a 1991 redistricting suit to force the state to comply with the 1965 Voting Rights Act. He is active on the boards of directors of several community-based organizations, and has been awarded numerous fellowships and awards. He founded and now directs Southern Echo in Jackson. Southern Echo is a leadership development, education, and training organization that works to develop grass-roots leadership across Mississippi and the Southern region.

p. 91

Hartman Turnbow (1904-1988) was one of a group of fourteen Holmes County Negroes who attempted to register to vote in 1963. Volunteering to lead, he became officially the first to make that attempt in the twentieth century. A month later, his house was fire-bombed. The local police arrested him for arson, but later dropped the charges. Despite the firebombing and legal harassment, he continued his work as a widely respected leader and went to Atlantic City for the MFDP challenge at the 1964 Democratic convention.

p. 93
Mayor Williford: William Oliver Williford (b. 1922) owned an insurance agency and still owns a real estate business in Drew. Elected mayor in 1957, he served for twenty-eight years. He now lives in Jackson.

p. 94
"Ain't going to let no jailing turn me around": A spiritual adapted to the freedom struggle by Reverend Ralph Abernathy in 1962, in Albany, Georgia.

p. 97
Robert J. Miles and his wife: Robert J. Miles (d. 1996) and his wife Mona. See note on p. 341.

p. 103
"I'm on My Way" (traditional)

p. 113
In White America: by Martin Duberman, who is now a Distinguished Professor of History at the City University of New York. He is well known for a biography of Paul Robeson and for his historical work in Queer studies. While a professor at Princeton University, he compiled *In White America*, one of the earliest documentary dramas, in order "to describe what it has been like to be a Negro in this country." The play had a successful run in New York in 1963; and, in August 1964, the Free Southern Theatre (conceived in 1964 by several SNCC workers) toured its production in Mississippi under the sponsorship of SNCC with an integrated company of eight.

p. 119

Staughton Lynd (b. 1929) the director of the freedom schools in 1964, a socialist Quaker, is the son of noted academics Helen and Robert S. Lynd. In the fall of 1964, he became an assistant professor at Yale University, a position he lost after he traveled to Hanoi in December 1965. A political activist, historian and a specialist in labor law, he has worked on landmark cases of labor organizing, both while he was with the Northeast Ohio Legal Services and since his retirement in 1997.

p. 122

11-year-old girl named Rita Mae: *"I remember her very well, she used to come into the office and was quite bright. I do wonder what happened to her."* (Joe Ellin note.)

p. 123

Laubach: Frank Charles Laubach (1884-1970) who began his career as a missionary, became a pioneer of teaching adult literacy as a means of empowering impoverished and disadvantaged peoples around the world.

p. 125

Langston Hughes (1902-1967) was the pre-eminent poet of the Harlem Renaissance.

Amistad: In 1839, a revolt by slaves on the Spanish ship *Amistad* became a cause célèbre when the slaves sued for their freedom in U. S. courts, in a case that reached the Supreme Court in 1841. The former slaves won their freedom. The incident, while not mentioned at all in standard U. S. history books of the 1960s, has since been the subject of many studies and a Hollywood film.

p. 128

a white man from California: Abe Osheroff (b. 1915) of Los Angeles, a self-described working-class intellectual, radical humanist and life-long social activist, a veteran of the Abraham

Lincoln Brigade in the Spanish Civil War, came from Los Angeles with $10,000 to build a community center which he donated to the Holmes County movement. Later, Osheroff went on to make award-winning films and to organize a brigade to build a village in Nicaragua in 1985. He lives now, still building, in Seattle.

p. 129

Lilies of the Field: a 1963 movie directed by Ralph Nelson and starring Sidney Poitier (who won an Oscar for this role) as an African-American handyman who helps a group of German nuns build a chapel.

p. 135

Dulles: Allen Welsh Dulles (1893-1969) was the director of the Central Intelligence Agency from 1953 until 1961. President Johnson designated Dulles to act as a liaison with Mississippi state authorities during the investigation after the murders of Chaney, Goodman and Schwerner. He was opposed to federal protection for civil rights workers.

p. 137

Mississippi Goddam: A 1964 song with words and music by Nina Simone. The song is printed in full in *Everybody Says Freedom* and can be heard on *Nina at Town Hall*, and subsequent collections of Simone's singing.

p. 138

Lawrence Guyot: Lawrence Guyot (b. 1939) was born in Pass Christian, Mississippi, and was recruited by Bob Moses to work with SNCC while he was a student at Tougaloo. He was elected chair of the Mississippi Freedom Democratic Party before the Atlantic City convention, but was in jail and unable to attend. He ran unsuccessfully for Congress on the MFDP ticket in 1966, and since the 1970s has been living as an activist in Washington, D. C.

p. 139

Curtis Hayes (b. 1943), now Curtis Muhammad, was recruited to SNCC by Bob Moses in Mississippi, spent some years in Africa after 1964; and for the past seven or eight years has been working with the Union of Needletrades Industrial and Textile Employees (UNITE) in Louisiana.

two white volunteers named Larry and Dave, and Rabbi Lelyveld: The volunteers were Larry Spears and Dave Owen. Rabbi Arthur Lelyveld (1913-1996) was rabbi at the Fairmount Temple in Cleveland, Ohio, 1958-1986, and was active in the Cleveland NAACP. He served as president of the American Jewish Congress (1966–1972), the Central Conference of American Rabbis (1975–1977), and the Synagogue Council of America (1979-1981). He is a recipient of the NAACP Distinguished Service Award.

On August 8, Clifton Archie Keys and Estus Keys were tried for the beating of Rabbi Lelyveld, pleaded *nolo contendere*, and were given suspended sentences.

p. 142

Professor Pease from Stanford University: Otis Pease was a professor of history at Stanford and later elected to the Board of Trustees. He is now retired from the University of Washington.

p. 147

Goldwater: Barry Goldwater (1909-1998) had just defeated New York governor Nelson Rockefeller for the Republican candidacy for president in the 1964 election.

p. 149

Bill ... Peter: Peter Werner; and Bill Jones, a schoolteacher from New York City.

p. 150
Kenneth Keating: Kenneth B. Keating (1900-1975) was elected to the U. S. Senate as a Republican from New York in 1958. Throughout the summer of 1964 he and his staff were accessible and supportive, responding quickly to requests for the official scrutiny that helped control and prevent violence. In November 1964, he was defeated in his bid for re-election by Robert F. Kennedy. He later served on the U. S. Court of Appeals and as ambassador to India and Israel.

His indefatigable aide in support of the civil rights workers was Pat Connell.

p. 152
Borstal Boy, Invisible Man, The Stranger: Brendan Behan's 1958 book *Borstal Boy* is an acount of his own experiences in a British juvenile prison. *Invisible Man* (1952) by Ralph Ellison, follows the experiences of a nameless black man through contemporary American society. *The Stranger* (1956) by Albert Camus, originally published as *L'Etranger* (1952), recounts the crime and punishment of an Algerian white man who kills an Arab.

p. 154
Eric Hoffer's *The True Believer*: Eric Hoffer (1902-1983) was a philosopher who wrote out of his working-class background, emphasizing the importance of self-respect. *The True Believer* was published in 1951.

B.F. Skinner and BBD&O: Burrhus Frederic Skinner (1904-1990) was a leading experimenter with behavioral psychology, in which animals and people reacted to mechanical stimuli. BBD&O was a leading Madison Avenue advertising firm.

p. 158
John Griffin's *Black Like Me*: A white man, John Howard Griffin (1920-1980) traveled throughout the South for a period of time disguised as a black man, and wrote about his

experiences in *Black Like Me* (1961) which was a powerful eye-opener for many white Americans, although old news to black people.

p. 161

Dylan's "Who Killed Davey Moore": In 1964, singer and songwriter Bob Dylan (b. 1941) had not yet recorded "Who Killed Davey Moore" himself, but Pete Seeger had sung the song at a Carnegie Hall concert on June 8, 1963, which was recorded on the album *We Shall Overcome* (Columbia 45312). It was at this concert and on this album also that the SNCC Freedom Singers made their recording debut. Davey Moore (1934-1963) was a featherweight boxing champion who died as a result of his fighting.

p. 167

The Harlem riots: The third set of "Harlem riots" (the first two had occurred in 1935 and 1943) took place after an off-duty policeman shot a fifteen-year-old black youth on July 16, 1964. A CORE protest two days later ended with a march on the police station, which in turn sparked four nights of street confrontations and rioting.

p. 176

Bob Beech: Robert L. Beech (b. 1935) a Presbyterian minister, directed the Ministers Project in Hattiesburg during the summer of 1964, stayed in Mississippi until 1968, then received a fellowship to study social conflict at Harvard. He headed the Midwest Training Network in Kansas City, and in 1972 returned to Minnesota, where he has recently retired from the formal ministry.

p. 177

George McClain (b. 1936) a Methodist minister from Indiana active in civil rights, went on to organize a chapter of Clergy and Laity Concerned about Vietnam during his pastorate on Staten Island, New York, and to resuscitate and lead (1974-1998) the Methodist Federation for Social Action.

Episcopal Chaplain: When James Meredith matriculated at the University of Mississippi in 1962, angry white students bombarded him with bricks and bottles. The Reverend Wofford Smith joined the rector of the local Episcopal church in walking among them in order to calm the violence.

Professor Russell Barrett of the Political Science department: Professor Barrett taught in the political science department of the University of Mississippi from 1954 to 1976. He was the author of *Integration at Ole Miss*, 1965.

p. 178

the home of a professor where we met Phil Patterson, and his wife: The professor was Tom J. Truss, Jr., who taught English, and his wife Suzanne was the organist and choirmaster at St. Peter's Episcopal Church in Oxford. The volunteers wound up staying overnight with Phil Patterson, originally from Memphis, who is now an optometrist in Tennessee.

Kathryn Webb: Actually, Katherine Houston Webb of Jackson, who edited the *Daily Mississippian* during the summer and fall of 1964. After graduation, she worked on the *Jackson Daily News*, then married and later moved to Maine, continuing to work in journalism and, more recently, to teach at the University of Maine. She is a regular columnist for the *Bangor Daily News*.

p. 187

Erskine Caldwell characters: Erskine Caldwell (1903-1987) wrote gritty, realistic novels of the rural South.

p. 190

"Take this hammer, Carry it to the captain": This traditional song is printed in full in *Carry It On*, by Pete Seeger and Bob Reiser (Simon & Schuster: New York, 1985).

p. 193

Byron de la Beckwith: see note on Medgar Evers, p. 319.

Sam Block, born and raised in Mississippi, became a beloved legend in the movement because of his pioneering courage in the face of great danger and hardship. He went on to attend Marlboro College in Vermont in fall 1964, and died of diabetic complications in California in 2000.

Willie: now Wazir — Peacock, born in Tallahatchie County, Mississippi, lived on a plantation as a boy. He won a four-year scholarship to Rust College in Holly Springs, where he was a student activist. By the early 1960s, he was working on voter registration with Sam Block, Bob Moses and others in the dangerous Delta counties and soon became a SNCC field secretary. He placed great emphasis on the importance of local leadership. Living in California since 1989, he has been working with Stepping Stones Growth Center, serving developmentally disabled children and adults. One of the original SNCC Freedom Singers, he still sings movement songs for audiences of all ages.

p. 194

Randolph Blackwell (1927-1981) had become Field Director of the Mississippi Voter Education Project in 1962. He helped to organize COFO and served as program director of SCLC from 1964 through 1966.

p. 198

Two snicks just got married: Paul Klein and Wendy Weiner. The wedding is described in Sally Belfrage's *Freedom Summer*.

p. 200

a 7-months pregnant woman: 15-year-old Annie Lee Turner was dragged across the pavement and arrested during the Freedom Day activities.

p. 201

Jim Bevel: The Reverend James Bevel was one of the students who organized the Nashville Student Movement that sparked the birth of SNCC. He had been influenced by the workshops at the Highlander Folk School founded by Myles and Zilphia Horton as an organizing center in Tennessee. By 1962, he was a staff member of the Southern Christian Leadership Conference, working closely with SNCC.

p. 203

Mrs. Victoria Gray of Hattiesburg: Victoria Jackson Gray Adams (1927-2006) raised in Hattiesburg, Mississippi, was one of the founders, national spokespersons, and leaders of the Mississippi Freedom Democratic Party. She was the first woman (of any color or community) in the history of Mississippi to run for the office of U.S. Senator. She has also served as a member of the National Board of the SCLC.

After the MFDP had finished its most historic work, Victoria Gray Adams lived abroad in Bangkok, Thailand and finally settled in Virginia. Recently Ms. Gray Adams taught for one semester in the History Department at the University of Southern Mississippi, in her hometown of Hattiesburg, Mississippi.

Bob Zellner, Phil M.: Robert Zellner (b. 1939) was the first white southerner to work as a SNCC field secretary. After 1964, he continued work as a student of sociology at Brandeis University, and became president of the Southern Christian Education Fund (SCEF), 1966-1979. Since then, he has been active as a teacher and lecturer, and is an Adjunct Professor of History at Southampton College of Long Island University. He is a founder and co-chair (with Julian Bond) of the National Civil Rights Coordinating Committee.

Phil M. is Phil Moore, a summer volunteer.

p. 205

Chief Larry: Curtis Lary (1909-1984) began as a streetcleaner in Greenwood in 1925, and remained in the city employ his entire working life. He served as a policeman for thirty-seven years, and as chief of the department from 1957 to 1975.

Robert Williams style: Robert Williams (1925-1996) was an African-American World War II veteran who became head of the NAACP in Monroe, N.C. Tired of the unending night-time attacks by whites, he organized local youth into a rifle club to defend the black community. Accused of kidnaping a white couple he had taken into protective custody during a black protest, he fled to Cuba. His story is told in *Negroes with Guns* (1962) a book which had a tremendous influence on the dialogue between proponents of nonviolence and militant defense in the Black communities. Williams subsequently moved from Cuba to China, then finally back to the United States and a profes-sorship at the University of Michigan.

p. 206

Slim Henderson: Alton Eugene Henderson (d. 1991) sold used cars as well as running his store.

p. 208

Dottie: Dorothy M. Zellner (b. 1938) was a staff member of SNCC from 1962 to 1967. In the Atlanta office she worked with Julian Bond, now Chairperson of the NAACP, as part of SNCC's communications department. She participated in and wrote about demonstrations in Danville, Virginia, and was in Greenwood, Mississippi during the summer of 1964. After spending twenty years in the South, Ms. Zellner returned to her home town, New York City, where she worked for the Center for Constitutional Rights for thirteen years, and now works for the City University of New York (CUNY) School of Law as Director of Institutional Advancement/Publications.

p. 209

Harry Belafonte (b. 1927) and **Sidney Poitier** (b. 1927) are two well-known black actors whose support of social activism has been one of the hallmarks of their careers. Belafonte in particular was one of the earliest and strongest public supporters of the Freedom Movement in Mississippi.

p. 211

Faulkner: William Faulkner (1897-1962) a Nobel Prize laureate, set all his major works in the fictional Yoknapatawpha County in Mississippi, located between Marshall and Panola Counties in real-life Mississippi.

p. 215

"We are soldiers in the army" was composed by James Cleveland as a gospel song, and was brought into the civil rights movement by the Montgomery Trio. The song is printed in full in *Everybody Says Freedom*.

Two bodies found in river: The bodies were later identified as those of Charles Moore, who had been a student at Alcorn A&M College, and Henry Hezekiah Dee. Both were from Meadville, and had been missing since May 1964. In January 2007, James Ford Seale was finally arrested for his role in their lynching by a local Klan.

p. 216

Pete Seeger (b. 1919) has been and continues to be the best known voice of activist folk music in the United States. In 1941 he helped organize the Almanac Singers, in 1948 the Weavers, and in the early 1960s he introduced the SNCC Freedom Singers to a national audience. More recently, he has focused his own banjo on environmental causes. He was awarded a Presidential Medal of the Arts in 1994, and inducted into the Rock and Roll Hall of Fame in 1996.

"No more lynchings ... before I'd be a slave": This traditional song, usually called "Oh Freedom," is more than 150 years old, and has been adapted by civil-rights and labor movements throughout the United States. A part of the history of the song is given in *Everybody Says Freedom*.

p. 226

Wayne Yancey, a black volunteer from Detroit, was killed in a head-on car collision on August 1, 1964 in a car driven by Charles Scales, apparently while they were being pursued by an unknown vehicle.

p. 234

Muslims: The Nation of Islam, led in 1964 by Elijah Muhammad (1897-1975) was commonly known as "The Black Muslims."

p. 239

"Go tell it on the mountain" was adapted as a freedom song from an old Christian hymn, "Go tell it on the mountain / That Jesus Christ is born."

p. 240

Bill Ryan: William Fitts Ryan (1922-1972) was a member of the United States House of Representatives, a Democrat from New York's 20th District, and one of the earliest and most radical supporters of civil rights. In 1968, he was a delegate to the nominating convention in Atlantic City, where he supported the MFDP challenge. Afterwards, he continued to support the FDP in its Congressional challenges.

p. 248

Ella Baker (1903-1986) was the central organizing force that brought the Student Nonviolent Coordinating Committee into being. Born in North Carolina, Baker graduated from Shaw University in Raleigh, then moved to New York City in 1927. She immediately began community organizing. She worked for the WPA, founded consumers' co-operatives in Philadelphia and Chicago in the 1930s, and became active with the NAACP and the Urban League. She was an organizer of the Southern Christian Leadership Council (SCLC), and, in 1960, organized the first national conferences of sit-in demonstrators, which established SNCC.

p. 249

"Ain't Gonna Let Nobody Turn Me Round," and **"This Little Light of Mine"**: All of these songs are printed in full in *Everybody Says Freedom*.

Joseph Rauh: Joseph Louis Rauh (1911-1992) was a New Deal attorney, a supporter of the NAACP and a lawyer who came to symbolize the uses and limitations of the white liberal establishment for the freedom movement.

Walter Reuther (1907-1970) was president of the United Auto Workers (1946-1970). He led the UAW in its liberal support of civil rights.

p. 255

Mr. Miles or C. J. Williams or Mrs. Lloyd or Reverend Middleton: The community in Batesville is illustrative of the kind of local organization the volunteers found when they came to work in Mississippi, and which continued to struggle after they left. Around 1960, Robert Miles had helped organize a Voters' League with a number of other local leaders: Edward Thomas, Willie Kuykendall, C. J. Williams, Jasper Williams, the Reverend Jesse Rudd and the Reverend W. G. Middleton. Miles said that he had been impelled by the experience of his brother, whom he felt had been chased out of Mississippi for his political activity after World War II. Robert himself said he didn't want to run. The legal argument the Voters' League made against the refusal of their voting registration applications led to a court challenge which, in May 1964, turned Panola County into a test case for the state of Mississippi. When SNCC worker Frank Smith first came to Panola County, he was directed immediately to the Miles', and Mona and Robert Miles were central in hosting and working with Summer Project volunteers.

After the summer of 1964, Mrs. Miles suffered what she herself called "a complete nervous breakdown." In 1965, Robert Miles directed an agricultural marketing co-operative to serve workers who had lost plantation jobs. The Miles' were also the first in Batesville to send their children to an integrated school. For the rest of their lives, Robert and Mona Miles struggled to hold onto their farm, even when Robert became a leading "elder statesman" in Panola County politics. After the death of Mona Miles, Robert remarried, and died in 1996.

Bull Connor: Theophilus Eugene "Bull" Connor (1897-1973). Elected to the Alabama legislature in 1934 and to the position of Commissioner of Public Safety in Birmingham in 1937. To the outside world, he became infamous for turning fire hoses and dogs on demonstrators. By 1962, a majority of Birmingham voters had grown tired of his reactionary politics and voted to change Birmingham's form of government from City Commission to Mayor-Council, primarily to oust Connor and his two fellow commissioners. In 1964, he won the first of two terms as President of the Alabama Public Service Commission. He retired after losing a race for a third term in 1972.

Green compromise: The compromise offered to the MFDP delegates was named after Congresswoman Edith S. Green (1910-1967) a Democrat from Oregon who served ten terms in Congress from 1955 to 1975.

p. 257

Roy Wilkins (1901-1981) served as Executive Secretary of the NAACP from 1949 until 1977.

p. 259

"This may be the last time" is an old church song. The song is printed in full in *Everybody Says Freedom*.

p. 262

Widener Library: the principal library of Harvard University.

p. 278

Emmett Till (1941-1955) was murdered in Money, Mississippi. J. W. Milam (d. 1980) and Roy Bryant (d. 1990) were acquitted by an all white jury. Thanks to the courage of Till's mother Mamie Till Mobley (d. 2003), the boy's murder became a national rallying point for Black and white awareness of Mississippi lynch law.

p. 279

Ida Ruth Griffin (O'Leary) graduated from Jackson State University, and has been a pre-school teacher at the Hudson Headstart Center for more than twenty years. She is married, with three children, and lives in Camden, Mississippi. A stirring account of her reading this poem out loud is given (p. 110) in *The Summer That Didn't End* by Len Holt.

p. 281

McComb Freedom School: The McComb Freedom House was bombed on July 8, the blast injuring the project leader and a volunteer. The Freedom School reopened with thirty-five students.

p. 301

Mr. Turnbow: Hartman Turnbow, see note on p. 328.

p. 302

Arelya J. Mitchell is now the publisher of *The Mid-South Tribune* and lives in Memphis, Tennessee.

p. 310

Jesse Harris: a native of Jackson, Mississippi, and a SNCC field secretary, directed the McComb Project in 1964 and was elected to the Executive Committee of SNCC in 1965. His burial in the poem is fictional. He is still living, working as a contractor and an interior designer, in Jackson.

p. 312

Elnora Fondren became the first African-American student to attend Clarksdale High School. She chose to go to the white school during her senior year in 1965-1966 because the local Black high school did not offer Latin courses. Emma Fondren followed her sister's lead and attended Clarksdale High during the 1966-1967 school year. These two were the only African-American students to attend the all-white high school before a court order in 1970.

100 Fifth Avenue, New York, N. Y.

Dear Parents:

U R G E N T !

We have been conferring with publishers about the publication of a book of letters sent to relatives or friends by the volunteers in the Mississippi Summer Project. COFO agrees with us that such a volume will be invaluable financially (the Mississippi Project will receive all royalties), and James Forman is enthusiastic about the possibilities of such a book and its certain benefits to the Project.

We know, too, that your sons and daughters will want to share their enthusiasm, knowledge, and deep, abiding commitment to the Project with all the people of our country.

We have obtained the (voluntary) services of a publisher's consultant who will advise us on the mechanics of publishing, and an editor selected by COFO will work with the publisher's editor to ensure that the letters are properly presented from COFO's viewpoint.

Speed in getting the letters to us is essential, since preparation and publication takes time, so we urge you to act quickly as follows:

(1) Send us copies of letters, stories, poems, snapshots, drawings, etc. (You or your child may edit out all personal material not pertinent to the Project.) Address to Parents Committee, Letter File, at above address.

(2) Sign (If your child is under 21 years of age) or instruct your child to sign the enclosed release which was prepared for us by COFO's lawyer.

We are sending a memo about the above to all the project centers in Mississippi.

Yours in Freedom,

Jacqueline Bernard

Jacqueline Bernard
Publications Committee

The Volunteers

The following is not a complete list of the volunteers to the Mississippi Summer Project of 1964, but only includes those who submitted letters for Letters from Mississippi. *In preparing the new edition, the editor and publisher have made every effort to find and make contact with the volunteers listed here, and that effort continues even as the book goes to press. Many of those we have been in touch with have provided biographical information, which we have also included.*

Joel Aber (b. 1943) went straight to Oxford, Ohio, to the training session for Freedom Summer from his graduation ceremony at Antioch College. Since 1964 in Mississippi, he has become a teacher and teachers' union activist. He once ran for mayor of New Orleans as a socialist, and has continued his teaching career while living in Maryland. He is active in the Howard County Friends of Latin America, which began in opposition to the contra war in Nicaragua and is now campaigning to end the embargo against Cuba.

Jeff Acorn (b. 1944) graduated from the University of Seattle in 1968 with a B.A. in English literature and creative writing. He received a Master of Divinity with a special interest in psychiatry and religion from the Union Theological Seminary in 1971, worked briefly as a church minister, then for five years as a child welfare caseworker for the state of Washington. Since 1979 he has been driving a school bus for the Seattle public school district with a particular interest in special education students. He has been married twice, divorced twice, with a child from each marriage — a daughter in San Francisco and a son in Guatemala.

Jim Adams (b. 1940) has worked with the Peace Corps in Chad and as a seventh-grade science teacher. For twenty years he has been part of two different intentional farming communities raising chickens, turkeys and lamb for the healthy food market. He is now also a massage therapist, and lives in Virginia.

Russell Allan

Kathie Amatniek (b. 1943) now Kathie Sarachild, had just graduated from Harvard/Radcliffe when she joined SNCC's Batesville Project in Mississippi as a volunteer in the summer of 1964, returning for the spring of 1965. In the years since, she has supported herself as a film editor and teacher. The guidance of some SNCC organizers to "fight your own oppressors" inspired her work in the anti-Viet Nam War and Labor Movements, but primarily the Women's Liberation Movement, in which she was one of the founding organizers. Currently, she is the director of the Women's Liberation Archives for Action project of Redstockings and lives in New York City.

Lawrence Archibald lives in Santa Fe, New Mexico.

Ellen Arguimbau (b. 1945) got involved in Civil Rights and anti-war activities as a student at Swarthmore. She now lives in Helena, Montana.

Doug Baer

Doug Baty, after graduation from Stanford in 1968, stayed for a year in California, involved in both the anti-war movement and the San Francisco Zen Center. Then he returned to Montana to his grandparent's homestead, which has become home for him and his wife (Antje, from Germany) and daughters. They make their income through organic farming. He stays actively involved in environmental and political/social issues. His short time in Mississippi remains a highly significant experience and he continues to draw inspiration from his memories — particularly of so many people's everyday courage.

Joel Bernard, after the summer of 1964, took the year off from college to continue working in the project in West Point, Mississippi. After going back to college, he kept in touch with the project (led by John Buffington), and visited in the summers of 1966 and 1967. He participated in the anti-war movement, and attended the National Conference for a New Politics in Chicago in 1967. After studying in England and working in France, he taught American history at the university level, continues to be involved in historical scholarship, and is now settled in Oregon.

Jacob Blum (b. 1946) helped with the development and distribution of the natural foods business in Vermont. For the past twenty years, he has worked in the computer business as a network services provider. He is also a volunteer firefighter and tree warden in Norwich, Vermont.

Bret Breneman obtained a BA degree in American literature from Stanford University in 1965 and an MA in English literature from the University of Sussex the following year. In 1969 he embraced the Baha'i Faith, and soon after enrolled in the National Teachers Corps. He obtained a Masters in Teaching degree in 1972. He has taught English in Honolulu, Singapore,

Japan, Micronesia, South Carolina and Virginia, and is currently teaching at Thomas Nelson Community College in Virginia. He has published several poems, a few articles, a children's novel, and is now writing an epic poem about the early days of the Baha'i Faith in the 19th century.

Virginia Brown

John Bundy (b. 1942) worked primarily in Jackson with the Freedom Democratic Party during summer 1964. He practiced commercial law from 1969 to 1983, and joined the Glacier Fish Company as Business Manager in 1993. In 1998 he became part owner and president. (Glacier Fish owns and operates two Bering Sea Pollock catcher-processors and two cod freezer-longliners.) He is a voting member of the North Pacific Fisheries Management Council. (Pollock is America's largest fishery, certified sustainable by Marine Stewardship Council.) He married the former Mattie Jackson of Jackson, Mississippi, who had worked at the NAACP office for Medgar Evers. They now live in Seattle, and have four children and eight grandchildren.

Jacques Calma (b. 1942) went from Mississippi to work as an organizer in the 19th ward of St. Louis, Missouri and on the staff of Eugene McCarthy's presidential campaign. For many years he taught political science, and is currently revising his political science dissertation — an analysis of military strategies from a pacifist point of view — for publication. He is a physician and a children's soccer coach in Oakland, California.

Wilfred Carney, after the summer of 1964 went directly to Jefferson Medical School. He has been engaged in the practice of vascular surgery since at the Rhode Island Hospital in Providence and has been teaching medical students and surgical residents at Brown University.

Virginia Chute

Barry Clemson stayed in Mississippi, returning to Penn State University in April 1965. He was active in the student movement and the anti-war movement for several years and then worked with the Order of the Ecumenical Institute, community organizing in Chicago and India. Eighteen years of university teaching and six years of software development followed. He recently was vice president of a group providing a "children's church" for young people in a large public housing project in Norfolk, Virginia. He practices aikido. He is now writing a novel, which, with its planned successors, is intended to help educate our collective imaginations on the use of nonviolence in large scale conflicts.

David Cleverdon is now a farmer, growing organic produce for Chicago restaurants and farmers' markets. Before becoming a farmer, he was a member of the Chicago Board of Trade and a political organizer in Chicago, most notably for Congressman Abner Mikva, whom he also served as administrative assistant; and for Governor Dan Walker. He was Executive Director of the Illinois Democratic Fund from 1974-1976, and director of the Illinois Link Deposit Program for Economic Development, 1989-91.

Michael Clurman (b. 1944) finished the Harvard University Graduate School of Economics and also earned a degree in educational counseling from the University of Massachusetts in Boston. Since then, he has been working in software development. He lives in Sudbury, Massachusetts.

Geoffrey Cowan, immediately after Mississippi Summer, entered Law School at Yale where he helped to found the *Southern Courier* newspaper in Alabama and to launch programs in political and corporate reform. In later years he became a public interest lawyer, a *Village Voice* columnist, an author (*See No Evil* and *The People v. Clarence Darrow*), a television producer (*Mark Twain and Me*), an advocate of ethics and campaign finance reform, owner of a minor league baseball team (the Stockton Ports) and the director of the Voice of America. Since 1997, he has been dean of the Annenberg School for Communication at the University of Southern California.

Paul Cowan, in the years after Mississippi Summer, continued to write about his experiences in the civil rights movement as a reporter for *The Village Voice* and the author of several books including *The Making of an Unamerican* and *An Orphan in History*. He died of leukemia in 1988 and is survived by his wife, Rabbi Rachel Cowan, and their children Matt and Lisa.

Dave Crittendon

Margaret (Peg) **Dobbie** (1943–2003), after Mississippi, returned to Brown University, then headed back South to work for the Southern Christian Leadership Conference for a year in various parts of Alabama. She spent eight years as an elementary school teacher. For twenty years she was the Executive Director of the National Abortion and Reproductive Rights Action League of New Hampshire (NARAL-NH), a pro-choice, grassroots political organization, retiring in October 2001.

Bryan (Joseph) Dunlap
Mary Edelen

Joseph Ellin (b. 1936) continues to teach philosophy at Western Michigan University. He has been active in the American Civil Liberties Union and anti-war movements.

Nancy Ellin (b. 1936) was an officer of the Democratic Party in Kalamazoo County for many years. She was also active in Planned Parenthood. She wrote a book on notable black women commissioned by the Michigan Department of Education.

Eugene Ericksen (b. 1941) graduated from the University of Chicago with a degree in Mathematics in June, 1963. He is now a professor of statistics and sociology at Temple University. A great deal of his research focuses on issues of race. Lately, he has concentrated on developing adjustments for the relative undercount of minority populations.

Gail Falk (b. 1943) was recruited into the Mississippi Summer Project as a Radcliffe student when Al Lowenstein gave a rousing speech. She remained with COFO in Meridian, Mississippi, until January, 1965, when she returned briefly to college. She spent two and a half more years in Mississippi and Alabama, working for the Southern Courier newspaper. In 1967 she went to Yale Law School, then to West Virginia, where she worked with the United Mine Workers. Later, when her first son developed severe disabilities, she was drawn into work with people with disabilities. Since then, she has worked professionally to support the closing of institutions and to support the rights of people with disabilities to live the lives they choose. She lives in Montpelier, Vermont with her husband and children Tom and Kate.

Bob Feinglass
Glenn Fetty

Tom Foner (1946-1999) grew up on an Old Left family deeply concerned about racial justice. After his summer in Mississippi he attended the School of General Studies at Columbia University and became an aspiring writer. He died of lung cancer in 1999.

William H. Forsyth

Hardy Frye (b. 1939) worked in rural and urban communities in Alabama, Mississippi and Tennessee with SNCC, CORE and other civil rights organizations. He has worked as an educational consultant to South Africa and on building community organizations in Nicaragua. He was a research sociologist at the Institute for the Study of Social Change, the University of California, Berkeley. In 1999, he retired from his professorship in 1999 on the Board of Studies in Sociology, at the University of California, Santa Cruz, in order to join the Peace Corps as the Country Director for Guyana. Among his many honors, he was nominated for an Oscar for the 1995 documentary film *Freedom on My Mind*, for which he was Associate Producer.

Aviva Futorian remained in Mississippi after the summer of 1964, as an organizer for SNCC in Benton County. After leaving Mississippi in 1966, she attended law school, then worked as a Legislative Assistant to (former) Congresswoman Elizabeth Holtzman and as Director of the Women's Law Project, a unit of the legal services program of Chicago. She currently represents death penalty defendants in their final appeals. She is a founder and vice-president of the Illinois Death Penalty Moratorium Project, and a board member of the Illinois Coalition against the Death Penalty, where she is coordinator of prisoner support services. Ms. Futorian is one of the authors of *A Broken System at Work: Report on the State of the Death Penalty in Illinois in the Year of the Moratorium.*

Lester Galt (b. 1943) returned from Mississippi to North Dakota, then moved afterwards to Minnesota and to New Orleans, where he now lives. From 1970 to 1972, he worked as a Vista supervisor. Over the years he has also worked in the anti-war movement and is now involved in opposing globalization and for proportional representation and instant run-off elections, with his ideas written into an as yet unpublished book, *Power Power Power Politics and Power.*

Robert (Reebee) **Garofalo** is a professor at the University of Massachusetts Boston, where he has taught since 1978. His most recent book is *Rockin' Out: Popular Music in the USA.* He is also editor of *Rockin' the Boat: Mass Music and Mass Movements*, and co-author of *Rock 'n' Roll is Here to Pay: The History and Politics of the Music Industry.* He also sits on the National Advisory Board of the Archives of African American Music and Culture. At the local level, Garofalo was a co-founder and past President of Massachusetts Rock Against Racism.

Clark Gardner

David Gelfand (b. 1944) after the summer of 1964, participated in the 1965 SCLC voter registration/education project in Columbia, South Carolina. He was involved in working at an off-base coffee shop in Oceanside, California started for Marine 'grunts,' draft counseling, and protesting the war in Viet Nam. He has worked in the biotechnology industry (molecular genetics) in the Bay Area since November 1976.

Mary Sue Gellatly
Marylou Gillard

Allan Gould
Bonnie Guy
Jan Louise Handke

Robert Hargreaves (b. 1939) was working on a Master's degree in Poultry Management at the time he went to Mississippi. He returned to Michigan State and finished his M.S., then went back to Mississippi for the first half of 1965. From there, he went to Viet Nam, working in agricultural development with International Voluntary Services for two years. He came home, got married, went to veterinary school, and has been working for the State of California in livestock and poultry disease control for the past twenty-nine years. He has returned to Viet Nam a number of times in the last ten years and assisted in their veterinary program.

Albert Hausfather emigrated to Canada and is now a psychologist on the faculty of McGill University in Montréal.

Kathleen Henderson
Gregory C. Hewlett
Philip Hocker

William Hodes graduated from Harvard College in 1966, and from Rutgers Law School in 1969. Upon graduation, he began practice in a small civil rights and personal injury firm in New Orleans. During the next eight years, he worked in Newark, New Jersey, first for the Kenneth Gibson administration as Assistant Corporation Counsel, and then as Senior Staff Attorney for the Education Law Center, a public interest law firm funded by the Ford Foundation. In 1978, Hodes returned to the legal academy, where he taught chiefly in the areas of Civil Procedure, Constitutional Law, and Professional Responsibility. Professor Hodes was the co-author (with Geoffrey Hazard) of the leading legal ethics treatise *The Law of Lawyering*, and in 1999 he retired from Indiana University to begin a solo law and consulting practice largely limited to lawyering and legal ethics issues.

Martha Honey (b. 1945) spent ten years in Africa after the Summer Project, getting her PhD and as a freelance reporter covering liberation movements from the movements' perspective for newspapers in the U.S. and England. She and her husband Tony Avirgan were the only western press to accompany the Tanzanian army and cover the overthrow of Idi Amin in Uganda. From 1983-91 they worked in Central America for ABC and other media, where they witnessed an attempt to assassinate Sandinista leader Eden Pastora at a press conference, during which her husband was wounded. In 1995 she became a fellow at the Institute for Policy Studies in Washington, D.C. directing a U.S. foreign policy project while also raising three children. She has published eight books including *Hostile Acts* (1994) about U.S. policies in Costa Rica in the 1980s.

Lucien Kabat died of cancer in 1966.

James Kates (b. 1945) returned to Mississippi in 1965, later became a public school teacher, nonviolence trainer, poet and literary translator. Since 1997, he has co-directed Zephyr Press.

Joe Keesecker (b. 1943) went on from Mississippi to work with the SCLC in Florida. He was ordained as a Presbyterian minister in 1969, and has since worked with community organization and community development in Chicago and Colorado, and with education and program administration for the Presbyterian Church in New York, New Mexico and in Central America. From 1987 to 1998 he directed the Ghost Ranch and Plaza Resolana Conference Centers in Abiquiu and Santa Fe, New Mexico. He is now co-coordinator (with his wife) of PRESGOV, a partnership program between the U. S. and Guatemalan Presbyterian churches.

Parrish Kelley (b. 1945) wanted to continue working for SNCC after the summer was over, but allowed his parents to persuade him to return to college. In 1966 he joined VISTA, and spent a year in Tulsa, Oklahoma, experimenting with community organizing, trying to get some indigenous groups started. In the

1970s he worked with the Bois d'Arc Patriots in Dallas, Texas, a group that was trying to organize low-income whites.

Richard Kelly

Paul Kendall earned a Master of Divinity degree from the Union Theological Seminary in 1968, worked as a caseworker for the New York City Department of Social Services in the mid-1960s, and later became the Director of the Manhattan office of the Department of City Planning. He is now the managing partner of a private consulting practice aiding not-for-profit organizations in the United States and Latin America.

Michael Kenney

Howard Kirschenbaum after Mississippi became a high school English and history teacher, then director of the National Humanistic Education Center, Values Associates, National Coalition for Democracy in Education, professor and chair of Counseling Program at the University of Rochester. He is the author of over twenty books in education, psychology and history, he was a national leader in values and character education and is a world authority on the life and work of Carl Rogers. He has also been a leader of historic preservation in the Adirondack Mountains. He was founder and president of the non-profit Adirondack Architectural Heritage and has helped save several historic properties from destruction.

Adam Kline (b. 1944) returned to college at Johns Hopkins, left college again to work with SDS in East Baltimore, and then finished law school. He went back to Mississippi for two years with the North Mississippi Rural Legal Services, and then moved to Seattle where he practiced as a personal injury lawyer and volunteer with the ACLU. He is now a Washington State senator.

Ruth Koenig (b. 1941) has worked as a teacher, a community education coordinator, and an environmental volunteer coordinator for the City of Eugene, Oregon. Her work has involved human needs: health clinic, mentoring programs, community garden, day care, senior citizen activities. Her travels, particularly to South Africa and Nicaragua, and work on the Sanctuary Movement, have extended her justice work, which continues today.

Rita Koplowitz

Ellen Lake (b. 1944) after Mississippi, finished college at Harvard, went to law school at Case Western Reserve University, moved to California, and practiced law, feeling that all her law practice has been an extension of the Mississippi project ideals: staff attorney for Cal. Supreme Court; Legal Aid Society of Alameda County; United Farm Workers Union; California Agricultural Labor Relations Board, private practice representing plaintiffs on appeal in employment and personal injury cases, including asbestos victims.

Ira Landess (b. 1939) taught from 1964 to 1979 in a New York City high school for boys who were socially delinquent and emotionally challenged, and who, in those years, were taken out of the mainstream and placed in "600 schools." He turned down an appointment at a plush city high school in order to teach there, a decision influenced in large measure by his work in Mississippi. He also trained to become a psychoanalyst, which he is now, with a practice in Manhattan, currently writing up a lengthy case history: his own.

Robert Lauen, after 1964, worked in civil rights actions in Minnesota, community organizing in Colombia (Peace Corps), community organizing in working class neighborhoods in Chicago (Saul Alinsky), community organizing for neighborhood health clinics in Denver, community organizing for and with Mexican farm workers in Ft. Lupton, Colorado, and then got involved in the issues of the criminal justice system. He has worked in adult corrections reform from 1973 and still continues mostly volunteer advocacy work.

Robert Lavelle
Brian Leekley

Sara Leiber

Joseph Leisner (b. 1942) worked at the New York City Welfare Department as a caseworker, then as a science teacher in Williamsburg, where he was nearly fatally stabbed. Later, he became a dance therapist and moved to California. For many years thereafter he worked as a carpenter and contractor, but in the past two years has moved into television production and video editing.

Betty Levy returned to work in the Jackson area in the summer of 1965. She received an MA from Harvard and an EdD from Columbia in elementary education. After teaching several years in Harlem, she joined the full-time faculty of the Women's Studies Department at SUNY/Old Westbury. She was 31 when she died in 1974.

Mark Levy returned to Mississippi in 1965 to work on voter registration and school desegregation. For eight years after that, he taught in junior high school and then college in New York City. Since that time, he has worked as a union organizer and administrator in the electrical manufacturing and healthcare industries.

Michael Lipsky (b. 1940) came to the Mississippi Summer Project after spending several weeks writing for and editing the *Mississippi Free Press*, and then organizing a Princeton Friends of SNCC during the winter. From 1966 to 1991 he taught political science at the University of Wisconsin, and then for twenty-one years at M.I.T. He was a founding member of the Legal Services Institute, a neighborhood legal clinic in Boston. He was also a member (1985-90) of the Committee on the Status of Black Americans for the National Academy of Sciences. He is now Senior Program Officer at the Ford Foundation in the Peace and Social Justice Program.

David Llorens (deceased)

Robert Mandel (b. 1944) is an ESL and history teacher, elected member of his union Executive Board, a Free Mumia activist, a Jew who believes in the right of Palestinians to return. For him, the Mississippi vision was that of a just society, and that vision evolved into a continuing belief in socialism.

Tom Manoff (b. 1945) is a composer, author and music critic. He has been the Classical Music Critic for NPR's *All Things Considered* since 1985. Manoff has written also for *The New York Times*, *The Christian Science Monitor*, and *The Oregonian*. His books include *The Music Kit* and *Music A Living Language*. Manoff's compositions in various styles include music for the Oscar-winning documentary film *Down and Out in the USA*.

Robert Masters
Marianne McKay

Ronald Meservey (b. 1943) graduated from Stanford University in 1965. He volunteered as an English teacher in a barrio in Peru, subsequently teaching Spanish in California until 1968. After working as a community service volunteer in Colombia in 1969, he earned an MACT in Political Science and returned to teaching, this time on the East Coast. He was active in the anti-Viet Nam War movement. From 1983 through 2003 he worked as an analyst for the Department of Defense, and has been active since retirement in Democratic Party electoral campaigns and the anti-Iraq War movement. He had not returned to Mississippi until 2007, for Hurricane Katrina relief work.

Judy Michalowski (b. 1943) worked with the State of California in a program promoting alternative technology when Jerry Brown was governor, and has been an organic gardener for the past twenty years. She helped to start the United Farmers Markets in Sacramento. She has maintained contact through the years with people she got to know in Cleveland, Mississippi in 1964.

Steven Miller
E. Beth Moore
Philip Moore
Grace Morton
Barbara Mutnick

Karol Nelson (McMahan) is a free-lance writer living in Austin, Texas.

William Ninde

James Ohls (b. 1945) finished his BA after his summer in Mississippi and then did graduate work in economics. He taught for a while at the college level and is now a Senior Fellow at Mathematica Policy Research, a social science research firm that focuses on conducting policy evaluation work. His specialty is federal nutrition policy, particularly the Food Stamp Program.

Joann Ooiman (Robinson) (b. 1942) remained in Mississippi until the spring of 1965. She then briefly attempted community organizing in San Francisco before entering graduate school at Johns Hopkins University, where she obtained a Ph. D. in History. She joined the history faculty at Morgan State University in 1969. Among the courses she teaches are histories of nonviolent protest, the civil rights movement, and affirmative action. Her publications include *Abraham Went Out*, a biography of A.J.Muste; *Affirmative Action*, a documentary History; *Education as My Agenda: Gertrude Williams, Race and the Baltimore Public Schools*.

David Owen (b. 1944) stayed in Mississippi until January 1965, returned to Oberlin College, was drafted into the army for a two-year hitch, and graduated from Oberlin in 1969. He finished Medical School at the University of California in 1973, and in 1974 moved to Urbana, Illinois, to work as a physician at the University of Illinois. He continues to live in Urbana.

Jerry Parker

Pam Parker (Chude Pamela Allen) (b. 1943) was a founding member of the women's liberation movement and in the late 70s, editor of the UNION WAGE newspaper. She is author of *Free Space, A Perspective on the Small Group in Women's Liberation* and contributed the chapter on the woman suffrage movement for *Reluctant Reformers: Racism and Social Reform*

Movements in the United States. Her writings about Mississippi are included in the anthology, *Freedom Is a Constant Struggle.* She is a member of the Veterans of the Civil Rights Movement of the Bay Area and has long been interested in helping activists write their own stories.

Susan Patterson Rigolo (Temple Weste), earned an MFA in painting in New York after she returned from Mississippi, and worked as a still photographer, artist and gofer with a couple of small film companies, and as an assistant art director with a computer animation company. She lived in Lahaina for 6 years (sunny west side white sand beaches), Hana for 3 (the rain forest) and then for nineteen years led a contemplative life on the slopes of Haleakala ("House of the Sun"), worked on her own books, poetry and animations, was a Feng Shui consultant, had a small graphics company and tutored for the Department of Education. In February 2006, she moved to Hilo, Hawaii.

Edna Perkins
Gitta Perl

Carl Pomerance (b. 1944) graduated from Brown University in 1966 and earned a PhD in mathematics from Harvard in 1972. He taught at the University of Georgia and was a researcher at Bell Labs. Currently a math professor at Dartmouth College, he is co-author of a popular text on prime numbers. Politically, he was active in the antiwar movement in the late 60s. The first two years of the 70s he spent as a middle school teacher in Massachusetts, and became less involved in organized movements. In 1997 he gave a talk on Freedom Summer to several history classes at the Batesville, Mississippi, high school.

Ann (Annie) **Popkin** (b. 1945) became one of the founders of the women's liberation movement in the Boston area, with Bread and Roses, among other groups. She studied in the Sociology Department at Brandeis University graduate school, moved west, and taught women's studies, ethnic studies, community studies as well as other disciplines at California universities. Trained in unlearning racism workshops, she continued to teach college students and teachers about oppression, in Oregon. More recently, she has taken up the practices of Qi Gong (a healing art form) and, Jin Shin Do (a form of acupressure), and Hakomi (a body centered counseling). She is now a licensed massage therapist. Her work includes counseling, massage, facilitating groups, unlearning racism and teaching in Oregon amidst a community of friends.

Than Porter (b. 1930) lives and works as a realtor in Gaithersburg, Maryland. He earned a doctorate at New York University in 1967, then taught mathematics at Roosevelt High School in the District of Columbia and Harren High School in New York City; and math and statistics at Silliman University in the Philippines and at NYU. He also taught mathematics at several universities in Puerto Rico but was repeatedly fired for protesting the sexual abuse and apparent murder of his son.

Kay Prickett (Michener) (b. 1942) graduated from Southern Illinois University in Carbondale in 1965. She worked in Mississippi off and on until October 1966. She taught school in Chicago for a while but finally got thrown out because of her political views. In 1975 she began the practice of Transcendental Meditation and in 1980 took the advanced course called the Sidhis. In 1982 she joined the faculty at Maharishi International University in Fairfield, Iowa.

Catherine Quinn

Peter Rabinowitz (b. 1944) earned three degrees from the University of Chicago (including a PhD in comparative literature), worked for five years in a community college, then came to teach at Hamilton College (coincidentally, Bob Moses's alma mater), where he has been for a quarter of a century. He has written much about narrative theory (including the book *Before Reading: Narrative Conventions and the Politics of Interpretation*), often (but not always) with a political edge. He has also been a classical music critic for a variety of publications. Active during the divestment movement at Hamilton, he has supported progressive political actions on campus through the years.

Deborah Rand became a social studies teacher after graduating from Carleton College and Harvard University, then went to law school, working later with the Equal Employment Opportunity Commission General Counsel's office, MFY Legal Services, the West Side SRO Law Project, and the Brooklyn Legal Services Corporation, concentrating on services for poor people and local organizations. She was the Deputy Chief/ Senior Counsel of the New York City Law Department for seventeen years and is now the Assistant Commissioner for Housing Litigation at the New York City Department of Housing Preservation and Development.

Marilyn Rapley

Peggy Reimann spent several years hitch-hiking, living, teaching, and drawing in South America and East Africa, learning Spanish and two African languages. Eventually, she and her daughter moved to rural western Pennsylvania, where she and her now deceased partner, the poet/journalist Bill Anderson, began to rethink how we teach and learn. They developed methods and curricula, called The Third Way, used by parents, tutors, and teachers to attack some of current gaps in how our children learn and think. She has worked in many settings, including rural, migrant, and immigrant communities and schools.

Ron Ridenour (b. 1939) continued with SNCC in Los Angeles and the anti-war movement; later with BPP, Chicano and Native America solidarity and for Central American liberation. The FBI blacklisted him from the mainstream media and he joined the left-underground media. He worked with the FSLN, was an organizer of the 1985 Central American Peace March and wrote *Yankee Sandinistas*. In 1988, Cuba's Culture Ministry invited him to work for Editorial José Martí, which published *Backfire: The CIA's Biggest Burn*. Later, he was a writer-translator for Prensa Latina. In 1996, he returned to Denmark, where he had first moved in 1980. His fifth book is *Cuba: Beyond the Crossroads*.

David Riley (b.1942) graduated from George Washington Law School; wrote three plays that have been produced by professional and community theaters; published many articles in newspapers and magazines; worked for Friends of the Earth, the National Nuclear Freeze Campaign; directed the National Campaign to Save the ABM Treaty; been a community activist since the civil rights days; and has had poems published in magazines and literary journals, as well as in a collection of five poets, *Summer Lines*, published in 2006.

Wally Roberts has worked primarily as a journalist and community organizer in New England. He is currently executive director of Rural Vermont, a statewide organization that works to preserve family farms and promote sustainable agriculture.

Margaret Rose
Tom Rowe

Susan Ryerson (Moon), a writer and activist, joined the Berkeley Zen Center in 1976 and has been studying and practicing Zen ever since. She is the editor of *Turning Wheel, the Journal of Socially Engaged Buddhism*, published by the Buddhist Peace Fellowship. She teaches creative writing workshops, both independently and through various cultural and Buddhist organizations. During the 1980s, she studied Russian and traveled repeatedly to the USSR as a "citizen diplomat." Recently, she was the dharma mentor for the Buddhist Peace Fellowship.

John Sawyer
Florence Sayer (deceased)
Nancy Schiffelin

Gretchen Schwarz (Hillard) (b. 1944) studied American Indian linguistics and urban planning after graduating from Swarthmore College. She has been working as an affordable housing and redevelopment program manager in local government most of the time since then, currently on the San Franciso Peninsula.

Linda Seese (b. 1942) stayed in Sunflower County for more than a year, then worked in an interracial project in Columbus, Ohio. In 1966 she lived and worked in northern Canada with Native Americans and became chairwoman of the Canadian New Left, helping start the women's liberation movement there. Later, she was active with Saul Alinsky and with women's liberation in Chicago; and in Portland, Oregon, with gay liberation, food co-ops, and a women's bookstore. She helped found women's land movements in Oregon, Denmark, and New Mexico. For more than two decades, she has lived in a small, predominantly Hispanic town in New Mexico, communally until two years ago. A Buddhist, she has never made much money.

Phil Sharpe

Terri Shaw (b. 1940) attended Antioch College and had worked as a journalist at the Buffalo (N. Y.) *Courier-Express* before going to Mississippi. In the fall of 1964 she attended the Columbia University Graduate School of Journalism, and subsequently worked for the Associated Press in New York, traveled as a free-lancer to South America, and then went to *The Washington Post*, where she was long active in the newspaper Guild. She has now retired from the *Post* to begin a new career as a translator, interpreter and ski instructor.

John (Jay) **Shetterly** (b. 1944) after college graduation, earned a Fulbright Scholarship to India where he taught English for a year. The War against Viet Nam steered him into the Peace Corps for a year in Libya and two in Iran. He finished law school in 1973. Opportunities for white lawyers in Mississippi, his original reason for studying law, had changed; and for family reasons as well, he became a lawyer in Boston. He now lives in Cambridge, Massachusetts, with two teenage daughters. He works on some progressive political issues and pursues lifelong hobbies studying birds and insects. He has been back to Mississippi several times.

Ellen Siegel

Lew Sitzer has since worked on fair-housing legislation in California, refugee relief in Laos, teacher corps with Latinos in southern California, and established a parentally run co-opera-tive school in northern California. He worked with high-risk youth for ten years in public and private schools and has been a history and photography teacher in private and public schools. He is now a history teacher and administrator at the American International School in Bucharest.

Mildred Smith
Nancy Smith
Douglas Sorenson
Soren Sorenson

Charles Sowerwine (b. 1943) after 1964 became active in the anti-war movement. He graduated from Oberlin in 1965. He went to Cuba in the spring of 1970 in the Venceremos Brigade. He taught in Paris and did his PhD thesis on women and the left in France. In Paris he translated for visiting US delegations, meeting with representatives of the Vietnamese. In 1974, he began teaching history at the University of Melbourne (Aus-tralia), where he has been ever since, more recently on a joint appointment with a French university.

Lawrence Spears (b. 1942) graduated from Union Theologi-cal Seminary and University of Chicago Law School, clerked for a federal judge in Chicago, was counsel to the mentally ill in North Carolina, was Assistant State Court Administrator for the North Dakota Judicial system, and founded the first Consensus Council to assist citizens and leaders in building agreements on difficult issues of public policy.

Virginia Steele (1922-2006) returned to her public school teach-ing job in Berkeley, California. After her retirement she moved to Friends House, Santa Rosa, California. In 1974 she bought an abandoned mountain farm adjacent to the Monongahela National Forest in Pocahontas County, West Virginia where she spent the summers writing and enjoying local activities.

She became a supporter, participant and subsequently a generous benefactor of High Rocks, a leadership training program located on her farm. Their summer program is named Camp Steele in her honor. Until her death she remained friends and exchanged visits with her Mississippi host, Ms. Lilly B. Royal of Greenwood.

Jane Steidemann
John Stevenson
Ruth Steward
Charles Stewart
Robert Stone

John Strand (b. 1942) moved from the civil rights movement into a career in urban public education. He taught in an inner city high school in New Haven, founded a school for dropouts in New York City, and served as the superintendent of schools in three different school districts. Since his retirement from public education, he has worked at the Efficacy Institute, at an urban charter school company, and is currently working at New Visions for Public Schools in New York City, where he helps educators and community organizations start new high schools to replace failing ones.

Howard Stromquist lives in Indianapolis, Indiana.

Richard Swanson was a graduate student active in the anti-war movement from 1964–1966. He then taught at Boggs Academy, a private, all-Black high school in Georgia for three years. After attending law school, he worked first as a legal services attorney, and now as a divorce attorney. He has four children.

Morton Thomas (b.1942) graduated from Harvard College in 1966 and from the University of Pennsylvania Law School in 1975. Since 1977 he has worked at various jobs, and is now semi-retired in Boston. His only child, Jesse Christopher, born deaf in 1975, is a student at Gallaudet University, where he has been very much involved in the recent (October 2006) successful student protests.

Eleanor Tideman (Aurthur) lives in Venice, California.

Heather Tobis (Booth) in 1973 started an organizer-training center called Midwest Academy that has helped to build large-scale grassroots efforts for such organizations as Sierra Club, NARAL, AARP, Childrens Defense Fund and thousands of others. She has directed a number of large-scale social change groups, including Citizen Action, the field effort for Sen. Carol Mosely Braun's successful 1992 election, the Illinois Coordinated Campaign in 1996, and she was the national Training Director and then the national Field Director for the Democratic National Committee between 1994-1998. She has also consulted for pro-democracy groups. The founding director of the NAACP National Voter Fund in 2000, she is now Vice President of USAction and consults with many social change organizations.

Roy Torkington (b. 1940), after the summer of 1964, returned to the UC Berkeley and completed a BA in history, then a masters degree in Library Science. He worked at the UC Berkeley Institute of Library Research, the Library of Congress, and internationally on library automation and automatic indexing projects. For the past twenty years, he has worked on mainframe banking and financial application systems development as well as consulting on microcomputer and network systems. He recently became interested in China and has made several trips to China, while learning Chinese. He now lives in Berkeley.

Karen Treusch (Lord), as a graduate student at Howard University School of Social Work 1964-1966, remained in the civil rights movement until it became Blacks Only. Then she went on to participate in the anti-war, Women's Liberation, and Back to the Land movements, marrying, divorcing and remarrying. She is a clinical social worker in private practice and a divorce mediator, and a therapist at Deerfield Academy since 1988.

David Trimble (b. 1945) went on to become a clinical psychologist. He participated in the 1973 formation of the Center for

Multicultural Training in Psychology at Boston Medical Center, the oldest psychology internship program to train psychologists for work with urban poor and working-class People of Color. He is now a Director and Past President of the Network for Multicultural Training in Psychology.

Bernard Wasow (b. 1944) graduated from Reed College, earned a PhD in economics from Stanford University and spent a student year as a DAAD Fellow in Berlin. He has taught at the University of British Columbia, the University of Nairobi, and New York University. Outside academia, he worked at the Federal Reserve in New York and at the Ford Foundation as a Program Officer. He spent a year each working in Puerto Rico and Bangladesh. These days, he is a Senior Fellow at The Century Foundation. He and his wife Eileen have two children, Omar, born in 1970, and Althea, 1974.

Tom Watts

Judy Werner

Grenville Whitman served with SNCC 1964-1966 in Mississippi, Baltimore and Cambridge, Md., and the Atlanta national office (research department with Jack Minnis). He was principal author of the SNCC anti-war statement issued by John Lewis that led to Julian Bond's legislative seating struggle. Since 1966 in Baltimore, he has worked as a political and community organizer, administrator, project planner, consultant, and journalist. He is currently employed as copy editor and proofreader for an Afro-American newspaper.

Christopher Williams (b. 1946) was probably the youngest of the summer volunteers, arriving right out of high school. He left Mississippi in September 1965 and spent the next 10 years learning the trades of carpentry and fine woodworking. He got married, had two kids, lived as a hippie outside the mainstream culture, opposed the Viet Nam War and sucessfully resisted being drafted. He attended architecture school at Pratt Institute in Brooklyn, New York, and then worked as a designer and contractor in New York City. In 1989 he moved back to Vermont. For the past nine years, he has been employed as the college architect at Williams College in western Massachusetts, and remains active in education and environmental issues in Vermont.

Edwin Wilson

George Winters (b. 1940) has been an organizer ever since Mississippi 1964 — for the National Farm Workers, for the unionization of cannery workers, for the homeless in Sacramento, for Jesse Jackson, and against the war in Viet Nam and intervention in Central America. He has worked in fields and factories, and raised thirteen children. He has been adopted as a member of the Tlingit people and now lives in Ketchikan, Alaska, where he is a member of the Tongas Conservation Society and engages in healing and environmental work, as well as carpentry.

Gloria Wise
Sylvia Woog
Larry Wright

Michael Yarrow failed as a carpenter and went on to do community organizing and to teach at an alternative school in working class North Philadelphia before teaching sociology at several colleges. His research was focused on the class and gender consciousness of Appalachian coal miners. After leaving the academy through early retirement he worked as a union organizer and now is organizer for the Western Washington Fellowship of Reconciliation, where he organizes against police shootings of black men, for lifting the sanctions on Iraq, and for a more just and less bloody U.S. foreign policy. He has written several articles about the Mississippi Summer Project.

Judy York

Selected Bibliography

The publishers listed for the following books are those that issued the most recent edition of the book. In some cases, earlier editions from other publishers exist.

Nonfiction:

Belfrage, Sally, *Freedom Summer*, Fawcett, 1965

Bloom, Alexander and Winnie Breines, *Takin' It to the Streets, a 60s Reader*, Oxford University Press, 1995

Blumberg, Rhoda Lois, *Civil Rights, the 1960s Freedom Struggle*, Twayne, 1991

Branch, Taylor, *Parting the Waters*, Simon and Schuster, 1988

——*Pillar of Fire*, Simon and Schuster, 1995

——*At Canaan's Edge*, Simon and Schuster, 2006

Burner, Eric C., *And Gently He Shall Lead Them: Robert Parris Moses and Civil Rights in Mississippi*, New York University Press, 1994

Cagin, Seth and Philip Dray, *We Are Not Afraid: The Mississippi Murder of Goodman, Schwerner and Chaney*, Bantam Books, 1989

Carawan, Guy and Candie, *We Shall Overcome! Songs of the Southern Freedom Movement*, Oak Publications, 1963

Carmichael, Stokely (Kwame Ture) and Ekwueme Michael Thelwell, *Ready for Revolution*, Scribner, 2003

Carson, Clayborne, *In Struggle: SNCC and the Black Awakening of the 1960s*, Harvard University Press, 1981

Carter, Hodding, *So the Hefners Left McComb*, Doubleday, 1965

Cash, W. J., *The Mind of the South*, Vintage, 1941

Cluster, Dick, *They Should Have Served That Cup of Coffee*, South End Press, 1979

Council of Federated Organizations, *mississippi BLACK PAPER*, Random House, 1965

Curry, Constance et al., *Deep in Our Hearts: Nine White Women in the Freedom Movement*, University of Georgia Press, 2000

Dallard, Shyrlee, *Ella Baker: A Leader Behind the Scenes*, Silver Burdett Press, 1990 (juvenile biography)

Dittmer, John, *Local People: The Struggle for Civil Rights in Mississippi*, University of Illinois, 1994

Du Bois, W. E. B., *The Souls of Black Folk*, 1903

East, P. D., *The Magnolia Jungle*, Simon and Schuster, 1960

Egerton, *Speak Now Against the Day: The Generation before the Civil Rights Movement in the South*, Alfred A. Knopf, 1995

Erenrich, Susie, *Freedom Is a Constant Struggle: An Anthology of the Mississippi Civil Rights Movement*, Black Belt Press, 1999

Fleming, Cynthia Griggs, *Soon We Will Not Cry: The Liberation of Ruby Doris Robinson*, Bowman and Littlefield, 1998

Forman, James, *The Making of Black Revolutionaries*, 3rd edition, University of Washington Press, 1997

Forman, James, *The Political Thought of James Forman*, Black Star Publishing, 1970

Good, Paul, *The Trouble I've Seen*, Howard University Press, 1975

Grant, Joanne, *Ella Baker: Freedom Bound*, John Wiley & Sons, 1998

Greenberg, Cheryl Lynn, editor, *A Circle of Trust: Remembering SNCC*, Rutgers University Press, 1998

Harrington, Michael, *The Other America*, Macmillan, 1962

Hoffman, Nicholas von, *Mississipi Notebook*, David White Company, 1964

Holt, Len, *The Summer That Didn't End*, William Morrow & Co., 1965

Jordan, June, *Fannie Lou Hamer*, Thomas Y. Crowell, 1972 (juvenile biography)

Key, V. O., Jr., *Southern Politics*, Vintage, 1949

King, Martin Luther, Jr. *Stride Toward Freedom*, Harper and Brothers, 1958

King, Mary, *Freedom Song: A Personal Story of the 1960s Civil Rights Movement*, William Morrow & Co., 1987

Lawson, Steven R., *Black Ballots: Voting Rights in the South, 1944-1969*, Columbia University Press, 1976

Lewis, John with Michael D'Orso, *Walking with the Wind: A Memoir of the Movement*, Harcourt Brace and Company, 1998

Loewen, James and Charles Sallis, *Mississippi: Conflict and Change*, rev. ed., Pantheon, 1980

Lyon, Danny, *Memories of the Southen Civil Rights Movement*, University of North Carolina Press, 1992 (photos)

MacLeod, Jay and the Youth of the Rural Organizing and Cultural Center, *Minds Stayed on Freedom: The Civil Rights Struggle in the Rural South*, Westview Press, 1991

McAdam, Douglas, *Freedom Summer*, Oxford University Press, 1988

McCord, William, *Mississippi, the Long Hot Summer*, W. W. Norton & Company, 1965

Mills, Kay, *This Little Light of Mine: The Life of Fannie Lou Hamer*, Plume, 1994

Mills, Nicolaus, *Like a Holy Crusade: Mississippi 1964: The Turning Point of the Civil Rights Movement in America*, Ivan R. Dee, 1992

Moses, Robert P. and Charles E. Cobb, Jr., *Radical Equations: Civil Rights from Mississippi to the Algebra Project*, Beacon, 2001

Payne, Charles M., *I've Got the Light of Freedom: The Organizing Tradition and the Mississippi Freedom Struggle*, University of California Press, 1995

Moody, Anne, *Coming of Age in Missisippi*, Dell, 1970

Myrdal, Gunnar, *An American Dilemma*, McGraw-Hill, 1964

Olson, Lynn, *Freedom's Daughters: The Unsung Heroines of the Civil Rights Movement from 1830 to 1970*, Scribner, 2001

Payne, Charles M., *I've Got the Light of Freedom*, University of California, 1995

Randall, Herbert and Bobs M. Tusa, *Faces of Freedom Summer*, University of Alabama, 2001 (photos)

Raines, Howell, *My Soul Is Rested: The Story of the Civil Rights Movement in the Deep South*, Penguin, 1977

Schultz, Debra L., *Going South: Jewish Women in the Civil Rights Movement*, New York University Press, 2001

Seeger, Pete and Bob Reiser, *Everybody Says Freedom*, Norton, 1989

Sellers, Cleveland and Robert Terrell, *The River of No Return: The Autobiography of a Black Militant and the Life and Death of SNCC*, University Press of Mississippi, 1990

Silberman, Charles E., *Crisis in Black and White*, Random House, 1964

Silver, James W., *Mississippi: The Closed Society*, Harcourt Brace, 1966

——*Running Scared: Silver in Mississippi*, University Press of Mississippi, 1984

Smith, Frank E., *Congressman from Mississippi*, Pantheon, 1964

Smith, Lillian, *Killers of the Dream*, Norton, 1949

Sugarman, Tracy, *Stranger at the Gates*, Hill and Wang, 1966

U. S. Commission on Civil Rights, *Hearings Held in Jackson, Mississippi, February 16-20, 1965*, Government Printing Office, 1965

Walter, Mildred Pitts, *Mississippi Challenge*, Bradbury Press, 1992 (juvenile)

Watters, Pat, *Down to Now*, University of Georgia Press, 1993

Zinn, Howard, *SNCC: The New Abolitionists*, Beacon, 1964

Fiction:

Golden, Marita, *And Do Remember Me*, Ballantine, 1992

Hall, Richard, *Long George Alley*, Delacorte, 1968

Heath, William, *The Children Bob Moses Led*, Milkweed, 1995

Marlette, Doug, *Magic Time*, Farrar, Straus & Giroux, 2006

Killens, John Oliver, *'Sippi*, Thunder's Mouth Press, 1967

Walker, Alice, *Meridian*, Pocket Books, 1976

Discography:

Freedom Is a Constant Struggle: Songs of the Mississippi Civil Rights Movement, Folk Era FE149CD

The Freedom Singers Sing of Freedom Now! Mercury, SR60924/MG 20924

Voices of the Civil Rights Movement: Black American Freedom Songs, Smithsonian Folkways, SF40084

We Shall Overcome: Pete Seeger Recorded Live at His Historic Carnegie Hall Concert June 8, 1963, Columbia 45312

"We Shall Overcome" (The Freedom Singers) Mercury, SR60879/MG 20879

About the Editor

Elizabeth Martínez has been a social justice activist for 40 years. She has published six books and numerous articles on popular struggles in the Americas including *The Youngest Revolution: A Personal Report on Cuba* and most recently *De Colores Means All of Us: Latina Views for a Multi-Colored Century.* Her anti-racist work began in 1960, and became full-time when she traveled to Mississippi for the 1964 Summer Project for the Student Non-Violent Coordinating Committee (SNCC), later joining its staff. She moved to New Mexico in 1968 to found a Chicano movement newspaper and later the Chicano Communications Center.

Also involved in the women's and anti-Viet Nam war movements, she went on to live in the Bay Area where she has been an anti-racist workshop organizer, adjunct professor of Women's and Ethnic Studies, mentor to youth groups, and director of the Institute for MultiRacial Justice to help develop alliances among peoples of color. She currently focuses on working to build a new movement for peace and justice here and abroad. Her daughter, Tessa, is an actress.